W9-APJ-357

Docker: Up and Running

Karl Matthias and Sean P. Kane

Beijing · Boston · Farnham · Sebastopol · Tokyo

Docker: Up and Running
by Karl Matthias and Sean P. Kane

Copyright © 2015 Karl Matthias, Sean P. Kane. All rights reserved.

Published by O'Reilly Media, Inc., 1005 Gravenstein Highway North, Sebastopol, CA 95472.

O'Reilly books may be purchased for educational, business, or sales promotional use. Online editions are also available for most titles (*http://safaribooksonline.com*). For more information, contact our corporate/institutional sales department: 800-998-9938 or *corporate@oreilly.com*.

Editor: Brian Anderson	**Indexer:** Wendy Catalano
Production Editor: Melanie Yarbrough	**Interior Designer:** David Futato
Copyeditor: Gillian McGarvey	**Cover Designer:** Ellie Volkhausen
Proofreader: Sonia Saruba	**Illustrator:** Rebecca Demarest

June 2015:   First Edition

Revision History for the First Edition
2015-06-09:   First Release
2015-07-22:   Second Release
2016-02-26   Third Release
2018-02-16   Fourth Release

See *http://oreilly.com/catalog/errata.csp?isbn=9781491917572* for release details.

The O'Reilly logo is a registered trademark of O'Reilly Media, Inc. *Docker: Up and Running,* the cover image, and related trade dress are trademarks of O'Reilly Media, Inc.

While the publisher and the authors have used good faith efforts to ensure that the information and instructions contained in this work are accurate, the publisher and the authors disclaim all responsibility for errors or omissions, including without limitation responsibility for damages resulting from the use of or reliance on this work. Use of the information and instructions contained in this work is at your own risk. If any code samples or other technology this work contains or describes is subject to open source licenses or the intellectual property rights of others, it is your responsibility to ensure that your use thereof complies with such licenses and/or rights.

978-1-491-91757-2

[LSI]

For my wife and children, who make everything worth it. And my parents, who pointed me towards the beautiful intersection between logic and passion.

—Sean P. Kane

For my Mom, who got me to read, and my Dad, who read to me. And for my wife and daughters, who are my bedrock.

—Karl Matthias

Table of Contents

Foreword

"Everything old is new again" is a commonly heard phrase that has described everything from fashion, to politics, to technology. It is also an apt statement when it comes to Linux containers, and I would expand upon it to say, "Everything old is new again—and nonetheless exciting."

Containers have been available for many years in Linux distributions but they've seldom been used because of the complexity required to build something that worked. Thus historically, Linux container implementations have been purpose-built with a single objective in mind, which made additional requirements like scaling and portability challenging—if not impossible—to implement.

Enter Docker, which has created phenomenal momentum in unlocking the value of Linux containers by combining a standardized packaging format with ease of use, to turn processes that were once esoteric and incomprehensible into consumable capabilities for developers and operations teams. Docker, in a sense, has created a Renaissance for Linux containers, driving an ever-growing wave of interest and possibility, leading to rapid adoption of the technology. It's helping technology teams everywhere realize the benefits of application portability, simplified integration, and streamlined development as promised by Linux containers for some time but historically trapped behind layers of complexity.

Through Docker, Linux containers have catapulted into an elite club of truly disruptive technologies with the power to transform the IT landscape, related ecosystems, and markets. In the wake of this emergence rises a wave of innovation that demonstrates Linux containers' potential to dramatically change application delivery across a variety of computing environments and platforms while leveraging a spectrum of technical skill sets.

Innovation doesn't necessarily mean the introduction of a completely new, world-altering technology. Like many of its predecessors, Docker's success stands on the shoulder of giants. It builds on years of technological innovation and Linux evolution that now provides the core capabilities which Docker makes easy to use.

The maturity of the Linux capabilities exploited by Docker can now be replicated in other operating systems, allowing Docker to function beyond its Linux roots.

Docker is facilitating a disruptive change in the minds of technology professionals. It has reshaped views on which aspects of application development and delivery, as well as infrastructure management should be considered "table stakes" versus complexity that requires technology or process solutions. As is typical for the early adoption phase of any disruptive technology, these perspective changes aim at what's right in front of us, often oversimplifying and ignoring relevant aspects – but the potential for Docker and Linux containers goes much deeper than simply redefining development. It is redefining the very nature of the application itself.

The obvious impact of Docker and the ease of use it brings to Linux containers is the possibility to redefine the organizational divide between business, application development, and IT infrastructure teams. In a sense, Docker provides a tangible technology for implementing DevOps, which is the merger (or at least an armistice) between the often competing teams of development and operations. Containerization modernizes IT environments and, at an organizational level, allows for "proper" ownership of the technology stack and processes, reducing handovers and the costly change coordination that comes with them.

Docker's role as both a packaging format for the application *and* a unifying interface and methodology enables the application team to own the Docker-formatted container image, including all dependencies, while allowing operations to retain infrastructure ownership. With a standardized container infrastructure in place, the IT organization can then focus on building and managing deployments, meeting their security standards, automation needs, skill levels and ultimately cost profile, all without losing the ability to hold the application team accountable for the security and cost impact of their code that is deployed inside the container.

Docker also brings with it greater efficiencies of scale and performance—by shrinking application footprints through Docker-formatted containers, system-level dependencies are reduced to a bare minimum, often dozens-to-hundreds of megabytes in size. Compare this to traditional virtual machine images, which typically consume gigabytes of storage…but when you factor in performance, it goes beyond simply being innovative and becomes truly disruptive.

Starting a container takes milliseconds—quite a difference compared to the minutes most users experience with virtual machines. Deploying container images is faster if less data needs to travel over networks and storage fabrics, so modern, elastic applications with frequent state changes and dynamic allocation of resources can be built far more efficiently if the rollout of changes can happen extremely quickly and resource needs can be fulfilled in real time.

But perhaps the greatest innovation and most significant impact delivered by Docker and Linux containers is the fundamental change to application consumption. The monolithic application stack as we know it can be broken into dozens or even hundreds of tiny, single-minded applications that, when woven together, perform the same function as the traditional application. The benefit, however, is that these pieces can be rewritten, reused, and managed far more efficiently than monolithic applications, delivering a truly composite application built entirely of microservices.

Containers represent the way forward for the application development world, but it's critical that we do not lose sight of the old as we bring in the new. Docker and Linux containers are not without challenges. Management, security, and certification are three of the most glaring challenges to enterprise adoption, and these concerns are not so dissimilar from more traditional applications. Obviously, containers must be deployed on a secure host, but, more importantly, container security will be defined by what is in a given container—is it free of vulnerabilities, malware, and known exploits? Having the appropriate signature on a given containerized application, from a trusted, certified source goes a long way towards effectively answering these questions.

Additionally, management is paramount when it comes to the new world of containerized applications and Docker. The potential for sheer sprawl with containers is exponentially greater than that of virtual machines. Managing all of the containers is one challenge, but just as important, much like security, will be managing the content inside these containers. How are updates and rollbacks handled? What of orchestration? What will define "sprawl"? When do containers need to be retired or archived, else spend a life of limbo on a aging server? These too are questions that the enterprise must see addressed before *mission critical* can be applied to containerized applications.

These challenges aside, Linux containers do represent a fundamental shift in how the enterprise world creates, consumes, and manages applications. While the traditional monolithic application is likely to remain (lots of old technology survives as a legacy still today), containers have huge potential to modernize the operational model for these traditional applications and, alongside new, container-based applications, allow for incredible flexibility, portability, and efficiency across the datacenter and hybrid clouds.

Sean and Karl have worked with Linux containers (and Docker) for years, and have, in this book, captured what the IT world needs to know about Docker and the *container Renaissance*. Leveraging their insights, the authors provide a solid overview of how Docker actually works in the real world and how developers and other IT professionals can best utilize Docker and Linux containers in a way that makes sense for them and their organization.

> — *Lars Herrmann, General Manager for Enterprise Linux, Enterprise Virtualization and Container Strategy, Red Hat*

Preface

This book will get you to the point where you have a running Docker environment and steer you towards good choices for a production environment. Along the way we'll explore building applications for Docker, testing, deploying, and debugging a running system. We'll stop by to see a few of the orchestration tools and platforms in the Docker ecosystem. And we'll round out with guidance on security and best practices for your container environment.

Who Should Read This Book

This book is intended for anyone who is looking to solve the complex workflow problems involved in developing and deploying software to production at scale. If you're interested in Docker, Linux containers, DevOps, and large, scalable, software infrastructures, then this book is for you.

Why Read This Book?

Today there are many conversations, projects, and articles on the Internet about Docker. So why should you devote precious hours to reading this book?

Even though there is a lot of information out there, Docker is a new technology and it is evolving very quickly. Even during the time that it took us to write the first release of this book, Docker, Inc., released four versions of Docker plus a few major tools into their ecosystem. Getting your arms around the scope of what Docker provides, understanding how it fits into your workflow, and getting integration right are not trivial tasks. Few companies or engineering teams have been running it in production for more than a year.

We have worked for over a year and a half building and operating a production Docker platform within the Site Engineering team at New Relic. We implemented Docker in production only months after its release and can share with you some of the experience we gained from evolving our production platform over the last year and a half. The goal is for you to enjoy the wins while avoiding many of the bumps in the road that we experienced. Even though the online documentation for the Docker project is useful, we attempt to give you a bigger picture and expose you to many of the best practices that we have learned along the way.

When you finish this book, you should have enough information to understand what Docker is, why it's important, how to get it running, how to deploy your applications with it, and be armed with a clear view of what you can do to get to production. It will hopefully be a quick trip through an interesting technology with some very practical applications.

Navigating This Book

This book is organized as follows:

- Chapters 1 and 2 provide an introduction to Docker, and explain what it is and how you can use it.
- Chapter 3 takes you through the steps required to install Docker.
- Chapters 4 through 6 dive into the Docker client, images, and containers, exploring what they are and how you can work with them.
- Chapters 7 and 8 discuss the flow for getting your containers into production and debugging them.
- Chapter 9 delves into deploying containers at scale in public and private clouds.
- Chapter 10 dives into advanced topics that require some familiarity with Docker and can be important as you start to use Docker in your production environment.
- Chapter 11 explores some of the core concepts that have started to solidify in the industry about how to design the next generation of Internet-scale production software.
- Chapter 12 wraps everything up and ties it with a bow. It includes a summary of what you have and how it should help you improve the way you deliver and scale software services.

We realize that many people don't read technical books front to back and that something like the preface is incredibly easy to skip, but if you're still with us, here is a quick guide to some different approaches to reading this book:

- If you are new to Linux containers, start at the beginning. The first two chapters are intended to get your head around the basics of Docker and Linux containers, including what they are, how they work, and why you should care.

- If you want to jump right in and install and run Docker on your workstation, then dive right into Chapters 3 and 4, which show you how to install Docker, create and download images, run containers, and much more.

- If you are already using Docker for development but need some help getting it into production, consider starting with Chapters 7 through 10, which delve into deploying and debugging containers, and many other advanced topics.

- If you are a software or platform architect, you might find Chapter 11 an interesting place to investigate, as we dive into some of the current thinking about designing containerized applications and horizontally scalable services.

Conventions Used in This Book

The following typographical conventions are used in this book:

Italic
: Indicates new terms, URLs, email addresses, filenames, and file extensions.

`Constant width`
: Used for program listings, as well as within paragraphs to refer to program elements such as variable or function names, databases, data types, environment variables, statements, and keywords.

`Constant width bold`
: Shows commands or other text that should be typed literally by the user.

`Constant width italic`
: Shows text that should be replaced with user-supplied values or by values determined by context.

This element signifies a tip or suggestion.

This element signifies a general note.

This element indicates a warning or caution.

Safari® Books Online

Safari *Safari Books Online* is an on-demand digital library that delivers expert content in both book and video form from the world's leading authors in technology and business.

Technology professionals, software developers, web designers, and business and creative professionals use Safari Books Online as their primary resource for research, problem solving, learning, and certification training.

Safari Books Online offers a range of plans and pricing for enterprise, government, education, and individuals.

Members have access to thousands of books, training videos, and prepublication manuscripts in one fully searchable database from publishers like O'Reilly Media, Prentice Hall Professional, Addison-Wesley Professional, Microsoft Press, Sams, Que, Peachpit Press, Focal Press, Cisco Press, John Wiley & Sons, Syngress, Morgan Kaufmann, IBM Redbooks, Packt, Adobe Press, FT Press, Apress, Manning, New Riders, McGraw-Hill, Jones & Bartlett, Course Technology, and hundreds more. For more information about Safari Books Online, please visit us online.

How to Contact Us

Please address comments and questions concerning this book to the publisher:

O'Reilly Media, Inc.
1005 Gravenstein Highway North
Sebastopol, CA 95472
800-998-9938 (in the United States or Canada)
707-829-0515 (international or local)
707-829-0104 (fax)

We have a web page for this book, where we list errata, examples, and any additional information. You can access this page at *http://bit.ly/docker-up-and-running*.

To comment or ask technical questions about this book, send email to *bookquestions@oreilly.com*.

For more information about our books, courses, conferences, and news, see our website at *http://www.oreilly.com*.

Find us on Facebook: *http://facebook.com/oreilly*

Follow us on Twitter: *http://twitter.com/oreillymedia*

Watch us on YouTube: *http://www.youtube.com/oreillymedia*

Acknowledgments

We'd like to send a heartfelt thanks to the many people who helped make this book possible:

- Nic Benders, Bjorn Freeman-Benson, and Dana Lawson at New Relic, who went far above and beyond in supporting this effort, and who ensured that we had time to pursue it.

- Laurel Ruma at O'Reilly who initially reached out to us about writing a Docker book, and Mike Loukides who helped get everything on track.

- Gillian McGarvey and Melanie Yarbrough, for their efforts copyediting the manuscript, and helping it appear like we were actually paying attention in our high school English classes. 464 commas added and counting…

- Wendy Catalano, who helped us ensure that the Index was useful to all of our readers.

- A special thanks to our editor, Brian Anderson, who ensured that we knew what we were getting into, and guided us along every step of the way.

- All of our peers at New Relic, who have been along for the whole Docker ride and provided us with much of the experience that's reflected here.

- World Cup Coffee, McMenamins Ringlers Pub, and Old Town Pizza in Portland, OR, who kindly let us use their tables and power long after our dishes were empty.

- Our draft reviewers, who helped ensure that we were on the right track at various points throughout the writing process: Ksenia Burlachenko, who gave us our very first review as well as a full tech review, Andrew T. Baker, Sébastien Goasguen, and Henri Gomez.

- A special callout is due to Alice Goldfuss and Tom Offermann who gave us detailed and consistently useful feedback.

- Our families, for being supportive and giving us the required quiet time when we needed it.

- And finally to everyone else who encouraged us, gave us advice, or supported us in any way throughout this process.

## CHAPTER 1

Introduction

The Birth of Docker

Docker was first introduced to the world—with no pre-announcement and little fanfare—by Solomon Hykes, founder and CEO of dotCloud, in a five-minute lightning talk (*http://youtu.be/wW9CAH9nSLs*) at the Python Developers Conference in Santa Clara, California, on March 15, 2013. At the time of this announcement, only about 40 people outside dotCloud been given the opportunity to play with Docker.

Within a few weeks of this announcement, there was a surprising amount of press. The project was quickly open-sourced and made publicly available on Git-Hub (*https://github.com/docker/docker*), where anyone could download and contribute to the project. Over the next few months, more and more people in the industry started hearing about Docker and how it was going to revolutionize the way software was built, delivered, and run. And within a year, almost no one in the industry was unaware of Docker, but many were still unsure what it was exactly, and why people were so excited about.

Docker is a tool that promises to easily encapsulate the process of creating a distributable artifact for any application, deploying it at scale into any environment, and streamlining the workflow and responsiveness of agile software organizations.

The Promise of Docker

While ostensibly viewed as a virtualization platform, Docker is far more than that. Docker's domain spans a few crowded segments of the industry that include technologies like KVM, Xen, OpenStack, Mesos, Capistrano, Fabric, Ansible, Chef, Puppet, SaltStack, and so on. There is something very telling about the list of products that Docker competes with, and maybe you've spotted it already. For example, most engineers would not say that virtualization products compete with configuration management tools, yet both technologies are being disrupted by Docker. The technologies in that list are also generally acclaimed for their ability to improve productivity and that's what is causing a great deal of the buzz. Docker sits right in the middle of some of the most enabling technologies of the last decade.

If you were to do a feature-by-feature comparison of Docker and the reigning champion in any of these areas, Docker would very likely look like a middling competitor. It's stronger in some areas than others, but what Docker brings to the table is a feature set that crosses a broad range of workflow challenges. By combining the ease of application deployment tools like Capistrano and Fabric, with the ease of administrating virtualization systems, and then providing hooks that make workflow automation and orchestration easy to implement, Docker provides a very enabling feature set.

Lots of new technologies come and go, and a dose of skepticism about the newest rage is always healthy. Without digging deeper, it would be easy to dismiss Docker as just another technology that solves a few very specific problems for developers or operations teams. If you look at Docker as a virtualization or deployment technology alone, it might not seem very compelling. But Docker is much more than it seems on the surface.

It is hard and often expensive to get communication and processes right between teams of people, even in smaller organizations. Yet we live in a world where the communication of detailed information between teams is increasingly required to be successful. A tool that reduces the complexity of that communication while aiding in the production of more robust software would be a big win. And that's exactly why Docker merits a deeper look. It's no panacea, and implementing Docker well requires some thought, but Docker is a good approach to solving some real-world organizational problems and helping enable companies to ship better software faster. Delivering a well-designed Docker workflow can lead to happier technical teams and real money for the organization's bottom line.

So where are companies feeling the most pain? Shipping software at the speed expected in today's world is hard to do well, and as companies grow from one or two developers to many teams of developers, the burden of communication around shipping new releases becomes much heavier and harder to manage. Developers have to understand a lot of complexity about the environment they will be shipping software into, and production operations teams need to increasingly understand the internals of the software they ship. These are all generally good skills to work on because they lead to a better understanding of the environment as a whole and therefore encourage the designing of robust software, but these same skills are very difficult to scale effectively as an organization's growth accelerates.

The details of each company's environment often require a lot of communication that doesn't directly build value in the teams involved. For example, requiring developers to ask an operations team for *release 1.2.1* of a particular library slows them down and provides no direct business value to the company. If developers could simply upgrade the version of the library they use, write their code, test with the new version, and ship it, the delivery time would be measurably shortened. If operations people could upgrade software on the host system without having to coordinate with multiple teams of application developers, they could move faster. Docker helps to build a layer of isolation in software that reduces the burden of communication in the world of humans.

Beyond helping with communication issues, Docker is opinionated about software architecture in a way that encourages more robustly crafted applications. Its architectural philosophy centers around atomic or throwaway containers. During deployment, the whole running environment of the old application is thrown away with it. Nothing in the environment of the application will live longer than the application itself and that's a simple idea with big repercussions. It means that applications are not likely to accidentally rely on artifacts left by a previous release. It means that ephemeral debugging changes are less likely to live on in future releases that picked them up from the local filesystem. And it means that applications are highly portable between servers because all state has to be included directly into the deployment artifact and be immutable, or sent to an external dependency like a database, cache, or file server.

This leads to applications that are not only more scalable, but more reliable. Instances of the application container can come and go with little repercussion on the uptime of the frontend site. These are proven architectural choices that have been successful for non-Docker applications, but the design choices included in Docker's own design mean that Dockerized applications will follow these best practices by requirement and that's a good thing.

Benefits of the Docker Workflow

It's hard to cohesively group into categories all of the things Docker brings to the table. When implemented well, it benefits organizations, teams, developers, and operations engineers in a multitude of ways. It makes architectural decisions simpler because all applications essentially look the same on the outside from the hosting system's perspective. It makes tooling easier to write and share between applications. Nothing in this world comes with benefits and no challenges, but Docker is surprisingly skewed toward the benefits. Here are some more of the things you get with Docker:

Packaging software in a way that leverages the skills developers already have.
    Many companies have had to create positions for release and build engineers
    in order to manage all the knowledge and tooling required to create software
    packages for their supported platforms. Tools like rpm, mock, dpkg, and
    pbuilder can be complicated to use, and each one must be learned independ-
    ently. Docker wraps up all your requirements together into one package that
    is defined in a single file.

*Bundling application software and required OS filesystems together in a single
standardized image format.*
    In the past, you typically needed to package not only your application, but
    many of the dependencies that it relied on, including libraries and daemons.
    However, you couldn't ever ensure that 100 percent of the execution environ-
    ment was identical. All of this made packaging difficult to master, and hard
    for many companies to accomplish reliably. Often someone running Scien-
    tific Linux would resort to trying to deploy a community package tested on
    Red Hat Linux, hoping that the package was close enough to what they
    needed. With Docker you deploy your application along with every single
    file required to run it. Docker's layered images make this an efficient process
    that ensures that your application is running in the expected environment.

*Using packaged artifacts to test and deliver the exact same artifact to all systems in
all environments.*
    When developers commit changes to a version control system, a new Docker
    image can be built, which can go through the whole testing process and be
    deployed to production without any need to recompile or repackage at any
    step in the process.

Abstracting software applications from the hardware without sacrificing resources.
    Traditional enterprise virtualization solutions like VMware are typically used
    when people need to create an abstraction layer between the physical hard-
    ware and the software applications that run on it, at the cost of resources.
    The hypervisors that manage the VMs and each VM's running kernel use a
    percentage of the hardware system's resources, which are then no longer
    available to the hosted applications. A container, on the other hand, is just
    another process that talks directly to the Linux kernel and therefore can uti-
    lize more resources, up until the system or quota-based limits are reached.

When Docker was first released, Linux containers had been around for quite a
few years, and many of the other technologies that it is built on are not entirely
new. However, Docker's unique mix of strong architectural and workflow choices
combine together into a whole that is much more powerful than the sum of its
parts. Docker finally makes Linux containers, which have been around for more
than a decade, approachable to the average technologist. It fits containers relatively easily into the existing workflow and processes of real companies. And the

problems discussed above have been felt by so many people that interest in the Docker project has been accelerating faster than anyone could have reasonably expected.

In the first year, newcomers to the project were surprised to find out that Docker wasn't already production-ready, but a steady stream of commits from the open source Docker community has moved the project forward at a very brisk pace. That pace seems to only pick up steam as time goes on. As Docker has now moved well into the 1.x release cycle, stability is good, production adoption is here, and many companies are looking to Docker as a solution to some of the serious complexity issues that they face in their application delivery processes.

What Docker Isn't

Docker can be used to solve a wide breadth of challenges that other categories of tools have traditionally been enlisted to fix; however, Docker's breadth of features often means that it lacks depth in specific functionality. For example, some organizations will find that they can completely remove their configuration management tool when they migrate to Docker, but the real power of Docker is that although it can replace some aspects of more traditional tools, it is usually compatible with them or even augmented by combining with them, as well. In the following list, we explore some of the tool categories that Docker doesn't directly replace but that can often be used in conjunction to achieve great results:

Enterprise Virtualization Platform (VMware, KVM, etc.)
A container is not a virtual machine in the traditional sense. Virtual machines contain a complete operating system, running on top of the host operating system. The biggest advantage is that it is easy to run many virtual machines with radically different operating systems on a single host. With containers, both the host and the containers share the same kernel. This means that containers utilize fewer system resources, but must be based on the same underlying operating system (i.e., Linux).

Cloud Platform (Openstack, CloudStack, etc.)
Like Enterprise virtualization, the container workflow shares a lot of similarities on the surface with cloud platforms. Both are traditionally leveraged to allow applications to be horizontally scaled in response to changing demand. Docker, however, is not a cloud platform. It only handles deploying, running, and managing containers on pre-existing Docker hosts. It doesn't allow you to create new host systems (instances), object stores, block storage, and the many other resources that are typically associated with a cloud platform.

Configuration Management (Puppet, Chef, etc.)
Although Docker can significantly improve an organization's ability to manage applications and their dependencies, it does not directly replace more

traditional configuration management. Dockerfiles are used to define how a container should look at build time, but they do not manage the container's ongoing state, and cannot be used to manage the Docker host system.

Deployment Framework (Capistrano, Fabric, etc.)

Docker eases many aspects of deployment by creating self-contained container images that encapsulate all the dependencies of an application and can be deployed, in all environments, without changes. However, Docker can't be used to automate a complex deployment process by itself. Other tools are usually still needed to stitch together the larger workflow automation.

Workload Management Tool (Mesos, Fleet, etc.)

The Docker server does not have any internal concept of a cluster. Additional orchestration tools (including Docker's own Swarm tool) must be used to coordinate work intelligently across a pool of Docker hosts, and track the current state of all the hosts and their resources, and keep an inventory of running containers.

Development Environment (Vagrant, etc.)

Vagrant is a virtual machine management tool for developers that is often used to simulate server stacks that closely resemble the production environment in which an application is destined to be deployed. Among other things, Vagrant makes it easy to run Linux software on Mac OS X and Windows-based workstations. Since the Docker server only runs on Linux, Docker originally provided a tool called Boot2Docker to allow developers to quickly launch Linux-based Docker machines on various platforms. Boot2Docker is sufficient for many standard Docker workflows, but it doesn't provide the breadth of features found in Docker Machine and Vagrant.

Wrapping your head around Docker can be challenging when you are coming at it without a strong frame of reference. In the next chapter we will lay down a broad overview of Docker, what it is, how it is intended to be used, and what advantages it brings to the table when implemented with all of this in mind.

## CHAPTER 2

Docker at a Glance

Before you dive into configuring and installing Docker, a quick survey is in order to explain what Docker is and what it can bring to the table. It is a powerful technology, but not a tremendously complicated one. In this chapter, we'll cover the generalities of how Docker works, what makes it powerful, and some of the reasons you might use it. If you're reading this, you probably have your own reasons to use Docker, but it never hurts to augment your understanding before you dive in.

Don't worry— this shouldn't hold you up for too long. In the next chapter, we'll dive right into getting Docker installed and running on your system.

Process Simplification

Docker can simplify both workflows and communication, and that usually starts with the deployment story. Traditionally, the cycle of getting an application to production often looks something like the following (illustrated in Figure 2-1):

1. Application developers request resources from operations engineers.
2. Resources are provisioned and handed over to developers.
3. Developers script and tool their deployment.
4. Operations engineers and developers tweak the deployment repeatedly.
5. Additional application dependencies are discovered by developers.
6. Operations engineers work to install the additional requirements.
7. Loop over steps 5 and 6 N more times.
8. The application is deployed.

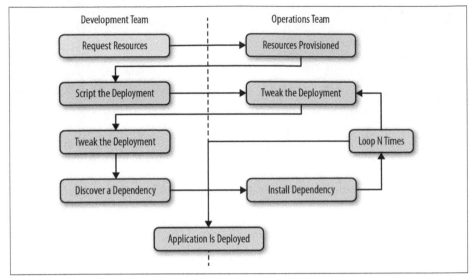

Figure 2-1. A traditional deployment workflow (without Docker)

Our experience has shown that deploying a brand new application into production can take the better part of a week for a complex new system. That's not very productive, and even though DevOps practices work to alleviate some of the barriers, it often requires a lot of effort and communication between teams of people. This process can often be both technically challenging and expensive, but even worse, it can limit the kinds of innovation that development teams will undertake in the future. If deploying software is hard, time-consuming, and requires resources from another team, then developers will often build everything into the existing application in order to avoid suffering the new deployment penalty.

Push-to-deploy systems like Heroku (*https://www.heroku.com*) have shown developers what the world can look like if you are in control of most of your dependencies as well as your application. Talking with developers about deployment will often turn up discussions of how easy that world is. If you're an operations engineer, you've probably heard complaints about how much slower your internal systems are compared with deploying on Heroku.

Docker doesn't try to be Heroku, but it provides a clean separation of responsibilities and encapsulation of dependencies, which results in a similar boost in productivity. It also allows even more fine-grained control than Heroku by putting developers in control of everything, down to the OS distribution on which they ship their application.

As a company, Docker preaches an approach of "batteries included but removable." Which means that they want their tools to come with everything most people need to get the job done, while still being built from interchangeable parts that can easily be swapped in and out to support custom solutions.

By using an image repository as the hand-off point, Docker allows the responsibility of building the application image to be separated from the deployment and operation of the container.

What this means in practice is that development teams can build their application with all of its dependencies, run it in development and test environments, and then just ship the exact same bundle of application and dependencies to production. Because those bundles all look the same from the outside, operations engineers can then build or install standard tooling to deploy and run the applications. The cycle described in Figure 2-1 then looks somewhat like this (illustrated in Figure 2-2):

1. Developers build the Docker image and ship it to the registry.

2. Operations engineers provide configuration details to the container and provision resources.

3. Developers trigger deployment.

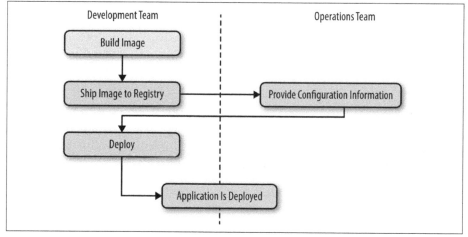

Figure 2-2. A Docker deployment workflow

This is possible because Docker allows all of the dependency issues to be discovered during the development and test cycles. By the time the application is ready for first deployment, that work is done. And it usually doesn't require as many handovers between the development and operations teams. That's a lot simpler and saves a lot of time. Better yet, it leads to more robust software through testing of the deployment environment before release.

Broad Support and Adoption

Docker is increasingly well supported, with the majority of the large public clouds announcing at least some direct support for it. For example, Docker runs on AWS Elastic Beanstalk, Google AppEngine, IBM Cloud, Microsoft Azure, Rackspace Cloud, and many more. At DockerCon 2014, Google's Eric Brewer announced that Google would be supporting Docker as its primary internal container format. Rather than just being good PR for these companies, what this means for the Docker community is that a lot of money is starting to back the stability and success of the Docker platform.

Further building its influence, Docker's containers are becoming the common format among cloud providers, offering the potential for "write once, run anywhere" cloud applications. When Docker released their `libswarm` development library at DockerCon 2014, an engineer from Orchard demonstrated deploying a Docker container to a heterogeneous mix of cloud providers at the same time. This kind of orchestration has not been easy before, and it seems likely that as these major companies continue to invest in the platform, the support and tooling will improve correspondingly.

So that covers Docker containers and tooling, but what about OS vendor support and adoption? The Docker client runs directly on most major operating systems, but because the Docker server uses Linux containers, it does not run on non-Linux systems. Docker has traditionally been developed on the Ubuntu Linux distribution, but most Linux distributions and other major operating systems are now supported where possible.

When Docker was barely two years old, it already had broad support across many platforms. With the creation of The Open Container Initiative (*https://www.opencontainers.org/*) in June of 2015, there is a lot of hope for a well-developed indsutry standard for containers and Docker's continued growth into the future.

Architecture

Docker is a powerful technology, and that often means something that comes with a high level of complexity. But the fundamental architecture of Docker is a simple client/server model, with only one executable that acts as both components, depending on how you invoke the `docker` command. Underneath this simple exterior, Docker heavily leverages kernel mechanisms such as iptables, virtual bridging, cgroups, namespaces, and various filesystem drivers. We'll talk about some of these in Chapter 10. For now, we'll go over how the client and server work and give a brief introduction to the network layer that sits underneath a Docker container.

Client/Server Model

Docker consists of at least two parts: the client and the server/daemon (see Figure 2-3). Optionally there is a third component called the registry, which stores Docker images and metadata about those images. The server does the ongoing work of running and managing your containers, and you use the client to tell the server what to do. The Docker daemon (*http://bit.ly/1Bttd5s*) can run on any number of servers in the infrastructure, and a single client can address any number of servers. Clients drive all of the communication, but Docker servers can talk directly to image registries when told to do so by the client. Clients are responsible for directing servers what to do, and servers focus on hosting containerized applications.

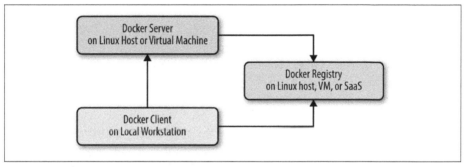

Figure 2-3. Docker client/server model

Docker is a little different in structure from some other client/server software. Instead of having separate client and server executables, it uses the same binary for both components. When you install Docker, you get both components, but the server will only launch on a supported Linux host. Launching the Docker server/daemon is as simple as running docker with the -d command-line argument, which tells it to act like a daemon and listen for incoming connections. Each Docker host will normally have one Docker daemon running that can manage a number of containers. You can then use the docker command-line tool client to talk to the server.

Network Ports and Unix Sockets

The docker command-line tool and docker -d daemon talk to each other over network sockets. You can choose to have the Docker daemon listen on one or more TCP or Unix sockets. It's possible, for example, to have Docker listen on both a local Unix socket and two different TCP ports (encrypted and nonencrypted). On many Linux distributions, that is actually the default. If you want to only be able to access Docker from the local system, listening only on the Unix socket would be the most secure option. However, most people want to talk to the docker daemon remotely, so it usually listens on at least one TCP port.

The original TCP port that docker was configured to use was 4243, but that port was never registered and in fact was already used by other tools such as the Mac OS X backup client CrashPlan. As a result, Docker registered its own TCP port with IANA and it's now generally configured to use TCP port 2375 when running un-encrypted, or 2376 when handling encrypted traffic.

In Docker 1.3 and later, the default is to use the encrypted port on 2376, but this is easily configurable. The Unix socket is located in different paths on different operating systems, so you should check where yours is located. If you have strong preferences, you can usually specify this at install time. If you don't, then the defaults will probably work for you.

Robust Tooling

Among the many things that have led to Docker's growing adoption is its simple and powerful tooling. This has been expanding ever wider since its initial release by Docker, and by the Docker community at large. The tooling that Docker ships with supports both building Docker images and basic deployment to individual Docker daemons, as well as all the functionality needed to actually manage a remote Docker server. Community efforts have focused on managing whole fleets (or clusters) of Docker servers and the scheduling and orchestrating of container deployments. Docker has also launched its own orchestration toolset, including Compose (*https://github.com/docker/compose*) (previously known as Fig), Machine (*https://github.com/docker/machine*), and Swarm (*https://github.com/docker/swarm/*), which promises to eventually create a cohesive deployment story across environments.

Because Docker provides both a command-line tool and a remote web API, it is easy to add additional tooling in any language. The command-line tool lends itself well to scripting, and a lot of power can easily be leveraged with simple shell script wrappers around the command-line tool.

Docker Command-Line Tool

The command-line tool docker is the main interface that most people will have with Docker. This is a Go program (*https://golang.org*) that compiles and runs on all common architectures and operating systems. The command-line tool is available as part of the main Docker distribution on various platforms and also compiles directly from the Go source. Some of the things you can do with the Docker command-line tool include, but are not limited to:

- Build a container image.
- Pull images from a registry to a Docker daemon or push them up to a registry from the Docker daemon.
- Start a container on a Docker server either in the foreground or background.

- Retrieve the Docker logs from a remote server.
- Start a command-line shell inside a running container on a remote server.

You can probably see how these can be composed into a workflow for building and deploying. But the Docker command-line tool is not the only way to interact with Docker, and it's not necessarily the most powerful.

Application Programming Interface (API)

Like many other pieces of modern software, the Docker daemon has a remote API. This is in fact what the Docker command-line tool uses to communicate with the daemon. But because the API is documented and public, it's quite common for external tooling to use the API directly. This enables all manners of tooling, from mapping deployed Docker containers to servers, to automated deployments, to distributed schedulers. While it's very likely that beginners will not initially want to talk directly to the Docker API, it's a great tool to have available. As your organization embraces Docker over time, it's likely that you will increasingly find the API to be a good integration point for this tooling.

Extensive documentation for the API (*https://docs.docker.com/reference/api/docker_remote_api/*) is on the Docker site. As the ecosystem has matured, robust implementations of Docker API libraries (*https://docs.docker.com/reference/api/remote_api_client_libraries/*) have begun to appear for many popular languages. We've used the Go and Ruby libraries, for example, and have found them to be both robust and rapidly updated as new versions of Docker are released.

Most of the things you can do with the Docker command-line tooling is supported relatively easily via the API. Two notable exceptions are the endpoints that require streaming or terminal access: running remote shells or executing the container in interactive mode. In these cases, it's often easier to use the command-line tool.

Container Networking

Even though Docker containers are largely made up of processes running on the host system itself, they behave quite differently from other processes at the network layer. If you think of each of your Docker containers as behaving on the network like a host on a private network, you'll be on the right path. The Docker server acts as a virtual bridge and the containers are clients behind it. A bridge is just a network device that repeats traffic from one side to another. So you can think of it like a mini virtual network with hosts attached.

The implementation is that each container has its own virtual Ethernet interface connected to the Docker bridge and its own IP address allocated to the virtual interface. Docker lets you bind ports on the host to the container so that the outside world can reach your container. That traffic passes over a proxy that is also part of the Docker daemon before getting to the container. See Chapter 10 for more detailed information.

Docker allocates the private subnet from an unused RFC 1918 (*https:// tools.ietf.org/html/rfc1918*) private subnet block. It detects which network blocks are unused on startup and allocates one to the virtual network. That is bridged to the host's local network through an interface on the server called docker0. This means that all of the containers are on a network together and can talk to each other directly. But to get to the host or the outside world, they go over the docker0 virtual bridge interface. As we mentioned, inbound traffic goes over the proxy. This proxy is fairly high performance but can be limiting if you run high throughput applications in containers. We talk more about this as well as other networking topics in Chapter 10, and offer some solutions.

There is a dizzying array of ways in which you can configure Docker's network layer, from allocating your own network blocks to configuring your own custom bridge interface. People often run with the default mechanisms, but there are times when something more complex or specific to your application is required. You can find much more detail about Docker networking in its documentation (*https://docs.docker.com/articles/networking/*), and we will cover more details about networking in the Advanced Topics chapter.

 When developing your Docker workflow, you should definitely get started with the default networking approach. You might later find that you don't want or need this default virtual network. You can disable all of this with a single switch at docker daemon startup time. It's not configurable per container, but you can turn it off for all containers using the --net host switch to docker -d. When running in that mode, Docker containers just use the host's own network devices and address.

Getting the Most from Docker

Like most tools, Docker has a number of great use cases, and others that aren't so good. You can, for example, open a glass jar with a hammer. But that has its downsides. Understanding how to best use the tool, or even simply determining if it's the right tool, can get you on the correct path much more quickly.

To begin with, Docker's architecture aims it squarely at applications that are either stateless or where the state is externalized into data stores like databases or caches. It enforces some good development principles for this class of application and we'll talk later about how that's powerful. But this means that doing things like putting a database engine inside Docker is basically like trying to swim against the current. It's not that you can't do it, or even that you shouldn't do it;

it's just that this is not the most obvious use case for Docker and if it's the one you start with, you may find yourself disappointed early on. Some good applications for Docker include web frontends, backend APIs, and short-running tasks, like maintenance scripts that might normally be handled by cron.

 Most traditional applications are stateful, which means that they keep track of important data in memory, files, or a database. If you restart a stateful service, you may lose any of the information that isn't written out of memory. Stateless applications, on the other hand, are normally designed to immediately answer a single self-contained request, and have no need to track information between requests from one or more clients.

If you focus first on building an understanding of running stateless or externalized-state applications inside containers, you will have a foundation on which to start considering other use cases. We strongly recommend starting with stateless applications and learning from that experience before tackling other use cases. It should be noted that the community is working hard on how to better support stateful applications in Docker, and there are likely to be many developments in this area over the next year or more.

Containers Are Not Virtual Machines

A good way to start shaping your understanding of how to leverage Docker is to think of containers not as virtual machines, but as very lightweight wrappers around a single Unix process. During actual implementation, that process might spawn others, but on the other hand, one statically compiled binary could be all that's inside your container (see "Outside Dependencies" on page 119 for more information). Containers are also ephemeral: they may come and go much more readily than a virtual machine.

Virtual machines are by design a stand-in for real hardware that you might throw in a rack and leave there for a few years. Because a real server is what they're abstracting, virtual machines are often long-lived in nature. Even in the cloud where companies often spin virtual machines up and down on demand, they usually have a running lifespan of days or more. On the other hand, a particular container might exist for months, or it may be created, run a task for a minute, and then be destroyed. All of that is OK, but it's a fundamentally different approach than virtual machines are typically used for.

Containers Are Lightweight

We'll get more into the details of how this works later, but creating a container takes very little space. A quick test on Docker 1.4.1 reveals that a newly created container from an existing image takes a whopping 12 kilobytes of disk space.

That's pretty lightweight. On the other hand, a new virtual machine created from a golden image might require hundreds or thousands of megabytes. The new container is so small because it is just a reference to a layered filesystem image and some metadata about the configuration.

The lightness of containers means that you can use them for things where creating another virtual machine would be too heavyweight, or in situations where you need something to be truly ephemeral. You probably wouldn't, for instance, spin up an entire virtual machine to run a curl command to a website from a remote location, but you might spin up a new container for this purpose.

Towards an Immutable Infrastructure

By deploying most of your applications within containers, it is possible to start simplifying your configuration management story by moving towards an immutable infrastructure. The idea of an immutable infrastructure has recently gained popularity in response to how difficult it is, in reality, to maintain a truly idempotent configuration management code base. As your configuration management code base grows, it can become as unwieldy and unmaintainable as large, monolithic legacy applications. With Docker it is possible to deploy a very lightweight Docker server that needs almost no configuration management, or in many cases, none at all. All of your application management is simply handled by deploying and redeploying containers to the server. When the server needs an important update to something like the Docker daemon or the Linux kernel, you can simply bring up a new server with the changes, deploy your containers there, and then decommission or reinstall the old server.

Limited Isolation

Containers are isolated from each other, but it's probably more limited than you might expect. While you can put limits on their resources, the default container configuration just has them all sharing CPU and memory on the host system, much as you would expect from colocated Unix processes. This means that unless you constrain them, containers can compete for resources on your production machines. That is sometimes what you want, but it impacts your design decisions. Limits on CPU and memory use are possible through Docker but, in most cases, they are not the default like they would be from a virtual machine.

It's often the case that many containers share one or more common filesystem layers. That's one of the more powerful design decisions in Docker, but it also means that if you update a shared image, you'll need to re-create a number of containers.

Containerized processes are also just processes on the Docker server itself. They are running on the same exact instance of the Linux kernel as the host operating system. They even show up in the ps output on the Docker server. That is utterly different from a hypervisor where the depth of process isolation usually includes running an entirely separate instance of the operating system for each virtual machine.

This light default containment can lead to the tempting option of exposing more resources from the host, such as shared filesystems to allow the storage of state. But you should think hard before further exposing resources from the host into the container unless they are used exclusively by the container. We'll talk about security of containers later, but generally you might consider helping to enforce isolation further through the application of SELinux or AppArmor policies rather than compromising the existing barriers.

 By default, many containers use UID 0 to launch processes. Because the container is *contained*, this seems safe, but in reality it isn't. Because everything is running on the same kernel, many types of security vulnerabilities or simple misconfiguration can give the container's *root* user unauthorized access to the host's system resources, files, and processes.

Stateless Applications

A good example of the kind of application that containerizes well is a web application that keeps its state in a database. You might also run something like ephemeral memcache instances in containers. If you think about your web application, though, it probably has local state that you rely on, like configuration files. That might not seem like a lot of state, but it means that you've limited the reusability of your container, and made it more challenging to deploy into different environments, without maintaining configuration data in your codebase.

In many cases, the process of containerizing your application means that you move configuration state into environment variables that can be passed to your application from the container. This allows you to easily do things like use the same container to run in either production or staging environments. In most companies, those environments would require many different configuration settings, from the names of databases to the hostnames of other service dependencies.

With containers, you might also find that you are always decreasing the size of your containerized application as you optimize it down to the bare essentials required to run. We have found that thinking of anything that you need to run in a distributed way as a container can lead to some interesting design decisions. If, for example, you have a service that collects some data, processes it, and returns the result, you might configure containers on many servers to run the job and then aggregate the response on another container.

Externalizing State

If Docker works best for stateless applications, how do you best store state when you need to? Configuration is best passed by environment variables, for example. Docker supports environment variables natively, and they are stored in the metadata that makes up a container configuration. This means that restarting the container will ensure that the same configuration is passed to your application each time.

Databases are often where scaled applications store state, and nothing in Docker interferes with doing that for containerized applications. Applications that need to store files, however, face some challenges. Storing things to the container's filesystem will not perform well, will be extremely limited by space, and will not preserve state across a container lifecycle. Applications that need to store filesystem state should be considered carefully before putting them into Docker. If you decide that you can benefit from Docker in these cases, it's best to design a solution where the state can be stored in a centralized location that could be accessed regardless of which host a container runs on. In certain cases, this might mean a service like Amazon S3, RiakCS, OpenStack Swift, a local block store, or even mounting iSCSI disks inside the container.

 Although it is possible to externalize state on an attached filesystem, it is not generally encouraged by the community, and should be considered an advanced use case. It is strongly recommended that you start with applications that don't need persistent state. There are multiple reasons why this is generally discouraged, but in almost all cases it is because it introduces dependencies between the container and the host that interfere with using Docker as a truly dynamic, horizontally scalable application delivery service. If your container relies on an attached filesystem, it can only be deployed to the system that contains this filesystem.

The Docker Workflow

Like many tools, Docker strongly encourages a particular workflow. It's a very enabling workflow that maps well to how many companies are organized, but it's probably a little different than what you or your team are doing now. Having adapted our own organization's workflow to the Docker approach, we can confidently say that this change is a benefit that touches many teams in the organization. If the workflow is implemented well, it can really help realize the promise of reduced communication overhead between teams.

Revision Control

The first thing that Docker gives you out of the box is two forms of revision control. One is used to track the filesystem layers that images are made up of, and the other is a tagging systems for built containers.

Filesystem layers

Docker containers are made up of stacked filesystem layers, each identified by a unique hash, where each new set of changes made during the build process is laid on top of the previous changes. That's great because it means that when you do a new build, you only have to rebuild the layers that include and build upon the change you're deploying. This saves time and bandwidth because containers are shipped around as layers and you don't have to ship layers that a server already has stored. If you've done deployments with many classic deployment tools, you know that you can end up shipping hundreds of megabytes of the same data to a server over and over at each deployment. That's slow, and worse, you can't really be sure exactly what changed between deployments. Because of the layering effect, and because Docker containers include all of the application dependencies, you can be quite sure where the changes happened.

To simplify this a bit, remember that a Docker image contains everything required to run your application. If you change one line of code, you certainly don't want to waste time rebuilding every dependency your code requires into a new image. Instead, Docker will use as many base layers as it can so that only the layers affected by the code change are rebuilt.

Image tags

The second kind of revision control offered by Docker is one that makes it easy to answer an important question: what was the previous version of the application that was deployed? That's not always easy to answer. There are a lot of solutions for non-Dockerized applications, from git tags for each release, to deployment logs, to tagged builds for deployment, and many more. If you're coordinating your deployment with Capistrano, for example, it will handle this for you by keeping a set number of previous releases on the server and then using symlinks to make one of them the current release.

But what you find in any scaled production environment is that each application has a unique way of handling deployment revisions. Or many do the same thing and one is different. Worse, in heterogeneous language environments, the deployment tools are often entirely different between applications and very little is shared. So the question of "What was the previous version?" can have many answers depending on whom you ask and about which application. Docker has a built-in mechanism for handling this: it provides image tagging at deployment time. You can leave multiple revisions of your application on the server and just tag them at release. This is not rocket science, and it's not functionality that is hard to find in other deployment tooling, as we mention. But it can easily be made standard across all of your applications, and everyone can have the same expectations about how things will be tagged for all applications.

 In many examples on the Internet and in this book, you will see people use the latest tag. This is useful when getting started and when writing examples, as it will always grab the most recent version of a image. But since this is a floating tag, it is a bad idea to use latest in most workflows, as your dependencies can get updated out from under you, and it is impossible to roll back to latest because the old version is no longer the one tagged latest.

Building

Building applications is a black art in many organizations, where a few people know all the levers to pull and knobs to turn in order to spit out a well-formed, shippable artifact. Part of the heavy cost of getting a new application deployed is getting the build right. Docker doesn't solve all the problems, but it does provide a standardized tool configuration and tool set for builds. That makes it a lot easier for people to learn to build your applications, and to get new builds up and running.

The Docker command-line tool contains a build flag that will consume a Dockerfile and produce a Docker image. Each command in a Dockerfile generates a new layer in the image, so it's easy to reason about what the build is going to do by looking at the Dockerfile itself. The great part of all of this standardization is that any engineer who has worked with a Dockerfile can dive right in and modify the build of any other application. Because the Docker image is a standardized artifact, all of the tooling behind the build will be the same regardless of the language being used, the OS distribution it's based on, or the number of layers needed.

Most Docker builds are a single invocation of the docker build command and generate a single artifact, the container image. Because it's usually the case that most of the logic about the build is wholly contained in the Dockerfile, it's easy to create standard build jobs for any team to use in build systems like Jenkins (*http://jenkins-ci.org*). As a further standardization of the build process, a few companies, including eBay, actually have standardized Docker containers to do the image builds from a Dockerfile.

Testing

While Docker itself does not include a built-in framework for testing, the way containers are built lends some advantages to testing with Docker containers.

Testing a production application can take many forms, from unit testing to full integration testing in a semi-live environment. Docker facilitates better testing by guaranteeing that the artifact that passed testing will be the one that ships to production. This can be guaranteed because we can either use the Docker SHA for the container, or a custom tag to make sure we're consistently shipping the same version of the application.

The second part of the testing story is that all testing that is run against the container will automatically include testing the application with all of the dependencies that it will ship with. If a unit test framework says tests were successful against a container image, you can be sure that you will not experience a problem with the versioning of an underlying library at deployment time, for example. That's not easy with most other technologies, and even Java WAR files, for example, don't include testing of the application server itself. That same Java application deployed in a Docker container will generally also include the application server, and the whole stack can be smoke tested before shipping to production.

A secondary benefit of shipping applications in Docker containers is that in places where there are multiple applications that talk to each other remotely via something like an API, developers of one application can easily develop against a version of the other service that is currently tagged for the environment they require, like production or staging. Developers on each team don't have to be experts in how the other service works or is deployed, just to do development on their own application. If you expand this to a service-oriented architecture with innumerable microservices, Docker containers can be a real lifeline to developers or QA engineers who need to wade into the swamp of inter-microservice API calls.

Packaging

Docker produces what for all intents and purposes is a single artifact from each build. No matter which language your application is written in, or which distribution of Linux you run it on, you get a multilayered Docker image as the result of your build. And it is all built and handled by the Docker tooling. That's the shipping container metaphor that Docker is named for: a single, transportable unit that universal tooling can handle, regardless of what it contains. Like the container port, or multimodal shipping hub, your Docker tooling will only ever have to deal with one kind of package: the Docker image. That's powerful because it's a huge facilitator of tooling reuse between applications, and it means that someone else's off-the-shelf tools will work with your build images. Applications that traditionally take a lot of custom configuration to deploy onto a new host or development system become incredibly portable with Docker. Once a container is built, it can easily be deployed on any system with a running Docker server.

Deploying

Deployments are handled by so many kinds of tools in different shops that it would be impossible to list them here. Some of these tools include shell scripting, Capistrano, Fabric, Ansible, or in-house custom tooling. In our experience with multi-team organizations, there are usually one or two people on each team who know the magic incantation to get deployments to work. When something goes wrong, the team is dependent on them to get it running again. As you probably expect by now, Docker makes most of that a nonissue. The built-in tooling supports a simple, one-line deployment strategy to get a build onto a host and up and running. The standard Docker client only handles deploying to a single host at a time, but there are other tools available that make it easy to deploy into a cluster of Docker hosts. Because of the standardization provided by Docker, your build can be deployed into any of these systems, with low complexity on the part of the development teams.

The Docker Ecosystem

There is a wide community forming around Docker, driven by both developers and system administrators. Like the DevOps movement, this has facilitated better tools by applying code to operations problems. Where there are gaps in the tooling provided by Docker, other companies and individuals have stepped up to the plate. Many of these tools are also open source. That means they are expandable and can be modified by any other company to fit their needs.

 Docker is a commercial company that has generously contributed much of the core Docker source code to the open source community. Companies are strongly encouraged to join the community and contribute back to the open source efforts. If you are looking for supported versions of the core Docker tools, you can find out more about their offerings at *https://www.docker.com/support*.

Orchestration

The first important category of tools that adds functionality to the core Docker distribution contains orchestration and mass deployment tools like Docker's Swarm (*https://github.com/docker/swarm/*), New Relic's Centurion (*https://github.com/newrelic/centurion/*) and Spotify's Helios (*https://github.com/spotify/helios*). All of these take a generally simple approach to orchestration. For more complex environments, Google's Kubernetes (*https://github.com/GoogleCloudPlatform/kubernetes*) and Apache Mesos (*http://mesos.apache.org*) are more powerful options. There are new tools shipping constantly as new adopters discover gaps and publish improvements.

Atomic hosts

One additional idea that can be leveraged to enhance your Docker experience is atomic hosts. Traditionally, servers and virtual machines are systems that an organization will carefully assemble, configure, and maintain to provide a wide variety of functionality that supports a broad range of usage patterns. Updates must often be applied via nonatomic operations, and there are many ways in which host configurations can diverge and introduce unexpected behavior into the system. Most running systems are patched and updated in place in today's world. Conversely, in the world of software deployments, most people deploy an entire copy of their application, rather than trying to apply patches to a running system. One of the appeals of containers is that they help make applications even more atomic than traditional deployment models.

What if you could extend that core container pattern all the way down into the operating system? Instead of relying on configuration management to try to update, patch, and coalesce changes to your OS components, what if you could simply pull down a new, thin OS image and reboot the server? And then if something breaks, easily roll back to the exact image you were previously using?

This is one of the core ideas behind Linux-based atomic host distributions, like CoreOS (*https://coreos.com*) and Project Atomic (*http://www.projectatomic.io*). Not only should you be able to easily tear down and redeploy your applications, but the same philosophy should apply for the whole software stack. This pattern helps provide incredible levels of consistency and resilience to the whole stack.

Some of the typical characteristics of an atomic host (*https://gist.github.com/jzb/0f336c6f23a0ba145b0a*) are a minimal footprint, a focused design towards supporting Linux containers and Docker, and providing atomic OS updates and rollbacks that can easily be controlled via multihost orchestration tools on both bare-metal and common virtualization platforms.

In Chapter 3, we will discuss how you can easily use atomic hosts in your development process. If you are also using atomic hosts as deployment targets, this process creates a previously unheard of amount of software stack symmetry between your development and production environments.

Additional tools

Additional categories include auditing, logging, network, mapping, and many other tools, the majority of which leverage the Docker API directly. Some of these tools and Docker-related features include CoreOS's flannel for Kubernetes; Weave, a virtual network for spanning containers across multiple Docker hosts;

and direct support for Docker logs in Mozilla's Heka (*https://github.com/mozilla-services/heka*) log router.

The results of the broad community that is rapidly evolving around Docker is anyone's guess, but it is likely that this support will only accelerate Docker's adoption and the development of robust tools that solve many of the problems that the community struggles with.

Wrap-Up

There you have it, a quick tour through Docker. We'll return to this discussion later on with a slightly deeper dive into the architecture of Docker, more examples of how to use the community tooling, and a deeper dive into some of the thinking behind designing robust container platforms. But you're probably itching to try it all out, so in the next chapter we'll get Docker installed and running.

## CHAPTER 3

Installing Docker

The steps required to install Docker vary depending on the primary platform you use for development and the Linux distribution that you use to host your applications in production. Since Docker is a technology built around Linux containers, people developing on non-Linux platforms will need to use some form of virtual machine or remote server for many parts of the process.

In this chapter, we discuss the steps required to get a fully working Docker development environment set up on most modern desktop operating systems. First we'll install the Docker client on your native development platform, then we'll get a Docker server running on Linux. Finally we'll test out the installation to make sure it works as expected.

Although the Docker client can run on Windows and Mac OS X to control a Docker Server, Docker containers can only be built and launched on Linux. Therefore, non-Linux systems will require a virtual machine or remote server to host the Linux-based Docker server.

Important Terminology

Below are a few terms that we will continue to use throughout the book and whose meanings you should become familiar with.

Docker client
> The docker command used to control most of the Docker workflow and talk to remote Docker servers.

Docker server
> The docker command run in daemon mode. This turns a Linux system into a Docker server that can have containers deployed, launched, and torn down via a remote client.

Docker images

Docker images consist of one or more filesystem layers and some important metadata that represent all the files required to run a Dockerized application. A single Docker image can be copied to numerous hosts. A container will typically have both a name and a tag. The tag is generally used to identify a particular release of an image.

Docker container

A Docker container is a Linux container that has been instantiated from a Docker image. A specific container can only exist once; however, you can easily create multiple containers from the same image.

Atomic host

An atomic host is a small, finely tuned operating system image, like CoreOS and Project Atomic, that supports container hosting and atomic OS upgrades.

The Docker ecosystem is changing very rapidly as the technology evolves to become more robust and solve a broader range of problems. Some features discussed in this book and elsewhere may become deprecated. To see what has been tagged for deprecation and eventual removal, visit this URL: *https:// docs.docker.com/engine/misc/deprecated/.*

Docker Client

The Docker client natively supports 64-bit versions of Linux and Mac OS X due to the Unix underpinnings of both operating systems. There have been reports of people getting Docker to run on 32-bit systems, but it is not currently supported.

The majority of popular Linux distributions can trace their origins to either Debian or Red Hat. Debian systems utilize the deb package format and Advanced Package Tool (apt) (*http://bit.ly/1Btzr5o*) to install most prepackaged software. On the other hand, Red Hat systems rely on rpm (Red Hat Package Manager) files and Yellowdog Updater, Modified (yum) (*http://red.ht/1AAMUZW*) to install similar software packages.

On Mac OS X and Microsoft Windows, native GUI installers provide the easiest method to install and maintain prepackaged software. On Mac OS X, Homebrew (*http://brew.sh*) is also a very popular option among technical users.

To develop with Docker on non-Linux platforms, you will need to leverage virtual machines or remote Linux hosts to provide a Docker server. Docker Machine, Boot2Docker, and Vagrant, which are discussed later in this chapter, provide some approaches to solving this issue.

Linux

It is strongly recommended that you run Docker on a modern release of your preferred Linux distribution. It is possible to run Docker on some older releases, but stability may be a significant issue. Generally a 3.8 or later kernel is required, and we advise you to use the newest stable version of your chosen distribution. The directions below assume you are using a recent, stable release.

Ubuntu Linux 14.04 (64-bit)

To install Docker on a current installation, run the following commands:

```
$ sudo apt-key adv \
  --keyserver hkp://p80.pool.sks-keyservers.net:80 \
  --recv-keys 58118E89F3A912897C070ADBF76221572C52609D
```

Next you will need to add the correct apt respository into your sources list.

```
$ sudo vim /etc/apt/sources.list.d/docker.list
```

Delete everything in /etc/apt/sources.list.d/docker.list and replace it with a single line from the list below, based on the version of Ubuntu that you are using:

```
# Debian Wheezy
deb https://apt.dockerproject.org/repo debian-wheezy main

# Debian Jessie
deb https://apt.dockerproject.org/repo debian-jessie main

# Debian Stretch/Sid
deb https://apt.dockerproject.org/repo debian-stretch main

# Ubuntu Precise
deb https://apt.dockerproject.org/repo ubuntu-precise main

# Ubuntu Trusty
deb https://apt.dockerproject.org/repo ubuntu-trusty main

# Ubuntu Utopic
deb https://apt.dockerproject.org/repo ubuntu-utopic main

# Ubuntu Vivid
deb https://apt.dockerproject.org/repo ubuntu-vivid main

# Ubuntu Wily
deb https://apt.dockerproject.org/repo ubuntu-wily main
```

Then run the following commands to install Docker.

```
$ sudo apt-get update
$ sudo apt-get purge lxc-docker* docker.io*  # Remove obsolete versions
$ sudo apt-get install docker-engine
```

Fedora Linux 21 (64-bit)

To install the correct Docker packages on your system, run the following command:

```
$ curl -sSL https://get.docker.com/ | sh
```

The easiest way to install the Docker Yum repositories on Red Hat–based systems is to use the script provided by Docker. Security-conscious people will however, prefer to create the repo file by hand.

 It is never a great idea to run a script from the Internet and pipe it into a shell. Even if it comes from a trusted source, sites get compromised frequently. If you are going to use this method, at least download the script and read it before piping it into a shell.

To create the required file by hand for Fedora 21, you would do the following:

```
cat >/etc/yum.repos.d/docker.repo <<-EOF
[dockerrepo]
name=Docker Repository
baseurl=https://yum.dockerproject.org/repo/main/fedora/21
enabled=1
gpgcheck=1
gpgkey=https://yum.dockerproject.org/gpg
EOF
```

If you are running another recent Red Hat–based distribution, you can replace the URL above with the correct entry from this list:

```
CentOS 6 & RHEL 6: https://yum.dockerproject.org/repo/main/centos/6

CentOS 7 & RHEL 7: https://yum.dockerproject.org/repo/main/centos/7

Fedora 20: https://yum.dockerproject.org/repo/main/fedora/20

Fedora 21: https://yum.dockerproject.org/repo/main/fedora/21

Fedora 22: https://yum.dockerproject.org/repo/main/fedora/22
```

Now you can install the current Docker release.

```
$ sudo yum erase docker* # Remove obsolete versions
$ sudo yum install docker-engine
```

 If you get a *Cannot start container* error, try running `sudo yum upgrade selinux-policy` and then reboot your system.

Older Fedora releases have a pre-existing package called docker, which is a KDE and GNOME2 system tray replacement docking application for WidowMaker. In newer versions of Fedora, this package has been renamed to wmdocker.

Mac OS X 10.10

To install Docker Machine on Mac OS X, you can use any one of the following methods, depending on your preferences and needs:

- GUI Installer
- Homebrew

New users may want to stick with the GUI installer for simplicity.

GUI installer

Download the latest Docker Toolbox installer (*https://goo.gl/39gmgE*) and then double-click on the downloaded program icon. Follow all of the installer prompts until the installation is finished.

On Mac OS X, the Docker Toolbox includes Docker Client, Machine, Compose, and Kitematic.

You will also need to download and install VirtualBox (*https://goo.gl/l3wrf*), which Mac OS X requires to launch Linux virtual machines that can build Docker images and run containers.

Homebrew installation

To install using the popular Homebrew package management system for Mac OS X, you must first install Homebrew. The Homebrew project suggests installing the software with the following command:

```
$ ruby -e \
"$(curl -fsSL \
https://raw.githubusercontent.com/Homebrew/install/master/install)"
```

Running random scripts from the Internet on your system is not considered wise. It is unlikely that this script has been altered in a malicious manner, but a wise soul would read through the script (*http://bit.ly/1LoavHJ*) first, or consider an alternative installation option (*http://bit.ly/1evu0PP*).

If you already have Homebrew installed on your system, you should update it and all the installed formulas by running:

```
$ brew update
```

To install VirtualBox via Homebrew, you need to add support for an additional Homebrew repository that contains many GUI and large binary applications for Mac OS X. This can be done with one simple command:

```
$ brew install caskroom/cask/brew-cask
```

You can find more information about Homebrew Casks at *cask-room.io*.

Now that you have Homebrew and Cask installed and the newest software formulas have been downloaded, you can install VirtualBox with the following command:

```
$ brew cask install virtualbox
```

And then installing Docker is as simple as running:

```
$ brew install docker
$ brew install docker-machine
```

Microsoft Windows 8

Download the latest Docker Toolbox installer (*https://goo.gl/39gmgE*) and then double-click on the downloaded program icon. Follow all of the installer prompts until the installation is finished.

On Windows, the Docker Toolbox includes Docker Client, Machine, and Compose.

You will also need to download and install VirtualBox (*https://goo.gl/l3wrf*), which Mac OS X requires to launch Linux virtual machines that can build Docker images and run containers.

Installation directions for additional operating systems can be found at docs.docker.com (*https://docs.docker.com/installation/*).

Docker Server

The Docker server is integrated into the same binary that you use as the client. It's not obvious that it's the same when you install it because all of the Linux init systems shield you from the command that is actually invoked to run the daemon. So it's useful to see that running the Docker daemon manually on a Linux system is a simple as typing something like this:

```
$ sudo docker daemon -H unix:///var/run/docker.sock -H tcp://0.0.0.0:2375
```

> In older versions of Docker, the server was started with `docker -d` or `docker --daemon`.

This command tells Docker to start in daemon mode (`-d`), create and listen to a Unix domain socket (`-H unix:///var/run/docker.sock`), and bind to all system IP addresses using the default unencrypted traffic port for docker (`-H tcp:// 0.0.0.0:2375`).

> If you already have Docker running, manually executing the daemon again, will fail because it can't use the same ports twice.

Of course, you're not likely to have to do this yourself. But that's what going on behind the scene. On non-Linux systems, you will need to set up a Linux-based virtual machine to host the Docker server.

Systemd-Based Linux

Current Fedora releases utilize `systemd` (*http://bit.ly/1Gj3KQT*) to manage processes on the system. Because you have already installed Docker, you can ensure that the server starts every time you boot the system by typing:

```
$ sudo systemctl enable docker
```

This tells systemd to enable the docker service and start it when the system boots or switches into the default runlevel.

To start the `docker` server, type the following:

```
$ sudo systemctl start docker
```

Upstart-Based Linux

Ubuntu uses the `upstart` (*http://upstart.ubuntu.com*) init daemon, although future versions are very likely going to be converting to `systemd`. Upstart replaces the traditional Unix init system with an event-driven model and supports vastly simplified init scripts, sometimes only a few lines long.

To enable the `docker` server to start when the system boots, type:

```
$ sudo update-rc.d docker.io defaults
```

To start the service immediately, you can use:

```
$ service docker.io start
```

init.d-Based Linux

Many Linux distributions used on production servers are still using a more tradi-tional init.d (*http://en.wikipedia.org/wiki/Init*) system. If you are running some-thing based on the Red Hat 6 ecosystem, among others, then you can likely use commands similar to the following to control when the docker server runs.

Enable the Docker service at boot with:

```
$ chkconfig docker on
```

Start the Docker service immediately:

```
$ service docker start
```

or:

```
$ /etc/init.d/docker start
```

Non-Linux VM-Based Server

If you are using Microsoft Windows or Mac OS X in your Docker workflow, you will need something like VirtualBox and Docker Machine, so that you can set up a Docker server for testing. These tools allow you to boot a Linux virtual machine on your local system. We'll focus on Docker Machine because it's more universal than other tools.

In addition to Docker Machine, it is also possible to use other tools to set up the Docker server, depending on your preferences and needs.

- Vagrant (*https://www.vagrantup.com/*)
- Manually maintained virtual machines
- Kitematic (*https://kitematic.com/*)
- Boot2Docker (*http://boot2docker.io/*)

Docker Machine

In early 2015, Docker announced the beta release of Docker Machine (*https:// github.com/docker/machine*), a tool that makes it much easier to set up Docker hosts on bare-metal, cloud, and virtual machine platforms.

The easiest way to install Docker Machine is to visit the GitHub releases page (*https://github.com/docker/machine/releases*) and download the correct binary for your operating system and architecture. Currently, there are variants for 32- and 64-bit versions of Linux, Windows, and Mac OS X.

For these demonstrations, you will also need to have a recent release of a hypervisor, like VirtualBox (*https://www.virtualbox.org/wiki/Downloads*), installed on your system.

For this section, you will use a Unix-based system with VirtualBox for the examples.

First, you need to download and install the `docker-machine` executable. The example below downloads v0.6.0, but you can determine the current release on GitHub (*https://github.com/docker/machine/releases/*).

```
$ mkdir ~/bin
$ curl -L https://github.com/docker/machine/releases/\
download/v0.6.0/docker-machine-`uname -s`-`uname -m` \
> ~/bin/docker-machine
$ export PATH=${PATH}:~/bin
$ chmod u+rx ~/bin/docker-machine
```

 We've had to line-wrap the URL to fit the format of this book. If you have trouble running that in your shell as-is, try removing the backslashes and joining it into one line without any spaces in the URL.

Once you have the `docker-machine` executable in your path, you can start to use it to set up Docker hosts. Here we've just put it temporarily into your path. If you want to keep running it in the future, you'll want to add it to your `.profile` or `.bash_profile` file. Now that we can run the tool, the next thing that you need to do is create a named Docker machine. You can do this using the `docker-machine create` command:

```
$ docker-machine create --driver virtualbox local
Running pre-create checks...
(local) ... Boot2Docker ISO is out-of-date, downloading the latest release...
(local) Latest release for github.com/boot2docker/boot2docker is v1.10.1
(local) Downloading ...boot2docker.iso from ...github.../boot2docker.iso...
(local) 0%...10%...20%...30%...40%...50%...60%...70%...80%...90%...100%
Creating machine...
(local) Copying .../cache/boot2docker.iso to .../local/boot2docker.iso...
(local) Creating VirtualBox VM...
(local) Creating SSH key...
(local) Starting the VM...
(local) Check network to re-create if needed...
(local) Waiting for an IP...
Waiting for machine to be running, this may take a few minutes...
Detecting operating system of created instance...
Waiting for SSH to be available...
Detecting the provisioner...
```

```
Provisioning with boot2docker...
Copying certs to the local machine directory...
Copying certs to the remote machine...
Setting Docker configuration on the remote daemon...
Checking connection to Docker...
Docker is up and running!
To see how to connect your Docker Client to the Docker Engine
    running on this virtual machine, run: docker-machine env local
```

 If you already have a docker-machine VM created, you can simply start it with the command: `docker-machine start local`.

This downloads a Boot2Docker image and then creates a VirtualBox virtual machine that you can use as a Docker host. If you look at the output from the `create` command, you will see that it instructs you to run the following command:

```
$ eval $(docker-machine env local)
```

This command has no output, so what does it do exactly? If you run it without `eval` and the surrounding `$()`, you will see that it sets a couple of environment variables in our current shell that tell the Docker client where to find the Docker server:

```
$ docker-machine env local
export DOCKER_TLS_VERIFY="1"
export DOCKER_HOST="tcp://172.17.42.10:2376"
export DOCKER_CERT_PATH="/Users/me/.docker/machine/machines/local"
export DOCKER_MACHINE_NAME="local"
# Run this command to configure your shell:
# eval $(docker-machine env local)
```

And now if you want to confirm what machines you have running, you can use the following command:

```
$ docker-machine ls
NAME   ACTIVE DRIVER      STATE    URL                       SWARM DOCKER   ERRORS
local *        virtualbox Running tcp://172.17.42.10:2376          v1.10.1
```

This tells you that you have one machine, named local, that is active and running.

Now you can pass commands to the new Docker machine by leveraging the regular `docker` command, since you have set the proper environment variables. If you did not want to set these environment variables, you could also use the `docker` and `docker-machine` commands in conjunction with one another, like so:

```
$ docker $(docker-machine config local) ps
CONTAINER ID  IMAGE  COMMAND  CREATED  STATUS  PORTS  NAMES
```

This command embeds the output from docker-machine into the middle of the docker command. If you run the docker-machine on its own, you can see what it is adding to the docker command:

```
$ docker-machine config local
--tlsverify
--tlscacert="/Users/me/.docker/machine/certs/ca.pem"
--tlscert="/Users/me/.docker/machine/certs/cert.pem"
--tlskey="/Users/me/.docker/machine/certs/key.pem"
-H=tcp://172.17.42.10:2376
```

Although you can see the Docker host's IP address in the output, you can ask for it explicitly with the following command:

```
$ docker-machine ip local
172.17.42.10
```

If you want to log in to the system, you can easily do this by running:

```
$ docker-machine ssh local
```

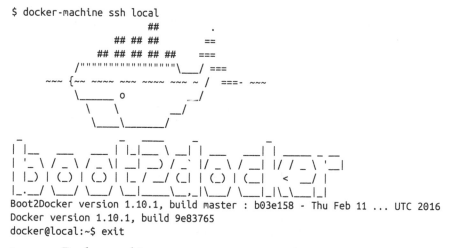

```
Boot2Docker version 1.10.1, build master : b03e158 - Thu Feb 11 ... UTC 2016
Docker version 1.10.1, build 9e83765
docker@local:~$ exit
```

To stop your Docker machine, you can run:

```
$ docker-machine stop local
```

And then you can run this to restart it (you need it to be running):

```
$ docker-machine start local
Stopping "local"...
Machine "local" was stopped.
```

> Some of the documentation states that if you run docker-machine stop without specifying a machine name, the command will execute on the active machine as identified in the output of docker-machine ls. This does not seem to actually be the case with all releases of docker-machine.

If you want to explore the other options that docker-machine provides, you can simply run docker-machine without any other options to see the command help.

Boot2Docker

 Boot2Docker was officially deprecated by Docker with the release of Docker 1.8, and replaced with Docker Machine. It is still documented here, as some people prefer to use Boot2Docker for simple local development workflows. It is currently community-maintained, and new ISO images for the VM have been released.

To install Boot2Docker, download the version for your operating system from bbot2docker.io (*http://boot2docker.io/*) and run the installer, following all the prompts.

Once you have Boot2Docker installed you will need to initialize Boot2Docker and download the required boot image. You can do this, by running the following command the first time you use Boot2Docker. You should see output similar to what is displayed below.

```
$ boot2docker init

WARNING: The 'boot2docker' command line interface (not to be confused with
'boot2docker' the operating system) is officially deprecated.

Please switch to Docker Machine (https://docs.docker.com/machine/) ASAP.

Docker Toolbox (https://docker.com/toolbox) is the recommended ... method.

Latest release for github.com/boot2docker/boot2docker is v1.10.1
Downloading boot2docker ISO image...
Success: downloaded https://.../releases/download/v1.10.1/boot2docker.iso
    to /Users/me/.boot2docker/boot2docker.iso
Initialization of virtual machine "boot2docker-vm" complete.
Use `boot2docker up` to start it.
```

Now you can start up a virtual machine with a running Docker daemon. By default, Boot2Docker will map port 2376 on your local host to the secure Docker port 2376 on the virtual machine to make it easier to interact with the Docker server from your local system.

```
$ boot2docker up

WARNING: The 'boot2docker' command line interface (not to be confused with
'boot2docker' the operating system) is officially deprecated.

Please switch to Docker Machine (https://docs.docker.com/machine/) ASAP.

Docker Toolbox (https://docker.com/toolbox) is the recommended ... method.
```

```
Waiting for VM and Docker daemon to start...
........................oooooooooooo
Started.
Writing /Users/me/.boot2docker/certs/boot2docker-vm/ca.pem
Writing /Users/me/.boot2docker/certs/boot2docker-vm/cert.pem
Writing /Users/me/.boot2docker/certs/boot2docker-vm/key.pem

To connect the Docker client to the Docker daemon, please set:
    export DOCKER_HOST=tcp://172.17.42.10:2376
    export DOCKER_CERT_PATH=/Users/me/.boot2docker/certs/boot2docker-vm
    export DOCKER_TLS_VERIFY=1

Or run: `eval "$(boot2docker shellinit)"`
```

To set up your shell environment so that you can easily use your local Docker client to talk to the Docker daemon on your virtual machine, you can run:

```
$ eval $(boot2docker shellinit)
Writing /Users/me/.boot2docker/certs/boot2docker-vm/ca.pem
Writing /Users/me/.boot2docker/certs/boot2docker-vm/cert.pem
Writing /Users/me/.boot2docker/certs/boot2docker-vm/key.pem
```

If everything is running properly, you should now be able to run the following to connect to the Docker daemon:

```
$ docker info
Containers: 0
Images: 0
Storage Driver: aufs
 Root Dir: /mnt/sda1/var/lib/docker/aufs
 Backing Filesystem: extfs
 Dirs: 0
 Dirperm1 Supported: true
Execution Driver: native-0.2
Logging Driver: json-file
Kernel Version: 4.1.17-boot2docker
Operating System: Boot2Docker 1.10.1 (TCL 6.4.1); master : b03e158 - ... 2016
CPUs: 8
Total Memory: 1.955 GiB
Name: boot2docker
ID: FZT2:SOXP:VWYZ:UAJO:PZV3:FTSD:E5I2:IFQP:2OU4:5NQH:YRXP:IOCF
Debug mode (server): true
File Descriptors: 10
Goroutines: 28
System Time: 2016-02-15T17:51:15.470080546Z
EventsListeners: 0
Init SHA1:
Init Path: /usr/local/bin/docker
Docker Root Dir: /mnt/sda1/var/lib/docker
Username: me
Registry: https://index.docker.io/v1/
```

To connect to a shell on your Boot2Docker-based virtual machine, you can use the following command:

```
$ boot2docker ssh
```

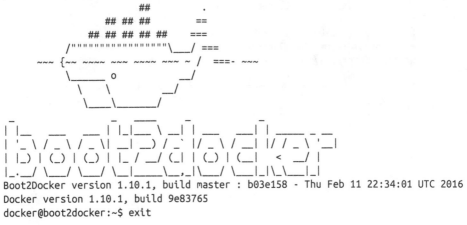

```
Boot2Docker version 1.10.1, build master : b03e158 - Thu Feb 11 22:34:01 UTC 2016
Docker version 1.10.1, build 9e83765
docker@boot2docker:~$ exit
```

You can stop your Boot2Docker image by running:

```
$ boot2docker stop
```

Vagrant

If you need more flexibility with the way your Docker development environment is set up, you might want to consider using Vagrant instead of Docker Machine or Boot2Docker. Like Docker Machine, Vagrant provides support for multiple hypervisors, but it is much more extensible, and can often be leveraged to mimic even the most complex environments.

A common use case for leveraging Vagrant during Docker development is to support testing on images that match your production environment. Vagrant supports everything from broad distributions like CentOS 7 and Ubuntu 14.04, to finely focused atomic host distributions like CoreOS (*https://coreos.com*) and Project Atomic (*http://www.projectatomic.io*).

Vagrant can be easily installed on most platforms by downloading a self-contained package from vagrantup.com (*https://www.vagrantup.com/down loads.html*). You will also need to have a hypervisor, like VirtualBox (*https://www.virtualbox.org/wiki/Downloads*), installed on your system.

In the following example, you will create a CoreOS-based Docker host running the Docker daemon on the unencrypted port 2375. You could use your favorite distribution here instead, but CoreOS ships with working Docker out of the box and the image is quite small.

In production, Docker should always be set up to only use encrypted remote connections. Although Docker Machine and Boot2Docker now use encrypted communications by default, setting up Vagrant to do this in CoreOS is currently a bit too complicated for this installation example.

After Vagrant is installed, create a host directory with a name similar to `docker-host` and then move into that directory:

```
$ mkdir docker-host
$ cd docker-host
```

To install the *coreos-vagrant* files, you need the version control tool named git. If you don't already have git, you can download and install it from git-scm.com (*http://git-scm.com/download*). When git is installed, you can grab the *coreos-vagrant* files and then change into the new directory with the following commands:

```
$ git clone https://github.com/coreos/coreos-vagrant.git
$ cd coreos-vagrant
```

Inside the *coreos-vagrant* directory, we need to create a new file called *config.rb* (that tells it to expose the Docker TCP port so we can connect):

```
echo "\$expose_docker_tcp=2375" > config.rb
```

Next you'll need to leverage the built-in `cloud-init` tool to add some `systemd` unit files that will enable the Docker daemon on TCP port 2375. You can do this by creating a file called *user-data* that contains all of the following, including `#cloud-config` at the beginning:

```
#cloud-config

coreos:
  units:
    - name: docker-tcp.socket
      command: start
      enable: yes
      content: |
        [Unit]
        Description=Docker Socket for the API

        [Socket]
        ListenStream=2375
        BindIPv6Only=both
        Service=docker.service

        [Install]
        WantedBy=sockets.target
    - name: enable-docker-tcp.service
      command: start
      content: |
```

```
[Unit]
Description=Enable the Docker Socket for the API

[Service]
Type=oneshot
ExecStart=/usr/bin/systemctl enable docker-tcp.socket
```

When you have saved both of these files, you can start up the Vagrant-based virtual machine by running:

```
$ vagrant up
Bringing machine 'core-01' up with 'virtualbox' provider...
==> core-01: Box 'coreos-alpha' could not be found. Attempting to find and
    install...
    core-01: Box Provider: virtualbox
    core-01: Box Version: >= 308.0.1
==> core-01: Loading metadata ... 'http://.../coreos_production_vagrant.json'
    core-01: URL: http://.../coreos_production_vagrant.json
==> core-01: Adding box 'coreos-alpha' (v472.0.0) for provider: virtualbox
    core-01: Downloading: http://.../coreos_production_vagrant.box
    core-01: Calculating and comparing box checksum...
==> core-01: Successfully added box 'coreos-alpha' (v472.0.0) for 'virtualbox'!
==> core-01: Importing base box 'coreos-alpha'...
==> core-01: Matching MAC address for NAT networking...
==> core-01: Checking if box 'coreos-alpha' is up to date...
==> core-01: Setting the name of the VM: coreos-vagrant_core-01
==> core-01: Clearing any previously set network interfaces...
==> core-01: Preparing network interfaces based on configuration...
    core-01: Adapter 1: nat
    core-01: Adapter 2: hostonly
==> core-01: Forwarding ports...
    core-01: 2375 => 2375 (adapter 1)
    core-01: 22 => 2222 (adapter 1)
==> core-01: Running 'pre-boot' VM customizations...
==> core-01: Booting VM...
==> core-01: Waiting for machine to boot. This may take a few minutes...
    core-01: SSH address: 127.0.0.1:2222
    core-01: SSH username: core
    core-01: SSH auth method: private key
    core-01: Warning: Connection timeout. Retrying...
==> core-01: Machine booted and ready!
==> core-01: Setting hostname...
==> core-01: Configuring network adapters within the VM...
==> core-01: Running provisioner: file...
==> core-01: Running provisioner: shell...
    core-01: Running: inline script
```

To set up your shell environment so that you can easily use your local Docker client to talk to the Docker daemon on your virtual machine, you can set the following variables:

```
$ unset DOCKER_TLS_VERIFY
$ unset DOCKER_CERT_PATH
$ export DOCKER_HOST=tcp://127.0.0.1:2375
```

If everything is running properly, you should now be able to run the following to connect to the Docker daemon:

```
$ docker info
Containers: 0
Images: 0
Storage Driver: btrfs
Execution Driver: native-0.2
Kernel Version: 3.16.2+
Operating System: CoreOS 472.0.0
```

To connect to a shell on the Vagrant-based virtual machine, you can run:

```
$ vagrant ssh
CoreOS (alpha)
core@core-01 ~ $ exit
```

You can stop your Vagrant-based VM by running:

```
$ vagrant halt
```

Test the Setup

You are now ready to test that everything is working. You should be able to run any one of the following commands on your local system to tell the Docker daemon to download the latest official container for that distribution and then launch it running an instance of bash.

This step is important to ensure that all the pieces are properly installed and communicating with each other as expected. It also shows off one of the features of Docker: we can run containers based on any distribution we like. In the next few steps we'll run Docker containers based on Ubuntu, Fedora, and CentOS. You don't need to run them all to prove that this works; running one of them will suffice.

If you want to run these commands on the server, be sure that you prepend each docker command with sudo. Alternatively you could add your user to the docker group directly.

Ubuntu

```
$ docker run --rm -ti ubuntu:latest /bin/bash
```

Fedora

```
$ docker run --rm -ti fedora:latest /bin/bash
```

CentOS

```
$ docker run --rm -ti centos:latest /bin/bash
```

 `ubuntu:latest`, `fedora:latest`, and `centos:latest` all represent a Docker image name followed by an image tag.

Wrap-Up

Now that you have a running Docker setup, you can start to look at more than the basic mechanics of getting it installed. In the next chapter, you'll explore some of the basic functionality of Docker with some hands-on work.

In the rest of the book, when you see `docker` on the command line, assume you will need to have the correct configuration in place either as environment variables or via the `-H` command-line flag to tell the `docker` client how to connect to your `docker` daemon.

## CHAPTER 4

Working with Docker Images

Every Docker container is based on an image, which provides the basis for everything that you will ever deploy and run with Docker. To launch a container, you must either download a public image or create your own. Every Docker image consists of one or more filesystem layers that generally have a direct one-to-one mapping to each individual build step used to create that image.

For image management, Docker relies heavily on its storage backend, which communicates with the underlying Linux filesystem to build and manage the multiple layers that combine into a single usable image. The primary storage backends that are supported include: AUFS (*http://bit.ly/1evu9D3*), BTRFS (*http://bit.ly/1PCwkQw*), Device-mapper (*http://bit.ly/1evughM*), and overlayfs (*http://bit.ly/1zFjGhH*). Each storage backend provides a fast copy-on-write (CoW) system for image management.

Anatomy of a Dockerfile

To create a custom Docker image with the default tools, you will need to become familiar with the Dockerfile. This file describes all the steps that are required to create one image and would usually be contained within the root directory of the source code repository for your application.

A typical Dockerfile might look something like the one shown here, which will create a container for a Node.js-based application:

```
FROM node:0.10

MAINTAINER Anna Doe <anna@example.com>

LABEL "rating"="Five Stars" "class"="First Class"

USER root
```

```
ENV AP /data/app
ENV SCPATH /etc/supervisor/conf.d

RUN apt-get -y update

# The daemons
RUN apt-get -y install supervisor
RUN mkdir -p /var/log/supervisor

# Supervisor Configuration
ADD ./supervisord/conf.d/* $SCPATH/

# Application Code
ADD *.js* $AP/

WORKDIR $AP

RUN npm install

CMD ["supervisord", "-n"]
```

Dissecting this Dockerfile will provide some initial exposure to a number of the possible instructions that you can use to control how an image is assembled. Each line in a Dockerfile creates a new image layer that is stored by Docker. This means that when you build new images, Docker will only need to build layers that deviate from previous builds.

Although you could build a Node instance from a plain, base Linux image, you can also explore the Docker Registry (*http://bit.ly/1evujdF*) for official images for Node. Node.js maintains a series of Docker images (*http://bit.ly/1evumGb*) and tags that allows you to quickly determine that you should tell the image to inherit from `node:0.10`, which will pull the most recent Node.js version 0.10 container. If you want to lock the image to a specific version of Node, you could instead point it at `node:0.10.33`. The base image that follows will provide you with an Ubuntu Linux image running Node 0.10.x:

```
FROM node:0.10
```

The `MAINTAINER` field provides contact information for the Dockerfile's author, which populates the Author field in all resulting images' metadata:

```
MAINTAINER Anna Doe <anna@example.com>
```

The ability to apply labels to images and containers was added to Docker in version 1.6. This means that you can now add metadata via key-value pairs that can later be used to search for and identify Docker images and containers. You can see the labels applied to any image using the `docker inspect` command:

```
LABEL "rating"="Five Stars" "class"="First Class"
```

By default, Docker runs all processes as root within the container, but you can use the USER instruction to change this:

```
USER root
```

Even though containers provide some isolation from the underlying operating system, they still run on the host kernel. Due to potential security risks, production containers should almost always be run under the context of a non-privileged user.

The ENV instruction allows you to set shell variables that can be used during the build process to simplify the Dockerfile and help keep it DRYer:[1]

```
ENV AP /data/app
ENV SCPATH /etc/supervisor/conf.d
```

In the following code, you'll use a collection of RUN instructions to start and create the required file structure that you need, and install some required software dependencies. You'll also start to use the build variables you defined in the previous section to save you a bit of work and help protect you from typos:

```
RUN apt-get -y update

# The daemons
RUN apt-get -y install supervisor
RUN mkdir -p /var/log/supervisor
```

It is generally considered a bad idea to run commands like apt-get -y update or yum -y update in your application Dockerfiles because it can significantly increase the time it takes for all of your builds to finish. Instead, consider basing your application image on another image that already has these updates applied to it.

Remember that every instruction creates a new Docker image layer, so it often makes sense to combine a few logically grouped commands onto a single line. It is even possible to use the ADD instruction in combination with the RUN instruction to copy a complex script to your image and then execute that script with only two commands in the Dockerfile.

The ADD instruction is used to copy files from the local filesystem into your image. Most often this will include your application code and any required support files:

---

1 Don't Repeat Yourself.

```
# Supervisor Configuration
ADD ./supervisord/conf.d/* $SCPATH/

# Application Code
ADD *.js* $AP/
```

 ADD allows you to include files from the local filesystem into the image. However, once the image is built, you can use the image without having access to the original files because they have been copied into the image.

With the WORKDIR instruction, you change the working directory in the image for the remaining build instructions:

```
WORKDIR $AP

RUN npm install
```

 The order of commands in a Dockerfile can have a very significant impact on ongoing build times. You should try to order commands so that things that change between every single build are closer to the bottom. This means that adding your code and similar steps should be held off until the end. When you rebuild an image, every single layer after the first introduced change will need to be rebuilt.

And finally you end with the CMD instruction, which defines the command that launches the process that you want to run within the container:

```
CMD ["supervisord", "-n"]
```

 It is generally considered best practice to only run a single process within a container, although there is debate about this within the community. The idea is that a container should provide a single function, so that it remains easy to horizontally scale individual functions within your architecture. In the example, you are using supervisord to manage the node application and ensure that it stays running within the container.

Building an Image

To build your first image, let's go ahead and clone a git repo that contains an example application called *docker-node-hello*, as shown here:[2]

---

2 This code was forked from GitHub (*https://github.com/enokd/docker-node-hello*).

```
$ git clone https://github.com/spkane/docker-node-hello.git
Cloning into 'docker-node-hello'...
remote: Counting objects: 20, done.
remote: Compressing objects: 100% (14/14), done.
remote: Total 20 (delta 6), reused 20 (delta 6)
Unpacking objects: 100% (20/20), done.
Checking connectivity... done.
$ cd docker-node-hello
```

Git is frequently installed on Linux and Mac OS X systems, but if you do not already have git available, you can download a simple installer from git-scm.com (*http://git-scm.com/downloads*).

This will download a working Dockerfile and related source code files into a directory called *docker-node-hello*. If you look at the contents while ignoring the git repo directory, you should see the following:

```
$ tree -a -I .git
.
├── .dockerignore
├── .gitignore
├── Dockerfile
├── Makefile
├── README.md
├── Vagrantfile
├── index.js
├── package.json
└── supervisord
    └── conf.d
        ├── node.conf
        └── supervisord.conf
```

Let's review the most relevant files in the repo.

The Dockerfile should be exactly the same as the one you just reviewed.

The *.dockerignore* file allows you to define files and directories that you do not want uploaded to the Docker host when you are building the image. In this instance, the *.dockerignore* file contains the following line:

```
.git
```

This instructs docker build to exclude the *.git* directory, which contains the whole source code repository. You do not need this directory to build the Docker image, and since it can grow quite large over time, you don't want to waste time copying it every time you do a build.

The *.git* directory contains git configuration data and every single change that you have ever made to your code. The rest of the files reflect the current state of your source code. This is why we can safely tell Docker to ignore the *.git* directory.

- *package.json* defines the Node.js application and lists any dependencies that it relies on.
- *index.js* is the main source code for the application.

The *supervisord* directory contains the configuration files for `supervisord` that you will need to start and monitor the application.

Using `supervisord` (*http://supervisord.org*) in this example to monitor the application is overkill, but it is intended to provide a bit of insight into some of the techniques you can use in a container to provide more control over your application and its running state.

As we discussed in Chapter 3, you will need to have your Docker server running and your client properly set up to communicate with it before you can build a Docker image. Assuming that this is all working, you should be able to initiate a new build by running the command below, which will build and tag an image based on the files in the current directory.

The first build that you run will take a few minutes because you have to download the base node image. Subsequent builds should be much faster unless a newer node 0.10 base image has been released.

Each step identified in the following output maps directly to a line in the Dockerfile, and each step creates a new image layer based on the previous step:

```
$ docker build -t example/docker-node-hello:latest .
Sending build context to Docker daemon 16.38 kB
Sending build context to Docker daemon
Step 0 : FROM node:0.10
node:0.10: The image you are pulling has been verified
511136ea3c5a: Pull complete
36fd425d7d8a: Pull complete
aaabd2b41e22: Pull complete
3c20e07c38ce: Pull complete
b6ef456c239c: Pull complete
b045b0cd49ad: Pull complete
210d9bc26f2f: Pull complete
27ecce8bd36c: Pull complete
```

```
fcac83abd52d: Pull complete
edc7d098628f: Pull complete
b5ac041b53f9: Pull complete
387247331d9c: Pull complete
Status: Downloaded newer image for node:0.10
 ---> 387247331d9c
Step 1 : MAINTAINER Anna Doe <anna@example.com>
 ---> Running in fd83efd2ecbd
 ---> a479befa0788
Removing intermediate container fd83efd2ecbd
Step 2 : LABEL "rating"="Five Stars" "class"="First Class"
 ---> Running in 30acbe0f1379
 ---> 3cbea27e857c
Removing intermediate container 30acbe0f1379
Step 3 : USER root
 ---> Running in 32dfbc0f0855
 ---> 9fada51b938d
Removing intermediate container 32dfbc0f0855
Step 4 : ENV AP /data/app
 ---> Running in 0e04f129d7f5
 ---> 818dafcc487a
Removing intermediate container 0e04f129d7f5
Step 5 : ENV SCPATH /etc/supervisor/conf.d
 ---> Running in f828cccc5038
 ---> b5f3a2dbc1a2
Removing intermediate container f828cccc5038
Step 6 : RUN apt-get -y update
 ---> Running in 51e0d361adfe
Get:1 http://security.debian.org jessie/updates InRelease [84.1 kB]
Get:2 http://http.debian.net jessie InRelease [191 kB]
Get:3 http://security.debian.org jessie/updates/main amd64 Packages [20 B]
Get:4 http://http.debian.net jessie-updates InRelease [117 kB]
Get:5 http://http.debian.net jessie/main amd64 Packages [9103 kB]
Get:6 http://http.debian.net jessie-updates/main amd64 Packages [20 B]
Fetched 9496 kB in 7s (1232 kB/s)
Reading package lists...
W: Size of file /var/lib/... is not what the server reported 9102955 9117278
 ---> 16c8639b44c9
Removing intermediate container 51e0d361adfe
Step 7 : RUN apt-get -y install supervisor
 ---> Running in fa79bc727362
Reading package lists...
Building dependency tree...
Reading state information...
The following extra packages will be installed:
  python-meld3
The following NEW packages will be installed:
  python-meld3 supervisor
0 upgraded, 2 newly installed, 0 to remove and 96 not upgraded.
Need to get 304 kB of archives.
After this operation, 1483 kB of additional disk space will be used.
Get:1 http://.../debian/ jessie/main python-meld3 amd64 1.0.0-1 [37.0 kB]
Get:2 http://.../debian/ jessie/main supervisor all 3.0r1-1 [267 kB]
```

```
debconf: delaying package configuration, since apt-utils is not installed
Fetched 304 kB in 1s (232 kB/s)
Selecting previously unselected package python-meld3.
(Reading database ... 29248 files and directories currently installed.)
Preparing to unpack .../python-meld3_1.0.0-1_amd64.deb ...
Unpacking python-meld3 (1.0.0-1) ...
Selecting previously unselected package supervisor.
Preparing to unpack .../supervisor_3.0r1-1_all.deb ...
Unpacking supervisor (3.0r1-1) ...
Setting up python-meld3 (1.0.0-1) ...
Setting up supervisor (3.0r1-1) ...
invoke-rc.d: policy-rc.d denied execution of start.
 ---> eabf485da230
Removing intermediate container fa79bc727362
Step 8 : RUN mkdir -p /var/log/supervisor
 ---> Running in 0bf6264625dd
 ---> 4bcba91d84e1
Removing intermediate container 0bf6264625dd
Step 9 : ADD ./supervisord/conf.d/* $SCPATH/
 ---> df0d938b53a3
Removing intermediate container dcfa16d0fec2
Step 10 : ADD *.js* $AP/
 ---> b21779fe3194
Removing intermediate container 00d2f6d10444
Step 11 : WORKDIR $AP
 ---> Running in f412220027b5
 ---> 0f84bc7ac153
Removing intermediate container f412220027b5
Step 12 : RUN npm install
 ---> Running in 7340a9041404
npm WARN engine formidable@1.0.13: wanted:
    {"node":"<0.9.0"} (current: {"node":"0.10.33","npm":"2.1.8"})
express@3.2.4 node_modules/express
├── methods@0.0.1
├── fresh@0.1.0
├── range-parser@0.0.4
├── cookie-signature@1.0.1
├── buffer-crc32@0.2.1
├── cookie@0.0.5
├── commander@0.6.1
├── mkdirp@0.3.4
├── debug@2.1.0 (ms@0.6.2)
├── send@0.1.0 (mime@1.2.6)
└── connect@2.7.9 (pause@0.0.1, qs@0.6.4, bytes@0.2.0, formidable@1.0.13)
 ---> 84f3a4bc2336
Removing intermediate container 7340a9041404
Step 13 : CMD supervisord -n
 ---> Running in 23671c2f57b7
 ---> 96eab440b7c8
Removing intermediate container 23671c2f57b7
Successfully built 96eab440b7c8
```

To improve the speed of builds, Docker will use a local cache when it thinks it is safe. This can sometimes lead to unexpected issues. In the output above you will notice lines like `---> Running in 23671c2f57b7`. If instead you see `---> Using cache`, you know that Docker decided to use the cache. You can disable the cache for a build by using the `--no-cache` argument to the `docker build` command.

If you are building your Docker images on a system that is used for other simultaneous processes, you can limit the resources avaliable to your builds by utilizing many of the same cgroup methods that we will discuss later in Chapter 5. You can find detailed documentation on the `docker build` arguments in the official documentation (*https://docs.docker.com/engine/reference/commandline/build/*).

Running Your Image

Once you have successfully built the image, you can run it on your Docker host with the following command:

```
$ docker run -d -p 8080:8080 example/docker-node-hello:latest
```

The above command tells Docker to create a running container in the background from the image with the `example/docker-node-hello:latest` tag, and then map port 8080 in the container to port 8080 on the Docker host.

If everything goes as expected, the new Node.js application should be running in a container on the host. You can verify this by running `docker ps`.

To see the running application in action, you will need to open up a web browser and point it at port 8080 on the Docker host.

You can usually determine the Docker host IP address by simply printing out the value of the `DOCKER_HOST` environment variable unless you are only running Docker locally, in which case 127.0.0.1 should work. Docker Machine or Boot2Docker users can also simply use `docker-machine ip` or `boot2docker ip`, respectively:

```
$ echo $DOCKER_HOST
tcp://172.17.42.10:2376
```

Get the IP address and enter something like *http://172.17.42.10:8080/* into your web browser address bar.

You should see the following text:

```
Hello World. Wish you were here.
```

Environment Variables

If you read the *index.js* file, you will notice that part of the file refers to the variable *$WHO*, which the application uses to determine who it is going to say Hello to:

```
var DEFAULT_WHO = "World";
var WHO = process.env.WHO || DEFAULT_WHO;

app.get('/', function (req, res) {
  res.send('Hello ' + WHO + '. Wish you were here.\n');
});
```

Let's quickly learn how you can configure this application by passing in environment variables when you start it.

First you need to stop the existing container using two commands. The first command will provide you with the container ID, which you will need to use in the second command:

```
$ docker ps
CONTAINER ID  IMAGE                          STATUS       ...
b7145e06083f  example/centos-node-hello:latest  Up 4 minutes ...
```

 With the release of Docker 1.8, it is now possible to format the output of docker ps by utilizing a Go template, so that you only see the information that you care about. In the above example you might decide to run something like docker ps --format "table {{.ID}}\t{{.Image}}\t{{.Status}}" to limit the output to the 3 fields you care about. Additionally, running docker ps --quiet with no format options will limit the output to only the container ID.

And then, using the container ID from the previous output, you can stop the running container by typing:

```
$ docker stop b7145e06083f
b7145e06083f
```

You can then restart the container by adding one argument to the previous docker run command:

```
$ docker run -d -p 8080:8080 -e WHO="Sean and Karl" \
example/docker-node-hello:latest
```

If you reload your web browser, you should see that the text on the web page now reads:

```
Hello Sean and Karl. Wish you were here.
```

Custom Base Images

Base images are the lowest-level images that other Docker images will build upon. Most often, these are based on minimal installs of Linux distributions like Ubuntu, Fedora, or CentOS, but they can also be much smaller, containing a single statically compiled binary. For most people, using the official base images for their favorite distribution or tool is a great option.

However, there are times when it is more preferable to build your own base images that are not based on an image created by someone else. One reason to do this would be to maintain a consistent OS image across all your deployment methods for hardware, VMs, and containers. Another would be to get the image size down substantially. There is no need to ship around an entire Ubuntu distribution, for example, if your application is a statically built C or Go application. You might find that you only need the tools you regularly use for debugging and some other shell commands and binaries. Making the effort to build such an image could pay off in better deployment times and easier application distribution.

In the official Docker documentation, there is some good information about how you can build base images on the various Linux distributions (*https:// docs.docker.com/articles/baseimages/*).

Storing Images

Now that you have created a Docker image that you're happy with, you'll want to store it somewhere so that it can be easily accessed by any Docker host that you want to deploy it to. This is also the clear hand-off point between building images and putting them somewhere to run. You don't normally build the images on the server and then run them. Ordinarily, deployment is the process of pulling an image from a repository and running it on one or more Docker servers. There are a few ways you can go about storing your images into a central repository for easy retrieval.

Public Registries

Docker provides an image registry (*https://registry.hub.docker.com*) for public images that the community wants to share. These include official images for Linux distributions, ready-to-go WordPress containers, and much more.

If you have images that can be published to the Internet, the best place for them is a public registry, like Docker Hub (*https://hub.docker.com/*). However, there are other options. When the core Docker tools were first gaining popularity, Docker Hub did not exist. To fill this obvious void in the community, Quay.io (*http:// quay.io/*) was created. Since then, Quay.io has been purchased by CoreOS and has been used to create the CoreOS Enterprise Registry product, which we will discuss in a moment.

Both Docker Hub and Quay.io provide centralized Docker image registries that can be accessed from anywhere on the Internet, and provide a method to store private images in addition to public ones. Both have nice user interfaces and the ability to separate team access permissions and manage users. Both also offer reasonable commercial options for private SaaS hosting of your images, much in the same way that GitHub sells private registries on their systems. This is probably the right first step if you're getting serious about Docker but are not yet shipping enough code to need an internally hosted solution.

For companies that use Docker heavily, the biggest downside to these registries is that they are not local to the network on which the application is being deployed. This means that every layer of every deployment might need to be dragged across the Internet in order to deploy an application. Internet latencies have a very real impact on software deployments, and outages that affect these registries could have a very detrimental impact on a company's ability to deploy smoothly and on schedule. This is mitigated by good image design where you make thin layers that are easy to move around the Internet.

 In December of 2015, Docker Hub dropped all support for version 1 of the image registry. If you still need to use Docker clients earlier than 1.6, you will need to run your own registry or use Quay.io.

Private Registries

The other option that many companies consider is to host some type of Docker image registry internally. Before the public registry existed for Docker, the Docker developers released the docker-registry (*http://bit.ly/1evuzJy*) project on GitHub. The docker-registry is a GUI-less Python daemon that can interact with the Docker client to support pushing, pulling, and searching images. The version 1 docker-registry has been deprecated and has now been replaced with the version 2 registry, called Docker Distribution.

Another strong contender in the private registry space is the CoreOS Enterprise Registry. When CoreOS bought Quay.io, it quickly took the codebase and made it avaliable as an easily deployable Docker container. This product basically offers all the same features at Quay.io, but can be deployed internally. It ships as a virtual machine that you run as an appliance, and supports the same UI and interfaces as the public Quay.io.

In April of 2015, Docker released the first version of the Docker Trusted Registry (*https://www.docker.com/products/docker-trusted-registry*), which had earlier been refered to as Docker Hub Enterprise. The Trusted Registry allows organizations to have a Docker-supported on-premise image registry in their data center or cloud environment.

Authenticating to a Registry

Communicating with a registry that stores container images is part of daily life with Docker. For many registries, this means you'll need to authenticate to gain access to images. But Docker also tries to make it easy to automate things so it can store your login information and use it on your behalf when you request things like pulling down a private image. By default, Docker assumes the registry will be Docker Hub, the public repository hosted by Docker, Inc.

Creating a Docker Hub account

For these examples, we will create an account on Docker Hub. You don't need an account to use publicly shared images, but you will need one to upload your own public or private containers.

To create your account, use your web browser of choice to navigate to Docker Hub (*https://hub.docker.com/account/signup/*).

From there, you can either log in via an existing GitHub account or create a new login based on your email address. When you first log in to your new account, you will land on the Docker welcome page (*https://hub.docker.com/account/welcome/*), which is where you can configure details about your account.

When you create your account, Docker Hub sends a verification email to the address that you provided during signup. You should immediately log in to your email account and click the verification link inside the email to finish the validation process.

At this point, you have created a public registry to which you can upload new images. The "Global settings" option in your account sidebar will allow you to change your registry into a private one if that is what you need.

Logging in to a registry

Now let's log in to the Docker Hub registry using our account:

```
$ docker login
Username: someuser
Password: <not shown>
Email: someone@example.com
Login Succeeded
```

When we get "Login Succeeded" back from the server, we know we're ready to pull images from the registry. But what happened under the covers? It turns out that Docker has written a dotfile for us in our home directory to cache this information. The permissions are set to 0600 as a security precaution against other users reading your credentials. You can inspect the file with something like:

```
$ ls -la ~/.dockercfg
-rw------- 1 someuser someuser 95 Mar  6 15:07 /home/someuser/.dockercfg
$ cat ~/.dockercfg
{"https://index.docker.io/v1/":{"auth":"cmVsaEXamPL3hElRmFCOUE=",
"email":"someone@example.com"}}
```

Here we can see the *.dockercfg* file, owned by someuser, and the stored credentials in JSON format. Note that this can support multiple registries at once. In this case, we just have one entry, for Docker Hub, but we could have more if we need it. From now on, when the registry needs authentication, Docker will look in *.dockercfg* to see if we have credentials stored for this hostname. If so, it will supply them. You will notice that one value is completely lacking here: a time-stamp. These credentials are cached forever or when we tell Docker to remove them, whichever comes first.

Just like logging in, we can also log out of a registry if we no longer want to cache the credentials:

```
$ docker logout
Remove login credentials for https://index.docker.io/v1/
$ ls -la ~/.dockercfg
ls: cannot access /home/someuser/.dockercfg: No such file or directory
```

Here we removed our cached credentials and they are no longer stored. But something else happened: the file is gone. That's because it was the only set of credentials that were cached, so Docker has simply removed the file.

If we were trying to log in to something other than the Docker Hub registry, we could supply the hostname on the command line:

```
$ docker login someregistry.example.com
```

This would then end up as just another line in our *.dockercfg* file.

Pushing images into a repository

The first step required to push your image is to ensure that you are logged into the Docker repository you intend to use. For this example we will focus on Docker Hub. So ensure that you are logged into Docker hub with your personal credentials.

```
$ docker login
Username: someuser
Password: <not shown>
Email: someone@example.com
Login Succeeded
```

Once you are logged in, you can upload an image. Earlier we used the command `docker build -t example/docker-node-hello:latest` . to build the docker-node-hello image.

The `example` portion of that command refers to a repository. When this is local, it can be anything that we want. However, when we are going to upload it to a real repository, we need that to match our login.

> You will need to replace `someuser` in all the examples with the user that you created in Docker Hub (or whatever repository you decided to use).

We can easily edit the tags on the image that we already created by running the following command:

```
$ docker tag example/docker-node-hello:latest someuser/docker-node-hello:latest
```

If you need to rebuild the image with the new naming convention or simply want to give it a try, you can accomplish this by running the following command in the `docker-node-hello` working directory that was generated when you performed the git checkout earlier in the chapter:

```
$ docker build -t someuser/docker-node-hello:latest .
...
```

> If you rebuild the image, you may find that it is very fast. This is because most, if not all, of the layers already exist on your Docker server from the previous build.

We can quickly verify that our image is indeed on the server by running `docker images`:

```
$ docker images
REPOSITORY                   TAG     IMAGE ID      CREATED         VIRTUAL SIZE
someuser/docker-node-hello   latest  69ddbcccd74f  31 minutes ago  649.2 MB
node                         0.10    38c02af29fa3  3 weeks ago     633.3 MB
```

> With the introduction of Docker 1.10, it is now possible to format the output of `docker images` to make it more concise by using the `--format` argument, like this: `docker images --format="table {{.ID }}\t {{.Repository }}"`.

At this point we can upload the image to our Docker repository by using the `docker push` command:

```
$ docker push someuser/docker-node-hello:latest
The push refers to a repository [docker.io/someuser/docker-node-hello] (len: 1)
6ad4dd20c832: Pushed
...
9ee13ca3b908: Pushed
latest: digest: sha256:55c0a161f8ec4af4e17a40ca057f97... size: 38338
```

If this image was uploaded to a public repository, it can now be easily downloaded by anyone in the world by running the `docker pull` command.

If you uploaded the image to a private repository, than users must log into the private repository using the `docker login` command before they will be able to pull the image down to their local system.

```
$ docker pull someuser/docker-node-hello:latest
latest: Pulling from someuser/docker-node-hello
69ddbcccd74f: Pull complete
Digest: sha256:55c0a161f8ec4af4e17a40ca057f97...
Status: Downloaded newer image for someuser/docker-node-hello:latest
```

Mirroring a Registry

It is possible to set up a local registry in your network that will mirror images from the upstream public registry so that you don't need to pull commonly used images all the way across the Internet every time you need them on a new host. This can even be useful on your development workstation so that you can keep a local stash of frequently used images that you might need to access offline.

Currently you can only mirror a registry using the older version 1 registry. This functionality is expected to be added into Docker Distribution with the release of version 2.4.

If you are considering setting up your own registry, you should investigate the Docker Distribution GitHub page (*http://bit.ly/ 1evuJAx*) and the official documentation for Docker Registry 2.0 (*http://bit.ly/1evuKo9*).

Configuring the Docker daemon

To do this, the first thing that you need to do is relaunch your Docker daemon with the `--registry-mirror` command-line argument, replacing `$ {YOUR_REGISTRY-MIRROR-HOST}` with your Docker server's IP address and port number (e.g., 172.17.42.10:5000).

If you plan to run the docker-registry container on your only Docker server, you can set ${YOUR_REGISTRY-MIRROR-HOST} to localhost:5000.

If you already have Docker running, you need to stop it first. This is distribution-specific. You should use the commands you normally use on your distribution, like initctl, service, or systemctl, to stop the daemon. Then we can invoke it manually with this registry mirroring option:

```
$ docker daemon --registry-mirror=http://${YOUR_REGISTRY-MIRROR-HOST}
```

If you would like to ensure that your Docker daemon always starts with this setup, you will need to edit the appropriate configuration file for your Linux distribution.

Boot2Docker ISO. This setup is for anything using a boot2docker.iso, like Docker Machine or the boot2docker command line interface.

Create */var/lib/boot2docker/profile* if it doesn't already exist:

```
$ sudo touch /var/lib/boot2docker/profile
```

Then edit */var/lib/boot2docker/profile* and append the argument to your EXTRA_ARGS:

```
EXTRA_ARGS="--registry-mirror=http://${YOUR_REGISTRY-MIRROR-HOST}"
```

And then restart the docker daemon:

```
sudo /etc/init.d/docker restart
```

Ubuntu. Edit */etc/default/docker* and append the argument to your DOCKER_OPTS:

```
DOCKER_OPTS="--registry-mirror=http://${YOUR_REGISTRY-MIRROR-HOST}"
```

And then restart the docker daemon:

```
sudo service docker.io restart
```

Fedora. Edit */etc/sysconfig/docker* and append the argument to your OPTIONS:

```
OPTIONS="--registry-mirror=http://${YOUR_REGISTRY-MIRROR-HOST}"
```

And then restart the docker daemon:

```
sudo systemctl daemon-reload
sudo systemctl restart docker
```

CoreOS. First copy the *systemd* unit file for Docker to a writeable filesystem:

```
$ sudo cp /usr/lib/systemd/system/docker.service /etc/systemd/system/
```

Then, as root, edit *etc/systemd/system/docker.service* and append the argument to the end of the `ExecStart` line:

```
ExecStart=/usr/lib/coreos/dockerd --daemon --host=fd:// \
$DOCKER_OPTS $DOCKER_OPT_BIP $DOCKER_OPT_MTU $DOCKER_OPT_IPMASQ \
--registry-mirror=http://${YOUR_REGISTRY-MIRROR-HOST}
```

And then restart the docker daemon:

```
sudo systemctl daemon-reload
sudo systemctl restart docker
```

Launching the local registry mirror service

You will now need to launch a container on your Docker host that will run the registry mirror service and provide you with a local cache of Docker images. You can accomplish this by running the `registry` image as a container with a few important environment variables (*http://bit.ly/1evuzJy*) defined and a storage volume mounted.

On your Docker server, ensure that you have a directory for storing the images:

```
$ mkdir -p /var/lib/registry
```

Then you can launch the container, with the following options defined:

```
$ docker run -d -p 5000:5000 \
    -v /var/lib/registry:/tmp/registry \
    -e SETTINGS_FLAVOR=dev \
    -e STANDALONE=false \
    -e MIRROR_SOURCE=https://registry-1.docker.io \
    -e MIRROR_SOURCE_INDEX=https://index.docker.io \
    registry
```

> The registry supports a lot of different storage backends, including S3, Swift, Glance, Azure Blob Storage, Google Cloud Storage, and more.

Testing the local registry mirror service

Now that the registry is running as a mirror, we can test it. On a Unix-based system, you can time how long it takes to download the newest CentOS image, using the following command:

```
$ time docker pull centos:latest
Pulling repository centos
88f9454e60dd: Download complete
511136ea3c5a: Download complete
5b12ef8fd570: Download complete
Status: Downloaded newer image for centos:latest
```

```
real    1m25.406s
user    0m0.019s
sys     0m0.014s
```

In this case, it took 1 minute and 25 seconds to pull the whole image. If we then go ahead and delete the image from the Docker host and then re-time fetching the image again, we will see a significant difference:

```
$ docker rmi centos:latest
Untagged: centos:latest
$ time docker pull centos:latest
Pulling repository centos
88f9454e60dd: Download complete
511136ea3c5a: Download complete
5b12ef8fd570: Download complete
Status: Image is up to date for centos:latest

real    0m2.042s
user    0m0.004s
sys     0m0.005s
```

Both times that you pulled the centos:latest image, the Docker server connected to the local registry mirror service and asked for the image. In the first case, the mirror service did not have the image so it had to pull it from the official docker-registry first, add it to its own storage, and then deliver it to the Docker server. After you delete the image from the Docker server and then request it again, you'll see that the time to pull the image will drop to be very low. In the previous code, it took only two seconds for the Docker server to receive the image. This is because the local registry mirror service had a copy of the image and could provide it directly to the server without pulling anything from the upstream public docker-registry.

Other Approaches to Image Delivery

Over the last two years, the community has explored many other approaches to managing Docker images and providing simple but reliable access to images when needed. Some of these projects, like dogestry (*https://github.com/dogestry/dogestry*), leverage the docker save and docker load commands to create and load images from cloud storage like Amazon S3 (*http://aws.amazon.com/s3*). Other people are exploring the possibilities of using torrents to distribute Docker images, with projects like torrent-docker (*http://bit.ly/1evuRQw*). Torrents seem like a natural fit because deployment is usually done to a group of servers on the same network all at the same time. Solomon Hykes recently committed that the Docker Distribution project (*http://bit.ly/1evuJAx*) will soon ship a command-line tool for importing and exporting image layers even without a Docker daemon. This will facilitate even more diverse methods of image distribution. As more and more companies and projects begin to use Docker seriously, even more robust solutions are likely to begin to appear to meet the needs of anyone's unique workflow and requirements.

If you have a scenario in which you can't use the off-the-shelf mechanisms, such as an isolated network for security concerns, you can leverage Docker's built-in importing and exporting features to dump and load new images. Unless you have a specific reason to do otherwise, you should use one of the off-the-shelf solutions and only considering changing your approach when needed. The available options will work for almost everyone.

## CHAPTER 5

Working with Docker Containers

In the previous chapter, we learned how to build a Docker image and the very basic steps required for running the resulting image within a container. In this chapter, we'll first take a look at where containers came from and then dive deeper into containers and the Docker commands that control the overall configuration, resources, and privileges that your container receives.

What Are Containers?

You might be familiar with virtualization systems like VMware or Xen that allow you to run a complete Linux kernel and operating system on top of a virtualized layer, commonly called a hypervisor. This approach provides very strong isolation between virtual machines because each hosted kernel sits in separate memory space and has defined entry points into the actual hardware, either through another kernel or something that looks like hardware.

Containers are a fundamentally different approach where all containers share a single kernel and isolation is implemented entirely within that single kernel. This is called operating system virtualization. The libcontainer project (*https:// github.com/docker/libcontainer*) gives a good, short definition of a container: "A container is a self-contained execution environment that shares the kernel of the host system and which is (optionally) isolated from other containers in the system." The major advantages are around efficiency of resources because you don't need a whole operating system for each isolated function. Since you are sharing a kernel, there is one less layer of indirection between the isolated task and the real hardware underneath. When a process is running inside a container, there is only a very little shim that sits inside the kernel rather than potentially calling up into a whole second kernel while bouncing in and out of privileged mode on the processor.

But the container approach means that you can only run processes that are compatible with the underlying kernel. Unlike hardware virtualization like that provided by VMware, for example, Windows applications cannot run inside a Linux container. So containers are best thought of as a Linux technology where, at least for now, you can run any of your favorite Linux applications or servers. When thinking of containers, you should try very hard to throw out what you might already know about virtual machines and instead conceptualize a container as a wrapper around a process that actually runs on the server.

History of Containers

It is often the case that a revolutionary technology is an older technology that has finally arrived in the spotlight. Technology goes in waves, and some of the ideas from the 1960s are back in vogue. Similarly, Docker is a new technology and it has an ease of use that has made it an instant hit, but it doesn't exist in a vacuum. Much of what underpins Docker comes from work done over the last 30 years in a few different arenas: from a system call added to the Unix kernel in the late 1970s, to tooling built on modern Linux. It's worth a quick tour through how we got to Docker because understanding that helps you place it within the context of other things you might be familiar with.

Containers are not a new idea. They are a way to isolate and encapsulate a part of the running system. The oldest technology in that area were the first batch processing systems. You'd run a program for a while, then switch to run another program. There was isolation: you could make sure your program didn't step on anyone else's program. That's all pretty crude now, but it's the very first step on the road to Linux containers and Docker.

Most people would argue that the seeds for today's containers were planted in 1979 with the addition of the *chroot* system call to Version 7 Unix. *chroot* restricts a process's view of the underlying filesystem. The *chroot* system call is commonly used to protect the operating system from untrusted server processes like FTP, BIND, and Sendmail, which are publicly exposed and susceptible to compromise.

In the 1980s and 1990s, various Unix variants were created with mandatory access controls for security reasons.[1] This meant you had tightly controlled domains running on the same Unix kernel. Processes in each domain had an extremely limited view of the system that precluded them from interacting across domains. A popular commercial version of Unix that implemented this idea was the Sidewinder firewall built on top of BSDI Unix. But this was not possible in most mainstream Unix implementations.

---

[1] SELinux is one current implementation.

That changed in 2000 when FreeBSD 4.0 was released with a new command, called jail, which was designed to allow shared-environment hosting providers to easily and securely create a separation between their processes and those of their individual customers. FreeBSD jail expanded *chroot's* capabilities, but restricted everything a process could do with the underlying system and processes in other jails.

In 2004, Sun released an early build of Solaris 10, which included Solaris Containers, and later evolved into Solaris Zones. This was the first major commercial implementation of container technology and is still used today to support many commercial container implementations. In 2007, HP released Secure Resource Partitions for HP-UX, later renamed to HP-UX Containers; and finally, in 2008, Linux Containers (LXC) were released in version 2.6.24 of the Linux kernel. The phenomenal growth of Linux Containers across the community did not really start to grow until 2013 with the inclusion of user namespaces in version 3.8 of the Linux Kernel and the release of Docker one month later.

Companies that had to deal with scaling applications to the size of the Internet, with Google being a very early example, started pushing container technology in the early 2000s in order to facilitate distributing their applications across data centers full of computers. A few companies maintained their own patched kernels with container support for internal use. Google contributed some of its work to support containers into the mainline Linux kernel, as understanding about the broader need for these features began to increase in the Linux community.

In late 2013, months after the Docker announcement, Google released lmctfy (*https://github.com/google/lmctfy*), the open source version of the internal container engine it had been running for some years. By this time, Docker was already widely discussed in the press. It was the right combination of ease of use and enabling technology just at the right time. Other promising container engines, like CoreOS Rocket, have been released since, but Docker seems to have built up a head of steam that is currently powering it to the forefront.

 If you haven't heard about CoreOS Rocket (*https://github.com/ coreos/rkt*), you might be wondering what it is. Rocket is an open source container runtime that CoreOS is designing to address what they see as serious deficiencies with the Docker approach to containerization and the supporting tool set. It is left as an exercise for the reader to determine whether the CoreOS approach and solution fits your needs.

Now let's turn back to Docker and take a closer look at modern containers.

Creating a Container

So far we've started containers using the handy docker run command. But docker run is really a convenience command that wraps two separate steps into one. The first thing it does is create a container from the underlying image. This is accomplished separately using the docker create command. The second thing docker run does is execute the container, which we can also do separately with the docker start command.

The docker create and docker run commands both contain all the options that pertain to how a container is initially set up. In Chapter 4, we demonstrated that with the docker run command you could map network ports in the underlying container to the host using the -p argument, and that -e could be used to pass environment variables into the container.

This only just begins to touch on the array of things that you can configure when you first create a container. So let's take a pass over some of the options that docker supports.

Basic Configuration

Now let's take a look at some of the ways we can tell Docker to configure our container when we create it.

Container name

When you create a container, it is built from the underlying image, but various command-line arguments can affect the final settings. Settings specified in the Dockerfile are always used as defaults, but you can override many of them at creation time.

By default, Docker randomly names your container (*http://bit.ly/1DUe0vi*) by combining an adjective with the name of a famous person. This results in names like *ecstatic-babbage* and *serene-albattani*. If you want to give your container a specific name, you can do so using the --name argument.

```
$ docker create --name="awesome-service" ubuntu:latest
```

 You can only have one container with any given name on a Docker host. If you run the above command twice in a row, you will get an error. You must either delete the previous container using docker rm or change the name of the new container.

Labels

As mentioned in Chapter 4, labels are key-value pairs that can be applied to Docker images and containers as metadata. When new Docker containers are created, they automatically inherit all the labels from their parent image.

It is also possible to add new labels to the containers so that you can apply metadata that might be specific to that single container.

```
docker run -d --name labels -l deployer=Ahmed -l tester=Asako \
    ubuntu:latest sleep 1000
```

You can then search for and filter containers based on this metadata, using commands like docker ps.

```
$ docker ps -a -f label=deployer=Ahmed
CONTAINER ID  IMAGE           COMMAND        ... NAMES
845731631ba4  ubuntu:latest  "sleep 1000"  ... labels
```

You can use the docker inspect command on the container to see all the labels that a container has.

```
$ docker inspect 845731631ba4
...
        "Labels": {
            "deployer": "Ahmed",
            "tester": "Asako"
        },
...
```

Hostname

By default, when you start a container, Docker will copy certain system files on the host, including */etc/hostname*, into the container's configuration directory on the host,[2] and then use a bind mount to link that copy of the file into the container. We can launch a default container with no special configuration like this:

```
$ docker run --rm -ti ubuntu:latest /bin/bash
```

This command uses the docker run command, which runs docker create and docker start in the background. Since we want to be able to interact with the container that we are going to create for demonstration purposes, we pass in a few useful arguments. The --rm argument tells Docker to delete the container when it exits, the -t argument tells Docker to allocate a psuedo-TTY, and the -i argument tells Docker that this is going to be an interactive session, and we want to keep STDIN open. The final argument in the command is the exectuable that we want to run within the container, which in this case is the ever useful /bin/bash.

---

2 Typically under */var/lib/docker/containers*.

If we now run the `mount` command from within the resulting container, we will see something similar to this:

```
root@ebc8cf2d8523:/# mount
overlay on / type overlay (rw,relatime,lowerdir=...,upperdir=...,workdir...)
proc on /proc type proc (rw,nosuid,nodev,noexec,relatime)
tmpfs on /dev type tmpfs (rw,nosuid,mode=755)
shm on /dev/shm type tmpfs (rw,nosuid,nodev,noexec,relatime,size=65536k)
mqueue on /dev/mqueue type mqueue (rw,nosuid,nodev,noexec,relatime)
devpts on /dev/pts type devpts (rw,nosuid,noexec,relatime,...,ptmxmode=666)
sysfs on /sys type sysfs (ro,nosuid,nodev,noexec,relatime)
/dev/sda9 on /etc/resolv.conf type ext4 (rw,relatime,data=ordered)
/dev/sda9 on /etc/hostname type ext4 (rw,relatime,data=ordered)
/dev/sda9 on /etc/hosts type ext4 (rw,relatime,data=ordered)
devpts on /dev/console type devpts (rw,nosuid,noexec,relatime,...,ptmxmode=000)
proc on /proc/sys type proc (ro,nosuid,nodev,noexec,relatime)
proc on /proc/sysrq-trigger type proc (ro,nosuid,nodev,noexec,relatime)
proc on /proc/irq type proc (ro,nosuid,nodev,noexec,relatime)
proc on /proc/bus type proc (ro,nosuid,nodev,noexec,relatime)
tmpfs on /proc/kcore type tmpfs (rw,nosuid,mode=755)
root@ebc8cf2d8523:/#
```

When you see any examples with a prompt that looks something like *root@hostname*, it means that you are running a command within the container instead of on the Docker host.

There are quite a few bind mounts in a container, but in this case we are interested in this one:

```
/dev/sda9 on /etc/hostname type ext4 (rw,relatime,data=ordered)
```

While the device number will be different for each container, the part we care about is that the mount point is */etc/hostname*. This links the container's */etc/hostname* to the hostname file that Docker has prepared for the container, which by default contains the container's ID and is not fully qualified with a domain name.

We can check this in the container by running the following:

```
root@ebc8cf2d8523:/# hostname -f
ebc8cf2d8523
root@ebc8cf2d8523:/# exit
```

Don't forget to `exit` the container shell so that we return to the Docker host when finished.

To set the hostname specifically, we can use the --hostname argument to pass in a more specific value.

```
$ docker run --rm -ti --hostname="mycontainer.example.com" ubuntu:latest /bin/bash
```

Then, from within the container, we will see that the fully-qualified hostname is defined as requested.

```
root@mycontainer:/# hostname -f
mycontainer.example.com
root@mycontainer:/# exit
```

Domain Name Service (DNS)

Just like */etc/hostname*, the *resolv.conf* file is managed via a bind mount between the host and container.

```
/dev/sda9 on /etc/resolv.conf type ext4 (rw,relatime,data=ordered)
```

By default, this is an exact copy of the Docker host's *resolv.conf* file. If we didn't want this, we could use a combination of the --dns and --dns-search arguments to override this behavior in the container:

```
$ docker run --rm -ti --dns=8.8.8.8 --dns=8.8.4.4 --dns-search=example1.com \
  --dns-search=example2.com ubuntu:latest /bin/bash
```

 If you want to leave the search domain completely unset, then use --dns-search=.

Within the container, we would still see a bind mount, but the file contents would no longer reflect the host's *resolv.conf*; instead, it now looks like this:

```
root@0f887071000a:/# more /etc/resolv.conf
nameserver 8.8.8.8
nameserver 8.8.4.4
search example1.com example2.com
root@0f887071000a:/# exit
```

Media Access Control (MAC) address

Another important piece of information that you can configure is the MAC address for the container.

Without any configuration, a container will receive a calculated MAC address that starts with the *02:42:ac:11* prefix.

If you need to specifically set this to a value, you can do this by running something similar to this:

```
$ docker run --rm -ti --mac-address="a2:11:aa:22:bb:33" ubuntu:latest /bin/bash
```

Normally you will not need to do that. But sometimes you want to reserve a particular set of MAC addresses for your containers in order to avoid other virtualization layers that use the same private block as Docker.

Be very careful when customizing the MAC address settings. It is possible to cause ARP contention on your network if two systems advertise the same MAC address. If you have a strong need to do this, try to keep your locally administered address ranges within some of the official ranges, like *x2-xx-xx-xx-xx-xx*, *x6-xx-xx-xx-xx-xx*, *xA-xx-xx-xx-xx-xx*, and *xE-xx-xx-xx-xx-xx* (with *x* being any valid hexidecimal character).

Storage Volumes

There are times when the default disk space allocated to a container or its ephemeral nature is not appropriate for the job at hand and it is necessary to have storage that can persist between container deployments.

Mounting storage from the Docker host is not a generally advisable pattern because it ties your container to a particular Docker host for its persistent state. But for cases like temporary cache files or other semi-ephemeral states, it can make sense.

For the times when we need to do this, we can leverage the -v command to mount filesystems from the host server into the container. In the following example, we are mounting */mnt/session_data* to */data* within the container:

```
$ docker run --rm -ti -v /mnt/session_data:/data ubuntu:latest /bin/bash
root@0f887071000a:/# mount | grep data
/dev/sda9 on /data type ext4 (rw,relatime,data=ordered)
root@0f887071000a:/# exit
```

If you have SELinux enabled on your Docker host, you may get a "Permission Denied" error when trying to mount a volume into your container. There are a few ways to handle this. The most direct method is to simply set the right context on the directory that you are trying to mount:

```
$ sudo chcon -Rt svirt_sandbox_file_t /var/lib/dhcpd
```

As of Docker 1.7, it is also possible to handle this directly from the Docker command line. If you are going to share a volume between containers, you can use the z option to the volume mount. This is identical to the above chcon command:

```
docker run -v /etc/dhcpd:/etc/dhcpd:z dhcpd
```

However, the best option is to actually utilize the Z option to the volume mount command, which will set the directory with the exact MCS label (e.g., chcon ... -l s0:c1,c2) that the container will be using. This provides for the best security and will only allow a single container to mount the volume:

```
docker run -v /etc/dhcpd:/etc/dhcpd:Z dhcpd
```

In the mount options, we can see that the filesystem was mounted read-write on /data as we expected.

The mount point in the container does not need to pre-exist for this command to work properly. However, the host mount point must exist. Auto creation of the host directory was deprecated in docker version 1.9.

If the container application is designed to write into /data, then this data will be visible on the host filesystem in /mnt/session_data and would remain available when this container was stopped and a new container started with the same volume mounted.

In Docker 1.5, a new command was added that allows the root volume of your container to be mounted read-only so that processes within the container cannot write anything to the root filesystem. This prevents things like logfiles, which a developer was unaware of, from filling up the container's allocated disk in production. When used in conjunction with a mounted volume, you can ensure that data is only written into expected locations.

In our previous example, we could accomplish this by simply adding --read-only=true to the command.

```
$ docker run --rm -ti --read-only=true -v /mnt/session_data:/data \
    ubuntu:latest /bin/bash
root@df542767bc17:/# mount | grep " / "
overlay on / type overlay (ro,relatime,lowerdir=...,upperdir=...,workdir=...)
```

```
root@df542767bc17:/# mount | grep data
/dev/sda9 on /data type ext4 (rw,relatime,data=ordered)
root@df542767bc17:/# exit
```

If we look closely at the mount options for the root directory, we will notice that they are mounted with the ro option, which makes it read-only. However, the /session_data mount is still mounted with the rw option so that our application can successfully write to the one volume to which we have designed it to write.

Sometimes it is necessary to make a directory like /tmp writeable, even when the rest of the container is read-only. In Docker 1.10, the --tmpfs attribute was added to docker run, so that you can mount a tmpfs filesystem into the container. Any data in these tmpfs directories will be lost when the container is stopped. The following command example shows a container being launched with a tmpfs filesystem mounted at /tmp with the rw, noexec, nodev, nosuid, and size=256M mount options set:

```
$ docker run --rm -ti --read-only=true --tmpfs \
  /tmp:rw,noexec,nodev,nosuid,size=256M ubuntu:latest /bin/bash
root@25b4f3632bbc:/# df -h /tmp
Filesystem      Size  Used Avail Use% Mounted on
tmpfs           256M     0  256M   0% /tmp
root@25b4f3632bbc:/# grep /tmp /etc/mtab
tmpfs /tmp tmpfs rw,seclabel,nosuid,nodev,noexec,relatime,size=262144k 0 0
root@25b4f3632bbc:/# exit
```

Containers should be designed to be stateless whenever possible. Managing storage creates undesirable dependencies and can easily make deployment scenarios much more complicated.

Resource Quotas

When people discuss the types of problems that you must often cope with when working in the cloud, the concept of the "noisy neighbor" is often near the top of the list. The basic problem this term refers to is that other applications, running on the same physical system as yours, can have a noticeable impact on your performance and resource availability.

Traditional virtual machines have the advantage that you can easily and very tightly control how much memory and CPU, among other resources, are allocated to the virtual machine. When using Docker, you must instead leverage the cgroup functionality in the Linux kernel to control the resources that are available to a Docker container. The docker create command directly supports configuring CPU and memory restrictions when you create a container.

Constraints are applied at the time of container creation. Constraints that you apply at creation time will exist for the life of the container. In most cases, if you need to change them, then you need to create a new container from the same image and change the constraints, unless you manipulate the kernel cgroups directly under the /sys filesystem.

There is an important caveat here. While Docker supports CPU and memory limits, as well as swap limits, you must have these capabilities enabled in your kernel in order for Docker to take advantage of them. You might need to add these as command-line parameters to your kernel on startup. To figure out if your kernel supports these limits, run docker info. If you are missing any support, you will get warning messages at the bottom, like:

```
WARNING: No swap limit support
```

The details regarding getting cgroup support configured for your kernel are distribution-specific, so you should consult the Docker documentation (*http://bit.ly/1DUrXth*) if you need help configuring things.

CPU shares

Docker thinks of CPU in terms of "cpu shares." The computing power of all the CPU cores in a system is considered to be the full pool of shares. 1024 is the number that Docker assigns to represent the full pool. By configuring a container's CPU shares, you can dictate how much time the container gets to use the CPU for. If you want the container to be able to use at most half of the computing power of the system, then you would allocate it 512 shares. Note that these are not exclusive shares, meaning that assigning all 1024 shares to a container does not prevent all other containers from running. Rather it's a hint to the scheduler about how long each container should be able to run each time it's scheduled. If we have one container that is allocated 1024 shares (the default) and two that are allocated 512, they will all get scheduled the same number of times. But if the normal amount of CPU time for each process is 100 microseconds, the containers with 512 shares will run for 50 microseconds each time, whereas the container with 1024 shares will run for 100 microseconds.

Let's explore a little bit how this works in practice. For the following examples, we are going to use a new Docker image that contains the stress command (*http://bit.ly/1evv1HK*) for pushing a system to its limits.

When we run stress without any cgroup constraints, it will use as many resources as we tell it to. The following command creates a load average of around 5 by creating two CPU-bound processes, one I/O-bound process, and two memory allocation processes:

```
$ docker run --rm -ti progrium/stress \
  --cpu 2 --io 1 --vm 2 --vm-bytes 128M --timeout 120s
```

This should be a reasonable command to run on any modern computer system, but be aware that it is going to stress the host system, so don't do this in a location that can't take the additional load, or even a possible failure, due to resource starvation.

If you run the `top` command on the Docker host, near the end of the two-minute run, you can see how the system is affected by the load created by the `stress` program.

In the following code, we are running on a system with two CPUs.

```
$ top -bn1 | head -n 15
top - 20:56:36 up 3 min,  2 users,  load average: 5.03, 2.02, 0.75
Tasks:  88 total,   5 running,  83 sleeping,   0 stopped,   0 zombie
%Cpu(s): 29.8 us, 35.2 sy,  0.0 ni, 32.0 id,  0.8 wa,  1.6 hi,  0.6 si,  0.0 st
KiB Mem:   1021856 total,   270148 used,   751708 free,    42716 buffers
KiB Swap:        0 total,        0 used,        0 free.    83764 cached Mem

  PID USER      PR  NI    VIRT    RES    SHR S  %CPU %MEM     TIME+ COMMAND
  810 root      20   0    7316     96      0 R  44.3  0.0   0:49.63 stress
  813 root      20   0    7316     96      0 R  44.3  0.0   0:49.18 stress
  812 root      20   0  138392  46936    996 R  31.7  4.6   0:46.42 stress
  814 root      20   0  138392  22360    996 R  31.7  2.2   0:46.89 stress
  811 root      20   0    7316     96      0 D  25.3  0.0   0:21.34 stress
    1 root      20   0  110024   4916   3632 S   0.0  0.5   0:07.32 systemd
    2 root      20   0       0      0      0 S   0.0  0.0   0:00.04 kthreadd
    3 root      20   0       0      0      0 S   0.0  0.0   0:00.11 ksofti...
```

If you want run the exact same `stress` command again, with only half the amount of available CPU time, you can run it like this:

```
$ docker run --rm -ti --cpu-shares 512 progrium/stress \
  --cpu 2 --io 1 --vm 2 --vm-bytes 128M --timeout 120s
```

The `--cpu-shares 512` is the flag that does the magic, allocating 512 CPU shares to this container. Note that the effect might not be noticeable on a system that is not very busy. That's because the container will continue to be scheduled for the same time-slice length whenever it has work to do, unless the system is constrained for resources. So in our case, the results of a `top` command on the host system will likely look exactly the same, unless you run a few more containers to give the CPU something else to do.

 Unlike virtual machines, Docker's cgroup-based constraints on CPU shares can have unexpected consequences. They are not hard limits; they are a relative limit, similar to the nice command. An example is a container that is constrained to half the CPU shares, but is on a system that is not very busy. Because the CPU is not busy, the limit on the CPU shares would have only a limited effect because there is no competition in the scheduler pool. When a second container that uses a lot of CPU is deployed to the same system, suddenly the effect of the constraint on the first container will be noticeable. Consider this carefully when constraining containers and allocating resources.

CPU pinning

It is also possible to pin a container to one or more CPU cores. This means that work for this container will only be scheduled on the cores that have been assigned to this container.

In the following example, we are running our stress container pinned to the first of two CPUs, with 512 CPU shares. Note that everything following the container image here are parameters to the stress command, not docker.

```
$ docker run --rm -ti --cpu-shares 512 --cpuset=0 progrium/stress \
  --cpu 2 --io 1 --vm 2 --vm-bytes 128M --timeout 120s
```

 The --cpuset argument is zero-indexed, so your first CPU core is 0. If you tell Docker to use a CPU core that does not exist on the host system, you will get a *Cannot start container* error. On our two-CPU example host, you could test this by using --cpuset=0,1,2.

If we run top again, we should notice that the percentage of CPU time spent in user space (us) is lower than it previously was, since we have restricted two CPU-bound processes to a single CPU.

```
%Cpu(s): 18.5 us, 22.0 sy,  0.0 ni, 57.6 id,  0.5 wa,  1.0 hi,  0.3 si,  0.0 st
```

 When you use CPU pinning, additional CPU sharing restrictions on the container only take into account other containers running on the same set of cores.

In Docker Engine 1.7, support was added for the CPU CFS (Completely Fair Scheduler) within the Linux kernel. You can alter the CPU quota a given container has by setting the `--cpu-quota` flag to a valid value when launching the container with `docker run`.

Memory

We can control how much memory a container can access in a manner similar to constraining the CPU. There is, however, one fundamental difference: while constraining the CPU only impacts the application's priority for CPU time, the memory limit is a *hard* limit. Even on an unconstrained system with 96 GB of free memory, if we tell a container that it may only have access to 24 GB, then it will only ever get to use 24 GB regardless of the free memory on the system. Because of the way the virtual memory system works on Linux, it's possible to allocate more memory to a container than the system has actual RAM. In this case, the container will resort to using swap in the event that actual memory is not available, just like a normal Linux process.

Let's start a container with a memory constraint by passing the `-m` option to the `docker run` command:

```
$ docker run --rm -ti -m 512m progrium/stress \
  --cpu 2 --io 1 --vm 2 --vm-bytes 128M --timeout 120s
```

When you use the `-m` option alone, you are setting both the amount of RAM and the amount of swap that the container will have access to. So here we've constrained the container to 512 MB of RAM and 512 MB of additional swap space. Docker supports b, k, m, or g, representing bytes, kilobytes, megabytes, or gigabytes, respectively. If your system somehow runs Linux and Docker and has mulitple terabytes of memory, then unfortunately you're going to have to specify it in gigabytes.

If you would like to set the swap separately or disable it altogether, then you need to also use the `--memory-swap` option. The `--memory-swap` option defines the total amount of memory and swap available to the container. If we rerun our previous command, like so:

```
$ docker run --rm -ti -m 512m --memory-swap=768m progrium/stress \
  --cpu 2 --io 1 --vm 2 --vm-bytes 128M --timeout 120s
```

Then we are telling the kernel that this container can have access to 512 MB of memory and 256 MB of additional swap space. Setting the `--memory-swap` option to -1 will disable the swap completely within the container.

Unlike CPU shares, memory is a hard limit! This is good because the constraint doesn't suddenly make a noticeable effect on the container when another container is deployed to the system. But it does mean that you need to be careful that the limit closely matches your container's needs because there is no wiggle room.

So, what happens if a container reaches its memory limit? Well, let's give it a try by modifying one of our previous commands and lowering the memory significantly:

```
$ docker run --rm -ti -m 100m progrium/stress --cpu 2 --io 1 \
    --vm 2 --vm-bytes 128M --timeout 120s
```

Where all our other runs of the `stress` container ended with the line:

```
stress: info: [1] successful run completed in 120s
```

We see that this run quickly fails with the line:

```
stress: FAIL: [1] (452) failed run completed in 1s
```

This is because the container tries to allocate more memory than it is allowed, and the Linux Out of Memory (OOM) killer is invoked and starts killing processes within the cgroup to reclaim memory. Since our container has only one running process, this kills the container.

Docker 1.10 has added features that allow you to tune and disable the Linux Out of Memory killer by using the `--oom-kill-disable` and the `--oom-score-adj` arguments to `docker run`

 As of Docker 1.9, it is also possible to specifically limit the amount of kernel memory available to a container by using the `--kernel-memory` argument to `docker run` or `docker create`.

Block I/O

In Docker 1.7, support was added to apply some prioritization to a container's use of block device I/O. This is managed by manipulating the default setting of the `blkio.weight` cgroup attribute, which can have a value of 10 to 1000, and defaults to 500. The system will divide all of the available I/O between every process within a cgroup slice, with the assigned weights impacting how much I/O each individual process receives.

To set this weight on a container, you need to pass the `--blkio-weight` to your `docker run` command with a valid value.

To read more technical details about this kernel feature, take a look at the blkio-controller kernel documentation (*https://www.kernel.org/doc/Documentation/cgroups/blkio-controller.txt*).

 The release of Docker 1.10, introduced even more block I/O tuning features, and added the docker update command, which can be used to dynamically adjust the resources limits of one of more containers. The following example shows how you could adjust the memory limit on 2 containers simultaneously: docker update --memory="1024M" 6b785f78b75e 92b797f12af1

ulimits

Another common way to limit resources avaliable to a process in Unix is through the application of user limits. The following code is a list of the types of things that can usually be configured by setting soft and hard limits via the ulimit command:

```
$ ulimit -a
core file size (blocks, -c) 0
data seg size (kbytes, -d) unlimited
scheduling priority (-e) 0
file size (blocks, -f) unlimited
pending signals (-i) 5835
max locked memory (kbytes, -l) 64
max memory size (kbytes, -m) unlimited
open files (-n) 1024
pipe size (512 bytes, -p) 8
POSIX message queues (bytes, -q) 819200
real-time priority (-r) 0
stack size (kbytes, -s) 10240
cpu time (seconds, -t) unlimited
max user processes (-u) 1024
virtual memory (kbytes, -v) unlimited
file locks (-x) unlimited
```

Before the release of Docker 1.6, all containers inherited the ulimits of the Docker daemon. This is usually not appropriate because the Docker server requires more resources to perform its job than any individual container.

It is now possible to configure the Docker daemon with the default user limits that you want to apply to every container. The following command would tell the Docker daemon to start all containers with a soft limit of 50 open files and a hard limit of 150 open files:

```
$ sudo docker daemon --default-ulimit nofile=50:150
```

You can then override these ulimits on a specific container by passing in values using the --ulimit argument.

```
$ docker run -d --ulimit nofile=150:300 nginx
```

There are some additional advanced commands that can be used when creating containers, but this covers many of the more common use cases. The Docker client documentation (*https://docs.docker.com/engine/reference/commandline/cli/*) lists all the available options and is kept current with each Docker release.

Starting a Container

Earlier in the chapter we used the `docker create` command to create our container. When we are ready to start the container, we can use the `docker start` command.

Let's say that we needed to run a copy of Redis, a common key-value store. We won't really do anything with this Redis container, but it's a long-lived process and serves as an example of something we might do in a real environment. We could first create the container using a command like the one shown here:

```
$ docker create -p 6379:6379 redis:2.8
Unable to find image 'redis:2.8' locally
30d39e59ffe2: Pull complete
...
868be653dea3: Pull complete
511136ea3c5a: Already exists
redis:2.8: The image you are pulling has been verified. Important: ...
Status: Downloaded newer image for redis:2.8
6b785f78b75ec2652f81d92721c416ae854bae085eba378e46e8ab54d7ff81d1
```

The command ends with the full hash that was generated for the container. However, if we didn't know the full or short hash for the container, we could list all the containers on the system, whether they are running or not, using:

```
$ docker ps -a
CONTAINER ID   IMAGE                   COMMAND                 ...
6b785f78b75e   redis:2.8               "/entrypoint.sh redi    ...
92b797f12af1   progrium/stress:latest  "/usr/bin/stress --v    ...
```

We can then start the container with the following command:

```
$ docker start 6b785f78b75e
```

 Most Docker commands will work with the full hash or a short hash. In the previous example, the full hash for the container is *6b785f78b75ec2652f81d92...bae085eba378e46e8ab54d7ff81d1*, but the short hash that is shown in most command output is *6b785f78b75e*. This short hash consists of the first 12 characters of the full hash.

To verify that it's running, we can run:

```
$ docker ps
CONTAINER ID   IMAGE      COMMAND             ... STATUS       ...
6b785f78b75e   redis:2.8  "/entrypoint.sh redi ... Up 2 minutes ...
```

Auto-Restarting a Container

In many cases, we want our containers to restart if they exit. Some containers are just very short-lived and come and go quickly. But for production applications, for instance, you expect them to be up after you've told them to run. We can tell Docker to do that on our behalf.

The way we tell Docker to do that is by passing the `--restart` argument to the `docker run` command. It takes three values: `no`, `always`, or `on-failure:#`. If restart is set to `no`, the container will never restart if it exits. If it is set to `always`, then the container will restart whenever the container exits with no regard to the exit code. If restart is set to `on-failure:3`, then whenever the container exits with a nonzero exit code, Docker will try to restart the container three times before giving up.

We can see this in action by rerunning our last memory-constrained stress container without the `--rm` argument, but with the `--restart` argument.

```
$ docker run -ti --restart=on-failure:3 -m 100m progrium/stress \
    --cpu 2 --io 1 --vm 2 --vm-bytes 128M --timeout 120s
```

In this example, we will see the output from the first run appear on the console before it dies. If we run a `docker ps` immediately after the container dies, we will see that Docker is attempting to restart the container.

```
$ docker ps
...  IMAGE                  ... STATUS                                ...
...  progrium/stress:latest ... Restarting (1) Less than a second ago ...
```

It will continue to fail because we have not given it enough memory to function properly. After three attempts, Docker will give up and we will see the container disappear from the the output of `docker ps`.

Stopping a Container

Containers can be stopped and started at will. You might think that starting and stopping are analogous to pausing and resuming a normal process. It's not quite the same, though. When stopped, the process is not paused; it actually exits. And when a container is stopped, it no longer shows up in the normal `docker ps` output. On reboot, docker will attempt to start all of the containers that were running at shutdown. It uses this same mechanism, and it's also useful when testing or for restarting a failed container. We can simply pause a Docker container with `docker pause` and unpause, discussed later. But let's stop our container now:

```
$ docker stop 6b785f78b75e
$ docker ps
CONTAINER ID IMAGE COMMAND CREATED STATUS PORTS NAMES
```

Now that we have stopped the container, nothing is in the ps list! We can start it back up with the container ID, but it would be really inconvenient to have to remember that. So docker ps has an additional option (-a) to show all containers, not just the running ones.

```
$ docker ps -a
CONTAINER ID   IMAGE                  STATUS              ...
6b785f78b75e   progrium/stress:latest Exited (0) 2 minutes ago ...
```

That STATUS field now shows that our container exited with a status code of 0 (no errors). We can start it back up with all of the same configuration it had before:

```
docker start 6b785f78b75e
6b785f78b75e
$ docker ps -a
CONTAINER ID IMAGE                  ... STATUS    ...
6b785f78b75e progrium/stress:latest  Up 15 seconds ...
```

Voila, our container is back up and running.

 Remember that containers exist even when they are not started, which means that you can always restart a container without needing to recreate it. Although memory contents will have been lost, all of the container's filesystem contents and metadata, including environment variables and port bindings, are saved and will still be in place when you restart the container.

We keep talking about the idea that containers are just a tree of processes that interact with the system in essentially the same way as any other process on the server. That means that we can send them Unix signals, which they can respond to. In the previous docker stop example, we're sending the container a SIGTERM signal and waiting for the container to exit gracefully. Containers follow the same process group signal propagation that any other process group would receive on Linux.

A normal docker stop sends a normal SIGTERM signal to the process. If you want to force a container to be killed if it hasn't stopped after a certain amount of time, you can use the -t argument, like this:

```
$ docker stop -t 25 6b785f78b75e
```

This tells Docker to initially send a SIGTERM signal as before, but then if the container has not stopped within 25 seconds, to send a SIGKILL signal to forcefully kill it.

Although `stop` is the best way to shut down your containers, there are times when it doesn't work and we need to forcefully kill a container.

Killing a Container

We saw what it looks like to use `docker stop` to stop a container, but often if a process is misbehaving, you just want it to exit immediately.

We have `docker kill` for that. It looks pretty much like `docker stop`:

```
$ docker kill 6b785f78b75e
6b785f78b75e
```

A `docker ps` nows shows that the container is no longer running, as expected:

```
$ docker ps
CONTAINER ID IMAGE COMMAND CREATED STATUS PORTS NAMES
```

Just because it was killed rather than stopped does not mean you can't start it again, though. You can just issue a `docker start` like you would for a nicely stopped container. Sometimes you might want to send another signal to a container, one that is not `stop` or `kill`. Like the Linux `kill` command, `docker kill` supports sending any Unix signal. Let's say we wanted to send a USR1 signal to our container to tell it to do something like reconnect a remote logging session. We could do the following:

```
$ docker kill --signal=USR1 6b785f78b75e
6b785f78b75e
```

If our container actually did something with the USR1 signal, it would now do it. Since we're just running a bash shell, though, it just continues on as if nothing happened. Try sending a HUP signal, though, and see what happens. Remember that a HUP is the signal that is sent when the terminal closes on a foreground process.

Pausing and Unpausing a Container

Sometimes we really just want to stop our container as described above. But there are a number of times when we just don't want our container to do anything for a while. That could be because we're taking a snapshot of its filesystem to create a new image, or just because we need some CPU on the host for a while. If you're used to normal Unix process handling, you might wonder how this actually works since containerized processes are just processes.

Pausing leverages the cgroups freezer (*https://www.kernel.org/doc/Documenta tion/cgroup-v1/freezer-subsystem.txt*), which essentially just prevents your process from being scheduled until you unfreeze it. This will prevent the container from doing anything while maintaining its overall state, including memory contents.

Unlike stopping a container, where the processes are made aware that they are stopping via the SIGSTOP signal, pausing a container doesn't send any information to the container about its state change. That's an important distinction. Several Docker commands use pausing and unpausing internally as well. Here's how we pause a container:

```
$ docker pause 6b785f78b75e
```

If we look at the list of running containers, we will now see that the Redis container status is listed as (Paused).

```
# docker ps
CONTAINER ID  IMAGE                  ...  STATUS                 ...
6b785f78b75e  progrium/stress:latest ...  Up 36 minutes (Paused) ...
```

Attempting to use the container in this paused state would fail. It's present, but nothing is running. We can now resume the container using the docker unpause command.

```
$ docker unpause 6b785f78b75e
6b785f78b75e
$ docker ps
CONTAINER ID  IMAGE                  ... STATUS ...
6b785f78b75e  progrium/stress:latest ... Up 1 second ...
```

It's back to running, and docker ps correctly reflects the new state. Note that it shows "Up 1 second" now, which is when we unpaused it, not when it was last run.

Cleaning Up Containers and Images

After running all these commands to build images, create containers, and run them, we have accumulated a lot of image layers and container folders on our system.

We can list all the containers on our system using the docker ps -a command and then delete any of the containers in the list, as follows:

```
$ docker ps -a
CONTAINER ID  IMAGE                  ...
92b797f12af1  progrium/stress:latest ...
...
$ docker rm 92b797f12af1
```

We can then list all the images on our system using:

```
$ docker images
REPOSITORY       TAG     IMAGE ID     CREATED       VIRTUAL SIZE
ubuntu           latest  5ba9dab47459 3 weeks ago   188.3 MB
redis            2.8     868be653dea3 3 weeks ago   110.7 MB
progrium/stress  latest  873c28292d23 7 months ago  281.8 MB
```

We can then delete an image and all associated filesystem layers by running:

```
$ docker rmi 873c28292d23
```

If you try to delete an image that is in use by a container, you will get a *Conflict, cannot delete* error. You should stop and delete the container(s) first.

There are times, especially during development cycles, when it makes sense to completely clean off all the images or containers from your system. There is no built-in command for doing this, but with a little creativity it can be accomplished reasonably easily.

To delete all of the containers on your Docker hosts, you can use the following command:

```
$ docker rm $(docker ps -a -q)
```

And to delete all the images on your Docker host, this command will get the job done:

```
$ docker rmi $(docker images -q -)
```

Newer versions of the docker ps and docker images commands both support a filter argument that can make it easy to fine-tune your delete commands for certain circumstances.

To remove all containers that exited with a nonzero state, you can use this filter:

```
$ docker rm $(docker ps -a -q --filter 'exited!=0')
```

And to remove all untagged images, you can type:

```
$ docker rmi $(docker images -q -f "dangling=true")
```

You can read the official Docker documentation to explore the filtering options. At the moment there are very few filters to choose from, but more will likely be added over time. And if you are really interested, Docker is an open source project, so they are always open to public code contributions.

It is also possible to make your own very creative filters by stringing together commands using pipes (|) and other similar techniques.

Next Steps

In the next chapter, we'll do more exploration of what Docker brings to the table. For now it's probably worth doing a little experimentation on your own. We suggest exercising some of the container control commands we covered here so that you're familiar with the command-line options and the overall syntax. Try interacting with stoppped or paused containers to see what you can see. Then when you're feeling confident, head on into Chapter 6!

Exploring Docker

Now that we have some experience working with Docker containers and images, we can explore some of its other capabilities. In this chapter, we'll continue to use the docker command-line tool to talk to the running docker daemon that you've configured, while visiting some of the other fundamental commands.

Docker provides commands to do a number of additional things easily:

- Printing the Docker version
- Viewing the server information
- Downloading image updates
- Inspecting containers
- Entering a running container
- Returning a result
- Viewing logs
- Monitoring statistics

Let's take a look at some of those and some community tooling that augments Docker's native capabilities.

Printing the Docker Version

If you completed the last chapter, you have a working Docker daemon on a Linux server or virtual machine, and you've started a base container to make sure it's all working. If you haven't set that up already and you want to try out the steps in the rest of the book, you'll want to follow the installation steps in Chapter 3 before you move on with this section.

The absolute simplest thing you can do with Docker is print the versions of the various components. It might not sound like much, but this is a useful tool to have in your belt because the server and API are often not backwards compatible with older clients. Knowing how to show the version will help you troubleshoot certain types of connection issues. Note that this command actually talks to the remote Docker server. If you can't connect to the server for any reason, the client will complain. If you find that you have a connectivity problem, you should probably revisit the steps in the last chapter.

You can always directly log in to the Docker server and run docker commands from a shell on the server if you are trouble-shooting issues or simply do not want to use the docker client to connect to a remote system.

Since we just installed all of the Docker components at the same time, when we run docker version, we should see that all of our versions match:

```
$ docker version
Client version: 1.3.1
Client API version: 1.15
Go version (client): go1.3.3
Git commit (client): 4e9bbfa
OS/Arch (client): linux/amd64
Server version: 1.3.1
Server API version: 1.15
Go version (server): go1.3.3
Git commit (server): 4e9bbfa
```

Notice how we have different lines representing the client, server, and API versions. It's important to note that different versions of the command-line tools might use the same Docker API version. Even when they do, sometimes Docker won't let you talk to a remote server that doesn't exactly match. Now you know how to verify this information.

In versions of Docker previous to 1.10, the docker client would error whenever you tried to connect to a server using a older version of the API. This situation can now be easily dealt with, as shown in this example:

```
$ docker ps
Error response from daemon: client is newer than server \
  (client API version: 1.22, server API version: 1.21)
$ export  DOCKER_API_VERSION="1.21"
$ docker ps
CONTAINER ID        IMAGE              COMMAND           \
CREATED             STATUS             PORTS             \
NAMES
```

Server Information

We can also find out a little bit about the Docker server itself via the Docker client. Later we'll talk more about what all of this means, but you can find out which filesystem backend the Docker server is running, which kernel version it is on, which operating system it is running on, and how many containers and images are currently stored there. If you run `docker info`, you will see something similar to this:

```
$ docker info
Containers: 22
Images: 180
Storage Driver: aufs
 Root Dir: /var/lib/docker/aufs
 Dirs: 224
Execution Driver: native-0.2
Kernel Version: 3.8.0-29-generic
Operating System: Ubuntu precise (12.04.3 LTS)
```

Depending on how your Docker daemon is set up, this might look somewhat different. Don't be concerned about that; this is just to give you an example. Here we can see that our server is an Ubuntu 12.04.3 LTS release running the 3.8.0 Linux kernel and backed with the AUFS filesystem driver. We also have a lot of images! With a fresh install, this number should be zero.

In most installations, */var/lib/docker* will be the default root directory used to store images and containers. If you need to change this, you can edit your Docker startup scripts to launch the daemon, with the `--graph` argument pointing to a new storage location. To test this by hand, you could run something like this:

```
$ sudo docker -d
-H unix:///var/run/docker.sock \
-H tcp://0.0.0.0:2375 --graph="/data/docker"
```

Downloading Image Updates

We're are going to use an Ubuntu base image for the following examples. Even if you have already grabbed the Ubuntu base image once, you can `pull` it again and it will automatically pick up any updates that have been published since you last ran it. That's because `latest` is a tag that, by convention, is always moved to the most recent version of the image that has been published to the image registry. Invoking the `pull` will look like this:

```
$ docker pull ubuntu:latest

Pulling repository ubuntu
5506de2b643b: Download complete
511136ea3c5a: Download complete
d497ad3926c8: Download complete
```

```
ccb62158e970: Download complete
e791be0477f2: Download complete
3680052c0f5c: Download complete
22093c35d77b: Download complete
```

That command pulled down only the layers that have changed since we last ran the command. You might see a longer or shorter list, or even an empty list, depending on when you ran it and what changes have been pushed to the registry since then.

 It's good to remember that even though you pulled latest, docker won't automatically keep the local image up-to-date for you. You'll be responsible for doing that yourself. However, if you deploy an image based on a newer copy of ubuntu:latest, Docker will download the missing layers during the deployment just like you would expect.

As of Docker 1.6, it is now possible to pull a specific version of an image from Docker Hub or any registry based on Docker's Registry 2.0 codebase by using the digest attached to the desired image. This is useful when you want to ensure that you are pulling a very specific image build and don't want to rely on a tag, which can potentially be moved.

```
docker pull ubuntu@sha256:2f9a...82cf
```

Inspecting a Container

Once you have a container created, running or not, you can now use docker to see how it was configured. This is often useful in debugging, and also has some other information that can be useful when identifying a container.

For this example, let's go ahead and start up a container.

```
$ docker run -d -t ubuntu /bin/bash
3c4f916619a5dfc420396d823b42e8bd30a2f94ab5b0f42f052357a68a67309b
```

We can list all our running containers with docker ps to ensure everything is running as expected, and to copy the container ID.

```
$ docker ps
CONTAINER ID  IMAGE          COMMAND        ... STATUS         ... NAMES
3c4f916619a5  ubuntu:latest  "/bin/bash" ... Up 31 seconds ... angry_mestorf
```

In this case, our ID is 3c4f916619a5. We could also use angry_mestorf, which is the dynamic name assigned to our container. Underlying tools all need the unique container ID, though, so it's useful to get into the habit of looking at that first. As is the case in many revision control systems, this hash is actually just the prefix of a much longer hash. Internally, the kernel uses a 64-byte hash to identify the container. But that's painful for humans to use, so Docker supports the shortened hash.

The output to `docker inspect` is pretty verbose, so we'll cut it down in the following code block to a few values worth pointing out. You should look at the full output to see what else you think is interesting:

```
$ docker inspect 3c4f916619a5
[{
    "Args": [],
    "Config": {
        "Cmd": [
            "/bin/bash"
        ],
        "Env": [
            "PATH=/usr/local/sbin:/usr/local/bin:/usr/sbin:/usr/bin:/sbin:/bin"
        ],
        "Hostname": "3c4f916619a5",
        "Image": "ubuntu",
    },
    "Created": "2014-11-07T22:06:32.229471304Z",
    "Id": "3c4f916619a5dfc420396d823b42e8bd30a2f94ab5b0f42f052357a68a67309b",
    "Image": "5506de2b643be1e6febbf3b8a240760c6843244c41e12aa2f60ccbb7153d1"
}
```

Note that long `"Id"` string. That's the full unique identifier of this container. Luckily we can use the short name, even if that's still not especially convenient. We can also see the exact time when the container was created in a much more precise way than `docker ps` gives us.

Some other interesting things are shown here as well: the top-level command in the container, the environment that was passed to it at creation time, the image on which it's based, and the hostname inside the container. All of these are configurable at container creation time if you need to do so. The usual method for passing configuration to containers, for example, is via environment variables, so being able to see how a container was configured via `docker inspect` can reveal a lot when debugging.

Getting Inside a Running Container

You can pretty easily get a shell running in a new container as we demonstrated above with `docker run`. But it's not the same as getting a new shell inside an existing container that is actively running your application. Every time you use `docker run`, you get a new container. But if you have an existing container that is running an application and you need to debug it from inside the container, you need something else.

Because Docker originally used the LXC (*https://linuxcontainers.org*) backend by default, the Linux `lxc-attach` command was the easiest way to enter a running container. But once Docker shifted to using libcontainer by default, this is no longer useful for most people. Since Docker containers are Linux namespaces, however, tools like the docker exec command and nsenter support this functionality more broadly.

The LXC driver was deprecated in Docker 1.8 and completely removed in Docker 1.10.

docker exec

First, let's look at the newest and best way to get inside a running container. From Docker 1.3 and up, the docker daemon and docker command-line tool support remotely executing a shell into a running container via docker exec. So let's start up a container in background mode, and then enter it using docker exec.

We'll need our container's ID, like we did above when we inspected it. I just did that, and my container's ID is 589f2ad30138. We can now use that to get inside the container. The command line to docker exec, unsurprisingly, looks a lot like the command line to docker run. We request a pseudo-tty and an interactive command:

```
$ docker exec -t -i 589f2ad30138 /bin/bash
root@589f2ad30138:/#
```

Note that we got a command line back that tells us the ID of the container we're running inside. That's pretty useful for keeping track of where we are. We can now run a ps to see what else is running inside our container. We should see our other bash process that we backgrounded earlier.

```
root@589f2ad30138:/# ps -ef
UID         PID  PPID  C STIME TTY          TIME CMD
root          1     0  0 23:13 ?        00:00:00 /bin/bash
root          9     0  1 23:14 ?        00:00:00 /bin/bash
root         17     9  0 23:14 ?        00:00:00 ps -ef
```

You can also run additional processes in the background via docker exec. You use the -d option just like with docker run. But you should think hard about doing that for anything but debugging because you lose the repeatability of the image deployment if you depend on this mechanism. Other people would then have to know what to pass to docker exec to get the desired functionality. If you're tempted to do this, you would probably reap bigger gains from rebuilding your container image to launch both processes in a repeatable way.

nsenter

Part of the core util-linux package from kernel.org (*http://bit.ly/1GpecsE*) is nsenter, short for "Namespace Enter," which allows you to enter any Linux namespace. In Chapter 10, we'll go into more detail on namespaces. But they are the core of what makes a container a container. Using nsenter, therefore, we can get into a Docker container from the server itself, even in situations where the Docker daemon is not responding and we can't use docker exec. nsenter can also be used to manipulate things in a container as *root* on the server that would otherwise be prevented by docker exec, for example. This can be really useful when debugging. Most of the time, docker exec is all you need. But you should have nsenter in your tool belt.

Most Linux distributions ship with the util-linux package that contains nsenter. But few ship with one that is new enough to have nsenter itself installed, because it's a recent addition to the package. So the easiest way to get ahold of nsenter is to install it via a third-party Docker container (*https://github.com/jpetazzo/nsenter*). This works by pulling a Docker image from the Docker Hub registry and then running a specially crafted Docker container that will install the nsenter command-line tool into */usr/local/bin*. This might seem strange at first, but it's a clever way to allow you to install nsenter to any Docker server remotely using nothing more than the docker command.

The following code shows how we install nsenter to */usr/local/bin* on your Docker server:

```
$ docker run --rm -v /usr/local/bin:/target jpetazzo/nsenter
Unable to find image 'jpetazzo/nsenter' locally
Pulling repository jpetazzo/nsenter
9e4ef84f476a: Download complete
511136ea3c5a: Download complete
71d9d77ae89e: Download complete
Status: Downloaded newer image for jpetazzo/nsenter:latest
Installing nsenter to /target
Installing docker-enter to /target
```

You should be very careful about doing this! It's always a good idea to check out what you are running, and particularly what you are exposing part of your filesystem to, before you run a third-party container on your system. With -v, we're telling Docker to expose the host's */usr/local/bin* directory into the running container as /target. When the container starts, it is then copying an executable into that directory on our host's filesystem. In Chapter 10, we will discuss some security frameworks and commands that can be leveraged to prevent potentially nefarious container activities.

Unlike docker exec, which can be run remotely, nsenter requires that you run it on the server itself. The README in the GitHub repo explains how to set this up to work over SSH automatically if you want to do that. For our purposes, we'll log in to our Docker server via SSH and then invoke the command from the server. In any case, like with docker exec, we need to have a container running. You should still have one running from above. If not, go back and start one, and then ssh into your server.

docker exec is pretty simple, but nsenter is a little inconvenient to use. It needs to have the PID of the actual top-level process in your container. That's less than obvious to find and requires a few steps. Luckily there's a convenience wrapper installed by that Docker container we just ran, called docker-enter, which takes away the pain. But before we jump to the convenience wrapper, let's run nsenter by hand so you can see what's going on.

First we need to find out the ID of the running container, because nsenter needs to know that to access it. This is the same as previously shown for docker inspect and docker exec:

```
$ docker ps
CONTAINER ID   IMAGE           COMMAND       ...   NAMES
3c4f916619a5   ubuntu:latest   "/bin/bash"   ...   grave_goldstine
```

The ID we want is that first field, 3c4f916619a5. Armed with that, we can now find the PID we need. We do that like this:

```
$ PID=$(docker inspect --format \{{.State.Pid\}} 3c4f916619a5)
```

This will store the PID we care about into the PID environment variable. We need to have root privilege to do what we're going to do. So you should either su to root or use sudo on the command line. Now we invoke nsenter:

```
$ sudo nsenter --target $PID --mount --uts --ipc --net --pid
root@3c4f916619a5:/#
```

If the end result looks a lot like docker exec, that's because it does almost exactly the same thing under the hood!

There are a lot of command-line options there, and what they're doing is telling nsenter which parts of the container we need access to. Generally you want all of them, so you might expect that to be the default, but it's not, so we specify them all.

Neither nsenter or docker exec work well for exploring a container that does not contain a Unix shell. In this case you usually need to explore the container from the Docker server by navigating directly to where the container filesystem resides on storage. This will typically look something like this */var/lib/docker/aufs/mnt/365c...87a3,*, but will vary based on the Docker setup, storage backend, and container hash. You can determine your Docker root directory by running docker info.

Back at the beginning of this section we mentioned that there is a convenience wrapper called docker-enter that gets installed by running the installation Docker container. Having now seen the mechanism involved with running nsenter, you can now appreciate that if you actually just want to enter all the namespaces for the container and skip several steps, you can do this:

```
$ sudo docker-enter 3c4f916619a5 /bin/bash
root@3c4f916619a5:/#
```

In Docker 1.9, a new volume subcommand was added to the docker client. Using this, it is possible to list all of the volumes stored in your root directory and then discover additional information about them, including where they are physically stored on the server.

```
# docker volume ls
DRIVER              VOLUME NAME
local               ca5ee542deefe42ad9004...
local               6680f5dabe4dcd73b89bd...
local               2be661504f3767227fd37...

# docker volume inspect 2be661504f3767227fd37...
[
    {
        "Name": "2be661504f3767227fd37...",
        "Driver": "local",
        "Mountpoint": "/var/lib/docker/volumes/2be661504f3767227f.../_data"
    }
]
```

The volume subcommand also allows you to create and remove volumes.

With these commands, you should be able to explore your containers in great detail. Once we've explained namespaces more in Chapter 10, you'll get a better understanding of exactly how all these pieces interact and combine to create a container.

Exploring the Shell

One way or another, either by launching a container with a foreground shell or via one of the other mechanisms above, we've got a shell running inside a container. So, let's look around a little bit. What processes are running?

```
$ ps -ef
UID        PID  PPID  C STIME TTY          TIME CMD
root         1     0  0 22:12 ?        00:00:00 /bin/bash
root        12     1  0 22:16 ?        00:00:00 ps -ef
```

Wow, that's not much, is it? It turns out that when we told docker to start bash, we didn't get anything but that. We're inside a whole Linux distribution image, but no other processes started for us automatically. We only got what we asked for. It's good to keep that in mind going forward.

 Docker containers don't, by default, start anything in the background like a full virtual machine would. They're a lot lighter weight than that and therefore don't start an init system. You can, of course, run a whole init system if you need to, but you have to ask for it. We'll talk about that in a later chapter.

That's how we get a shell running in a container. You should feel free to poke around and see what else looks interesting inside the container. Note that you might have a pretty limited set of commands available. You're in an Ubuntu distribution, though, so you can fix that by using apt-get to install more packages. Note that these are only going to be around for the life of this container. You're modifying the top layer of the container, not the base image!

Returning a Result

Most people would not think of spinning up a virtual machine to run a single process and then return the result because doing so would be very time consuming and require booting a whole operating system to simply execute one command. But Docker doesn't work the same way as virtual machines: containers are very lightweight and don't have to boot up like an operating system. Running something like a quick background job and waiting for the exit code is a normal use case for a Docker container. You can think of it as a way to get remote access to a containerized system and have access to any of the individual commands inside that container with the ability to pipe data to and from them and return exit codes.

This can be useful in lots of scenarios: you might, for instance, have system health checks run this way remotely, or have a series of machines with processes that you spin up via Docker to process a workload and then return. The docker command-line tools proxy the results to the local machine. If you run the remote command in foreground mode and don't specify doing otherwise, docker will redirect its stdin to the remote process, and the remote process's stdout and stderr to your terminal. The only things we have to do to get this functionality are to run the command in the foreground and not allocate a TTY on the remote. This is actually the default configuration! No command-line options are required. We do need to have a container configured and ready to run.

The following code shows what you can do:

```
$ docker run 8d12decc75fe /bin/false
$ echo $?
1
$ docker run 8d12decc75fe /bin/true
$ echo $?
0
$ docker run 8d12decc75fe /bin/cat /etc/passwd
root:x:0:0:root:/root:/bin/bash
bin:x:1:1:bin:/bin:/sbin/nologin
daemon:x:2:2:daemon:/sbin:/sbin/nologin
adm:x:3:4:adm:/var/adm:/sbin/nologin
lp:x:4:7:lp:/var/spool/lpd:/sbin/nologin
sync:x:5:0:sync:/sbin:/bin/sync
shutdown:x:6:0:shutdown:/sbin:/sbin/shutdown
nobody:x:99:99:Nobody:/:/sbin/nologin
$ docker run 8d12decc75fe /bin/cat /etc/passwd | wc -l
8
```

Here we executed /bin/false on the remote server, which will always exit with a status of 1. Notice how docker proxied that result to us in the local terminal. Just to prove that it returns other results, we also run /bin/true, which will always return a 0. And there it is.

Then we actually ask docker to run cat /etc/passwd on the remote container. What we get is the result of that container's version of the /etc/passwd file. Because that's just regular output on stdout, we can pipe it into local commands just like we would anything else.

 The previous code pipes the output into the local wc command, not a wc command in the container. The pipe itself is not passed to the container. If you want to pass the whole command, including the pipes, to the server, you need to invoke a complete shell on the remote side and pass a quoted command, like bash -c "<your command> | <something else>". In the previous code, that would be: docker run 8d12decc75fe /bin/bash -c "/bin/cat /etc/passwd | wc -l".

Docker Logs

Logging is a critical part of any production application. There are common ways we expect to interact with application logs on Linux systems. If you're running a process on a box, you might expect the output to go to a local logfile that you could read through. Or perhaps you might expect the output to simply be logged to the kernel buffer where it can be read from dmesg. Because of the container's restrictions, neither of these will work without some gyrations to do so. But that's OK, because logging is first class in Docker. First we'll talk about the simple case, using the default logging mechanism. There are limitations to this mechanism, which we'll explain in a minute, but for the simple case it works well. The mechanism is docker logs.

The way this works is that anything sent to stdout or stderr in the container is captured by the Docker daemon and streamed into a configurable backend, which is by default a JSON file for each container. We'll cover that first, then talk about other options. The default logging mechanism lets us retrieve logs for any container at any time like this, showing some logs from a container running nginx:

```
$ docker logs 3c4f916619a5
nginx stderr | 2014/11/20 00:34:56 [notice] 12#0: using the "epoll" ...
nginx stderr | 2014/11/20 00:34:56 [notice] 12#0: nginx/1.0.15
nginx stderr | 2014/11/20 00:34:56 [notice] 12#0: built by gcc 4.4.7 ...
nginx stderr | 2014/11/20 00:34:56 [notice] 12#0: OS: Linux 3.8.0-35-generic
```

This is nice because Docker allows you to get the logs remotely, right from the command line, on demand. That's really useful for low-volume logging.

 To limit the log output to more recent logs, you can use the --since option to only display logs after a specified RFC 3339 date (e.g., 2002-10-02T10:00:00-05:00), Unix timestamp (e.g., 1450071961), or Go duration string (e.g., 5m45s). You may also use --tail followed by a number of lines to tail.

The actual files backing this logging are on the Docker server itself, by default in */var/lib/docker/containers/<container_id>/* where the *<container_id>* is replaced by the actual container ID. If you take a look at one of those files, you'll see it's a file with each line representing a JSON object. It will look something like this:

```
{"log":"2015-01-02 23:58:51,003 INFO success: running.\r\n",
"stream":"stdout",
"time":"2015-01-02T23:58:51.0040362382Z"}
```

That *log* field is exactly what was sent to stdout on the process in question; the *stream* field tells us that this was stdout and not stderr; and the precise time that the Docker daemon received it is provided in the *time* field. It's an uncommon format for logging, but it's structured rather than just a raw stream, which is beneficial if you want to do anything with the logs later.

Like a logfile, you can also tail the Docker logs live with `docker logs -f`:

```
$ docker logs -f 3c4f916619a5
nginx stderr | 2014/11/20 00:34:56 [notice] 12#0: using the "epoll" ...
nginx stderr | 2014/11/20 00:34:56 [notice] 12#0: nginx/1.0.15
nginx stderr | 2014/11/20 00:34:56 [notice] 12#0: built by gcc 4.4.7 ...
nginx stderr | 2014/11/20 00:34:56 [notice] 12#0: OS: Linux 3.8.0-35-generic
```

By configuring the tag log option similar to `--log-opt tag="{{.ImageName }}/ {{.ID }}"`, it is possible to change the default log tag (which every log line will start with) to something more useful. By default, Docker logs will be tagged with the first 12 characters of the container ID.

This looks identical to the usual `docker logs`, but the client then blocks, waiting on and displaying any new logs to appear, much like the Linux command line `tail -f`.

The default settings do not currently enable log rotation. You'll want to make sure you specify the `--log-opt max-size` and `--log-opt max-file` settings if running in production. Those limit the largest file size before rotation and the maximum number of log files to keep, respectively. `max-file` does not do anything unless you've also set `max-size` to tell Docker when to rotate the logs. Note that when this is enabled, the `docker logs` mechanism will only return data from the current log file.

For single host logging, this mechanism is pretty good. Its shortcomings are around log rotation, access to the logs remotely once they've been rotated, and disk space usage for high-volume logging. For when this isn't enough—and in production it's probably not—Docker also supports configurable logging backends. Currently supported are the native `json-file` we described above and `syslog`, `fluentd`, `journald`, `gelf`, `awslogs`, and `splunk` which are used for sending logs to various remote logging frameworks. The supported option that currently is the simplest, but not the best as we'll describe, for running Docker at scale is the option to send your container logs to `syslog` directly from Docker. You can specify this on the Docker command line with the `--log-driver=syslog` option.

If you change the log driver to anything other than the default (json-file), then you will no longer be able to use the docker logs command. It is assumed that you will have another means of accessing your logs in that case.

Secondly, the Docker daemon itself will now be writing to /dev/log. This is usually read by the syslog daemon. If that blocks, the logging will buffer into memory in the Docker process. At the time of this writing, further work is being done on this feature to mitigate that effect. As a result of this deficiency, we can't currently recommend this solution at scale. This shortcoming affects the other remote mechanisms as well.

You can also log directly to a remote syslog server by setting the log option syslog-address similar to this: --log-opt syslog-address=tcp://192.168.42.42:123.

It was a long time from the beginning of the Docker project to when logging by other than the json-file method was supported. So there are community contributions with many alternate ways of getting you logging at scale. It should be noted that many of these mechanisms are also incompatible with docker logs. The most common solution is to use a method to send your logs directly to syslog. There are several mechanisms in use:

- Log directly from your application.
- Have a process manager in your container relay the logs (e.g., systemd, upstart, supervisor, or runit).
- Run a logging relay in the container that wraps stdout/stderr from the container.
- Relay the Docker JSON logs themselves to a remote logging framework from the server or another container.

Some third-party libraries and programs, like supervisor, write to the file system for various (and sometimes unexpected) reasons. If you are trying to design clean containers that do not write directly into the container filesystem, you should consider utilizing the --read-only and --tmpfs options to docker run that we discussed in Chapter 5.

Many of these options share the drawbacks of changing the logging driver in Docker itself: they hide logs from docker logs so you can see them on an individual container during debugging as easily without relying on an external application. So let's take a look at how these options stack up.

Logging directly from your application to syslog might make sense, but if you're running any third-party applications, that probably won't work and it's inflexible to changes once deployed inside tens of production applications. And unless you also emit logs on stdout and stderr, they will not be visible in docker logs.

Spotify has released a simple, statically linked Go relay (*https://github.com/spotify/syslog-redirector*) to handle logging your stderr and stdout to syslog for one process inside the container. Generally you run this from the CMD line in the Dockerfile. Because it's statically compiled, it has no dependencies, which makes it very flexible. It swallows the loglines, however, so they are not visible in docker logs.

Although controversial in the Docker community, running a process manager in the container is a reasonably easy way to capture output and direct it to a central logging service. New Relic released a logging plug-in for supervisor (*http://github.com/newrelic/supervisor-remote-logging*) that does exactly that. This mechanism is nice because there is no additional machinery in the container other than what you'd already include. You do need Python installed, though, and it writes a certain amount of data to the container filesystem which can have deleterious effects on performance and container longevity. You can also emit the logs to stdout and stderr, which makes them available both locally with docker logs and remotely.

If you want to have one system to support all your containers, a popular option is Logspout (*https://github.com/progrium/logspout*), which runs in a separate container, talks to docker, and logs all the containers' logs to syslog (UDP only). The advantage of this approach is that it does not preclude docker logs but it does require that you set up log rotation.

Probably the best current option is to run Heka (*https://github.com/mozilla-services/heka*), from Mozilla. This is a mature and very robust logging framework with extensive filtering and routing options for your logs. It also has first-class support for Docker logging. You can run a single Heka daemon in either a container or natively on the Docker host and, like Logspout, it will attach to and follow all the logs from all of your containers. It's much more flexible than Logspout, however, and supports a wide array of outputs and transformations. It is pretty simple to set up the first time but can scale to the limits of whatever you might want to do. This is what we currently recommend.

Finally, while you really should be capturing your logs somewhere, there are rare situations in which you simply don't want any logging. You can use the --log-driver=none switch to turn them off completely.

Monitoring Docker

Running something in production is not a good idea unless you can tell what's going on. In the modern world, we monitor everyting and report as many statistics as we can. Docker supports some nice, basic reporting capabilities via `docker stats` and `docker events`. We'll show you those and then look at a community offering from Google that does some nice graphing output as well.

Container Stats

In version 1.5.0, Docker added an endpoint for viewing stats of running containers. The command-line tool can stream from this endpoint and every few seconds report back on one or more listed containers, giving basic statistics information about what's happening. `docker stats`, like the Linux `top` command, takes over the current terminal and updates the same lines on the screen with the current information. It's hard to show that in print, so we'll just give an example, but this updates every few seconds by default.

```
$ docker stats e64a279663aa
CONTAINER      CPU %    MEM USAGE/LIMIT      MEM %    NET I/O
e64a279663aa   0.00%    7.227 MiB/987.9 MiB  0.73%    936 B/468 B
```

Here we can see the container ID (but not the name), the amount of CPU it's currently consuming, the amout of memory it has in use, and the limit of what it's allowed to use. The percentage of memory utilized is also provided to make it easier for the user to quickly determine how much free memory the container has available. And stats are provided for both in and out network bytes.

These are all of basic interest, but what they provide is not all that exciting. It turns out, though, that the Docker API provides a *lot* more information on the stats endpoint than is shown in the client. We've steered away from hitting the API in this book so far, but in this case the data provided by the API is so much richer that we'll use `curl` to call it and see what our container is doing. It's nowhere near as nice to read, but there is a lot more detail. This is a good intro to calling the API yourself as well.

The `/stats/` endpoint that we'll hit on the API will continue to stream stats to us as long as we keep the connection open. Since as humans we can't really parse usefully, we'll just ask for one line and then use Python to "pretty print" it. In order for this command to work, you'll need to have Python installed (version 2.6 or later). If you don't and you still want to see the JSON output, you can skip the pipe to Python, but you'll get plain, ugly JSON back.

Here we call `localhost`, but you'll want to use the hostname of your Docker server. Port 2375 is usually the right port. Note that we also pass the ID of our container in the URL we send to `curl`.

You can usually inspect the contents of the DOCKER_HOST environment variable, using something like echo $DOCKER_HOST, to discover the hostname or IP address of the Docker server that you are using.

It is easiest to run through the following example if you are running Docker on a full Linux distribution, with the Docker server bound to the default unencrypted port 2375.

First, let's go ahead and start up a container that you can read stats from:

```
$ docker run -d ubuntu:latest sleep 1000
91c86ec7b33f37da9917d2f67177ebfaa3a95a78796e33139e1b7561dc4f244a
```

Now that the container is running, we can get an ongoing stream of statistics information about the container in JSON format by running something like curl with your container's hash.

```
$ curl -s http://localhost:2375/v1/containers/91c8...244a/stats
```

This JSON stream of statistics will not stop on its own. So for now, we can use the Ctrl-C key combination to stop it.

To get a single group of statistics, we can run something similar to this:

```
$ curl -s http://localhost:2375/v1/containers/91c8...244a/stats | head -1
```

And finally, if we have Python or another tool capable of "pretty printing" JSON, we can make this output human-readable, as shown here:

```
$ curl -s http://localhost:2375/v1/containers/91c8...244a/stats \
| head -1 | python -m json.tool
{
    "blkio_stats": {
        "io_merged_recursive": [],
        "io_queue_recursive": [],
        "io_service_bytes_recursive": [
            {
                "major": 8,
                "minor": 0,
                "op": "Read",
                "value": 6098944
            },
...snip...
        ],
        "io_service_time_recursive": [],
        "io_serviced_recursive": [
            {
                "major": 8,
```

```json
                    "minor": 0,
                    "op": "Read",
                    "value": 213
                },
    ...snip...
            ],
            "io_time_recursive": [],
            "io_wait_time_recursive": [],
            "sectors_recursive": []
        },
        "cpu_stats": {
            "cpu_usage": {
                "percpu_usage": [
                    37320425
                ],
                "total_usage": 37320425,
                "usage_in_kernelmode": 20000000,
                "usage_in_usermode": 0
            },
            "system_cpu_usage": 1884140000000,
            "throttling_data": {
                "periods": 0,
                "throttled_periods": 0,
                "throttled_time": 0
            }
        },
        "memory_stats": {
            "failcnt": 0,
            "limit": 1035853824,
            "max_usage": 7577600,
            "stats": {
                "active_anon": 1368064,
                "active_file": 221184,
                "cache": 6148096,
                "hierarchical_memory_limit": 9223372036854775807,
                "inactive_anon": 24576,
                "inactive_file": 5890048,
                "mapped_file": 2215936,
                "pgfault": 2601,
                "pgmajfault": 46,
                "pgpgin": 2222,
                "pgpgout": 390,
                "rss": 1355776,
                "total_active_anon": 1368064,
                "total_active_file": 221184,
                "total_cache": 6148096,
                "total_inactive_anon": 24576,
                "total_inactive_file": 5890048,
                "total_mapped_file": 2215936,
                "total_pgfault": 2601,
                "total_pgmajfault": 46,
                "total_pgpgin": 2222,
                "total_pgpgout": 390,
```

```
            "total_rss": 1355776,
            "total_unevictable": 0,
            "unevictable": 0
        },
        "usage": 7577600
    },
    "network": {
        "rx_bytes": 936,
        "rx_dropped": 0,
        "rx_errors": 0,
        "rx_packets": 12,
        "tx_bytes": 468,
        "tx_dropped": 0,
        "tx_errors": 0,
        "tx_packets": 6
    },
    "read": "2015-02-11T15:20:22.930379289-08:00"
}
```

There is *a lot* of information in there. We won't spend much time going into the details, but you can get quite detailed memory usage information, as well as blkio and CPU usage information. If you are using CPU or memory limits in your containers, this endpoint is very useful for finding out when you are hitting them.

If you are doing your own monitoring, this is a great endpoint to hit as well. Note that one drawback is that it's one endpoint per container, so you can't get the stats about all containers from a single call.

Docker Events

The docker daemon internally generates an events stream around the container life cycle. This is how various parts of the system find out what is going on in other parts. You can also tap into this stream to see what life cycle events are happening for containers on your Docker server. This, as you probably expect by now, is implemented in the docker CLI tool as another command-line argument. When you run this command, it will block and continually stream messages to you. Behind the scenes, this is a long-lived HTTP request to the Docker API that returns messages in JSON blobs as they occur. The docker CLI tool decodes them and prints some data to the terminal.

This event stream is useful in monitoring scenarios or in triggering additional actions, like wanting to be alerted when a job completes. For debugging purposes, it allows you see when a container died even if Docker restarts it later. Down the road, this is a place where you might also find yourself directly implementing some tooling against the API. Here's how we use it on the command line:

```
$ docker events
2015-02-18T14:00:39-08:00 1b3295bf300f: (from 0415448f2cc2) die

2015-02-18T14:00:39-08:00 1b3295bf300f: (from 0415448f2cc2) stop

2015-02-18T14:00:42-08:00 1b3295bf300f: (from 0415448f2cc2) start
```

In this example, we initiated a stop signal with docker stop, and the events stream logs this as a "die" message. The "die" message actually marks the beginning of the shutdown of the container. It doesn't stop instantaneously. So, following the "die" message is a "stop" message, which is what Docker says when a container has actually stopped execution. Docker also helpfully tells us the ID of the image that the container is running on. This can be useful for tying deployments to events, for example, because a deployment usually involves a new image.

Once the container was completely down, we initiated a docker start to tell it to run again. Unlike the "die/stop" operations, this is a single command that marks the point at which the container is actually running. We don't get a message telling us that someone explicitly started it. So what happens when we try to start a container that fails?

```
2015-02-18T14:03:31-08:00 e64a279663aa: (from e426f6ef897e) die
```

Note that here the container was actually asked to start, but it failed. Rather than seeing a "start" and a "die," all we see is a "die."

If you have a server where containers are not staying up, the docker events stream is pretty helpful in seeing what's going on and when. But if you're not watching it at the time, Docker very helpfully caches some of the events and you can still get at them for some time afterward. You can ask it to display events after a time with the --since option, or before with the --until option. You can also use both to limit the window to a narrow scope of time when an issue you are investigating may have occurred. Both options take ISO time formats like those in the previous example (e.g., 2015-02-18T14:03:31-08:00).

cAdvisor

docker stats and docker events are useful but don't yet get us graphs to look at. And graphs are pretty helpful when trying to see trends. Of course, other people have filled some of this gap. When you begin to explore the options for monitoring Docker, you will find that many of the major monitoring tools now provide some functionality to help you improve the visibility into your containers' performance and ongoing state.

In addition to the commercial tooling provided by companies like DataDog, GroundWork, and New Relic, there are plenty of options for open source tools like Nagios.

One of the best open source options today comes from Google, which released its own internal container advisor as an open source project on GitHub, called cAdvisor (*https://github.com/google/cadvisor*). Although cAdvisor can be run outside of Docker, the easiest implementation is to simply run it as a Docker container.

To install cAdvisor on an Ubuntu-based system, all you need to do is run this code:

```
$ docker run \
  --volume=/:/rootfs:ro \
  --volume=/var/run:/var/run:rw \
  --volume=/sys:/sys:ro \
  --volume=/var/lib/docker/:/var/lib/docker:ro \
  --publish=8080:8080 \
  --detach=true \
  --name=cadvisor \
  google/cadvisor:latest

Unable to find image 'google/cadvisor:latest' locally
Pulling repository google/cadvisor
f0643dafd7f5: Download complete
...
ba9b663a8908: Download complete
Status: Downloaded newer image for google/cadvisor:latest
f54e6bc0469f60fd74ddf30770039f1a7aa36a5eda6ef5100cddd9ad5fda350b
```

 On RHEL- and CentOS-based systems, you will need to add the following line to the docker run command shown here: --volume=/cgroup:/cgroup \.

Once you have done this, you will be able to navigate to your Docker host on port 8080 to see the cAdvisor web interface (i.e., *http://172.17.42.10:8080/*) and the various detailed charts it has for the host and individual containers (see Figure 6-1).

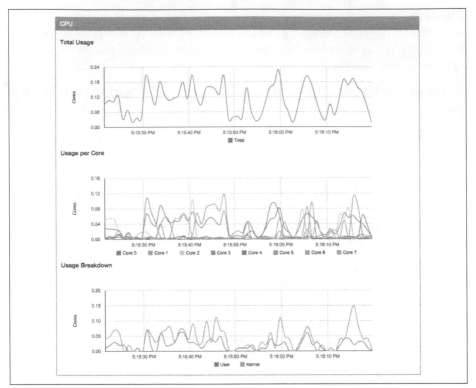

Figure 6-1. cAdvisor CPU graphs

cAdvisor provides a REST API endpoint, which can easily be queried for detailed information by your monitoring systems:

```
$ curl http://172.17.42.10:8080/api/v1.3/containers/

{
  "name": "/",
  "subcontainers": [
    {
      "name": "/docker"
    }
  ],
  "spec": {
    "creation_time": "2015-04-05T00:05:40.249999996Z",
    "has_cpu": true,
    "cpu": {
      "limit": 1024,
      "max_limit": 0,
      "mask": "0-7"
    },
    "has_memory": true,
    "memory": {
      "limit": 18446744073709551615,
```

```
        "swap_limit": 18446744073709551615
      },
      "has_network": true,
      "has_filesystem": true,
      "has_diskio": true
    },
    "stats": [
      {
        "timestamp": "2015-04-05T00:26:50.679218419Z",
        "cpu": {
          "usage": {
            "total": 123375166639,
            "per_cpu_usage": [
              41967365270,
              8589893874,
              11289461032,
              14350545587,
              11866977873,
              13414428349,
              12667210966,
              9229283688
            ],
            "user": 22990000000,
            "system": 43890000000
          },
          "load_average": 0
        },
        "diskio": {},
        "memory": {
          "usage": 394575872,
          "working_set": 227770368,
          "container_data": {
            "pgfault": 91617,
            "pgmajfault": 0
          },
          "hierarchical_data": {
            "pgfault": 91617,
            "pgmajfault": 0
          }
        },
        "network": {
          "rx_bytes": 0,
          "rx_packets": 0,
          "rx_errors": 0,
          "rx_dropped": 0,
          "tx_bytes": 0,
          "tx_packets": 0,
          "tx_errors": 0,
          "tx_dropped": 0
        },
        "filesystem": [
          {
            "device": "/dev/sda1",
```

```
            "capacity": 19507089408,
            "usage": 2070806528,
            "reads_completed": 1302,
            "reads_merged": 9,
            "sectors_read": 10706,
            "read_time": 1590,
            "writes_completed": 1283,
            "writes_merged": 1115,
            "sectors_written": 509824,
            "write_time": 4150,
            "io_in_progress": 0,
            "io_time": 590,
            "weighted_io_time": 5670
          }
        ],
        "task_stats": {
          "nr_sleeping": 0,
          "nr_running": 0,
          "nr_stopped": 0,
          "nr_uninterruptible": 0,
          "nr_io_wait": 0
        }
      },
      ...
      }
    ]
  }
```

As you can see, the amount of detail provided here should be sufficient for many of your graphing and monitoring needs.

Exploration

That gives you all the basics you need to start running containers. It's probably worth downloading a container or two from the Docker Hub registry and exploring a bit on your own to get used to the commands we just learned. There are many other things you can do with Docker, including:

- Copying files in and out of the container with `docker cp`
- Saving a container's filesystem to a tarball with `docker export`
- Saving an image to a tarball with `docker save`
- Loading an image from a tarball with `docker import`

Docker has a huge feature set that you will likely grow into over time. Each new release adds more functionality as well. We'll get into a lot more detail later on many other commands and features, but you should keep in mind that Docker's whole feature set is huge.

## CHAPTER 7

The Path to Production Containers

In this chapter, we cover some of the ideas around deploying and testing containers in production. This chapter is intended to show you how you might take containers to production based on our experience doing so. There are a myriad of ways in which you will probably need to tailor this to your own application and environment. The purpose of this chapter is really to provide a starting point and to help you understand the Docker philosophy in practical terms.

Deploying

Deployment, which is often the most mine-ridden of the steps in getting to production, is made vastly simpler by the shipping container model. If you can imagine what it was once like to load goods into a ship to take across the ocean before shipping containers existed, you can get a sense of what most deployment systems look like. In that old shipping model, random-sized boxes, crates, barrels, and all manner of other packaging were all loaded by hand onto ships. They then had to be manually unloaded by someone who could tell which pieces needed to be unloaded first so that the whole pile wouldn't collapse like a Jenga puzzle.

Shipping containers changed all that: we have a standardized box with well-known dimensions. These containers can be packed and unloaded in a logical order and whole groups of items arrive together when expected. This is the Docker deployment model. All Docker containers support the same external interface, and the tooling just drops them on the servers they are supposed to be on without any concern for what's inside.

Now that we have a running build of our application, we don't have to write much custom tooling to kick off deployment. If we only want to ship it to one server, the docker command-line tooling will handle most of that for us. If we want to send it to more, then we might look to some community tooling.

There is a progression you will follow while getting your applications to production on Docker:

1. Locally build and test a Docker image on your development box.
2. Build your official image for testing and deployment.
3. Deploy your Docker image to your server.

As your workflow evolves, you will eventually collapse all of those steps into a single fluid workflow:

1. Orchestrate the deployment of images and creation of containers on production servers.

We talked about some of those steps already, but it is worthwhile to look at them again to see where deployment fits into the life cycle of getting Docker up and running.

If you don't already have an application to ship, you don't need to spend too much time on deployment. But it's good to know ahead of time what you'll encounter when you do get there, so let's look at how that is done.

Classes of Tooling

Deployment by hand is the simplest, but often the least reliable, way to get an application into production. You can just take your image and docker pull and docker run it on the servers in question. That may be good enough for testing and development. But for production, you will want something more robust.

At the most basic level, a deployment story must encompass two things:

1. It must be a repeatable process. Each time you invoke it, it needs to do the same thing.
2. It needs to handle container configuration for you. You must be able to define your application's configuration in a particular environment and then guarantee that it will ship that configuration for each container on each deployment.

The Docker client itself can only talk to one server, so you need some kind of orchestration tool to support deployment at any scale. Docker's Swarm tool, which we talk about in "Docker Swarm" on page 134, solves the problem of talking to multiple servers, but you would still need additional tools to support items one and two above. You could script that behavior with shell scripting or your

---

favorite dynamic language. As we mentioned earlier, you could also talk directly to the Docker Remote API, which is the API exposed by the docker daemon. If you have complicated needs, the Remote API might be the right solution since it exposes much of the power of the docker command line in a programmatically accessible way.

But for most people, there are already a large number of community contributions that can address your needs. These are already being used in production environments in many cases and thus are far more battle-hardened than anything you'll cook up in-house. There are really two classes of community tooling for deployment:

1. Tools that treat this as an orchestration or deployment problem, replacing things like Capistrano, Fabric, and shell scripts.

2. Tools that treat your network like a larger computer, implementing automatic scheduling and/or fleet management policies, typically replacing manual processes.

Orchestration Tools

We'll call the first set of tools "orchestration tools" because they allow you to coordinate the configuration and deployment of your application onto multiple Docker daemons in a more or less synchronous fashion. You tell them what to do, then they do it at scale while you wait, much like the deployment model of Capistrano, for example. These tools generally provide the simplest way to get into production with Docker.

In this category are tools like:

- New Relic's Centurion (*https://github.com/newrelic/centurion*)
- Spotify's Helios (*https://github.com/spotify/helios*)
- Ansible's Docker tooling (*https://www.ansible.com/docker*)

This class of tools in many cases requires the least infrastructure or modification to your existing system. Setup time is pretty minimal and the standardized nature of the Docker interface means that a lot of functionality is already packed into the tooling. You can get important processes like zero-down-time deployment right out of the box.

The first two concentrate on orchestration of the application and Docker alone, while Ansible is also a system-configuration management platform and so can also configure and manage your servers if you wish. Centurion and Ansible require no external resources other than a docker-registry. Helios requires an Apache Zookeeper (*http://zookeeper.apache.org*) cluster.

Distributed Schedulers

The second set of tools looks at Docker as a way to turn your network into a single computer by using a distributed scheduler. The idea here is that you define some policies about how you want your application to run and you let the system figure out where to run it and how many instances of it to run. If something goes wrong on a server or with the application, you let the scheduler start it up again on resources that are healthy. This fits more into Solomon's original vision for Docker: a way to run your application anywhere without worrying about how it gets there. Generally, zero downtime deployment in this model is done in the blue-green style (*http://bit.ly/1Gph4FZ*) where you launch the new generation of an application alongside the old generation, and then slowly filter new work to the new generation.

Probably the first publicly available tool in this arena is Fleet (*https://github.com/coreos/fleet*) from CoreOS, which works with systemd on the hosts to act as a distributed init system. It is by far the easiest to use on CoreOS, CentOS/RHEL 7, or any version of Linux with systemd. It requires etcd (*https://github.com/coreos/etcd*) for coordination, and also needs SSH access to all of your Docker servers.

The tool in this category with the most press right now is Google's Kubernetes (*http://kubernetes.io*). It makes fewer assumptions about your OS distribution than Fleet and therefore runs on more OS and provider options. It does, however, require that your hosts be set up in a very specific way and has a whole network layer of its own. If your data center happens to have its networks laid out like Google's, you can skip the network overlay. If not, you must run Flannel, an IP-over-UDP layer that sits on top of your real network. Like Fleet, it requires etcd. It supports a number of backends, everything from the Docker daemon, to Google Compute Engine, Rackspace, and Azure. It's a powerful system with a good API and growing community support.

Apache Mesos (*http://mesos.apache.org*), which was originally written at the University of California, Berkeley, and most publicly adopted by Twitter and Airbnb, is the most mature option. At DockerCon EU in December 2014, Solomon described Mesos as the gold standard (*http://bit.ly/1PC5Lel*) for clustered containers. Mesos is a framework abstraction that lets you run multiple frameworks on the same cluster of hosts. You can, for example, run Docker applications and Hadoop jobs on the same compute cluster. Mesos uses Zookeeper and has been around for much longer than most of the other options because it actually predates Docker. First-class support for Docker appeared in recent versions of Mesos. Some of the popular Mesos frameworks like Marathon and Aurora have good support for Docker. It's arguably the most powerful Docker platform right now, but requires more decisions to implement than Kubernetes. Work is in progress to allow Kubernetes to run as a Mesos framework as well.

A deep dive into Mesos is out of the scope of this book. But when you are ready for serious at-scale deployment, this is where you should look. It's an impressive and very mature technology that has been used at scale by a number of high-profile organizations. Mesosphere's Marathon framework and the Apache Aurora project are two frameworks actively engaging with the Docker community.

In December 2014, Docker, Inc., announced the beta release of a Docker native clustering tool called Swarm (*https://github.com/docker/swarm/*), which presents a large collection of Docker hosts as a single resource pool. It's a lightweight clustering tool with a narrower scope than Kubernetes or Mesos. It can, in fact, work on top of other tools as needed. But it's reasonably powerful: a single Docker Swarm container can be used to create and coordinate the deployments of containers across a large Docker cluster. We will take a deeper dive into this tool in "Docker Swarm" on page 134.

 If you are interested in diving deeper into orchestration and distributed schedulers for Docker, consider reading the *Docker Cookbook* by Sébastien Goasguen.

Deployment Wrap-Up

Many people will start by using simple Docker orchestration tools. However, as the number of containers and frequency with which you deploy containers grow, the appeal of distributed schedulers will quickly become apparent. Tools like Mesos allow you to abstract individual servers and whole data centers into large pools of resources in which to run container-based tasks.

There are undoubtedly many other worthy projects out there in the deployment space. But these are the most commonly cited and have the most publicly available information at the time of this writing. It's a fast-evolving space, so it's worth taking a look around to see what new tools are being shipped.

In any case, you should start by getting a Docker infrastructure up and running and then look at outside tooling. Docker's built-in tooling might be enough for you. We suggest using the lightest weight tool for the job, but having flexibility is a great place to be, and Docker is increasingly supported by more and more powerful tooling.

Testing Containers

One of the key promises of Docker is the ability to test your application and all of its dependencies in exactly the operating environment it would have in production. It can't guarantee that you have properly tested external dependencies like databases, nor does it provide any magical test framework, but it can make sure that your libraries and other code dependencies are all tested together. Changing underlying dependencies is a critical place where things go wrong, even for organizations with strong testing discipline. With Docker, you can build your image, run it in on your development box, and then test the exact same image with the same application version and dependencies before shipping it to production servers.

Testing your Dockerized application is not really much more complicated than testing your application itself, but you need to make sure that your test environment has a Docker server you can run things on and that your application will allow you to use environment variables or command-line arguments to switch on the correct testing behavior. Here's one example of how you might do this.

Quick Overview

Let's draw up an example production environment for a fictional company. We'll try to describe something that is similar to the environment at a lot of companies, with Docker thrown into the mix for illustration purposes.

Our fictional company's environment has a pool of production servers that run Docker daemons, and an assortment of applications deployed there. There is a build server and test worker boxes that are tied to the test server. We'll ignore deployment for now and talk about it once we have our fictional application tested and ready to ship.

Figure 7-1 shows what a common workflow looks like for testing Dockerized applications, including the following steps:

1. A build is triggered by some outside means.

2. The build server kicks off a Docker build.

3. The image is created on the local docker.

4. The image is tagged with a build number or commit hash.

5. A container is configured to run the test suite based on the newly built image.

6. The test suite is run against the container and the result is captured by the build server.

7. The build is marked as passing or failing.

8. Passed builds are shipped to an image store (registry, etc.).

You'll notice that this isn't too different from common patterns for testing applications. At a minimum you need to have a job that can kick off a test suite. The steps we're adding here are just to create a Docker image first and invoke the test suite inside the container rather than on the raw system itself.

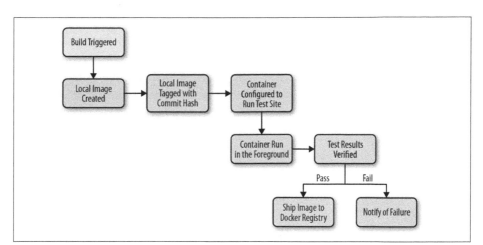

Figure 7-1. Docker testing workflow chart

Let's look at how this works for the application we're deploying at our fictional company. We just updated our application and pushed the latest code to our git repository. We have a post-commit hook that triggers a build on each commit, so that job is kicked off on the build server. The job on the test server is set up to talk to a docker on a particular test worker server. Our test server doesn't have docker running, but it has the docker command-line tool installed. So we run our docker build against that remote Docker server and it runs our Dockerfile, generating a new image on the remote Docker server. We could run docker on the test server itself if we had a smaller environment.

 You should build your container image exactly as you'll ship it to production. If you need to make concessions for testing, they should be externally provided switches, either via environment variables or through command-line arguments. The whole idea is to test the exact build that you'll ship, so this is a critical point.

Once the image has been built, our test job will create and run a new container based on our new production image. Our image is configured to run the application in production, but we need to run a different command for testing. That's OK! Docker lets us do that simply by providing the command at the end of the docker run command. In production, we'd start supervisor and it would start up an nginx instance and some Ruby unicorn web server instances behind that. But for testing, we don't need that nginx and we don't need to run our web application. Instead, our build job invokes the container like this:

```
$ docker run -e ENVIRONMENT=testing -e API_KEY=12345 \
  -i -t awesome_app:version1 /opt/awesome_app/test.sh
```

We called docker run, but we did a couple of extra things here, too. We passed a couple of environment variables into the container: ENVIRONMENT and API_KEY. These can either be new or overrides for the ones Docker already exports for us. We also asked for a particular tag; in this case, version1. That will make sure we build on top of the correct image even if another build is running simultaneously. Then we override the command that our container was configured to start in the Dockerfile's CMD line. Instead, we call our test script, /opt/awesome_app/test.sh.

Always pass the exact Docker tag for your image into the test job. If you always use *latest*, then you won't be able to guarantee that another job has not moved that tag just after your build was kicked off. If you use the exact tag, you can be sure you're testing the right version of the application.

A critical point to make here is that docker run will not exit with the exit status of the command that was invoked in the container. That means we can't just look at the exit status to see if our tests were successful. One way to handle this is to capture all of the output of the test run into a file and then look at the last line of the file to see if it resulted in success. Our fictional build system does just that. We write out the output from the test suite and our test.sh echoes either "Result: SUCCESS!" or "Result: FAILURE!" on the last line to signify if our tests passed.

Be sure to look for some output string that won't appear by happenstance in your normal test suite output. If we need to look for "success," for example, we had best limit it to looking at the last line of the file, and maybe also anchored to the beginning of the line.

In this case, we look at just the last line of the file and find our success string, so we mark the build as passed. There is one more Docker-specific step. We want to take our passed build and push that image to our registry. The registry is the interchange point between builds and deployments. It also allows us to share the image with other builds that might be stacked on top of it. But for now, let's just think of it as the place where we put and tag successful builds. Our build script will now do a docker tag to give the image the right build tag(s), including latest, and then a docker push to push the build to the registry.

That's it! As you can see, there is not much to this compared with testing a normal application. We take advantage of the client/server model of Docker to invoke the test on a different server from the test master server, and we have to wrap up our test output in a shell script to generate our output status. But other than that, it's a lot like a common build system anywhere.

But, critically, our fictional company's system makes sure they only ship applications whose test suite has passed on the same Linux distribution, with the same libraries and the same exact build settings. That doesn't guarantee success, but it gets them a lot closer to that guarantee than the dependency roulette often experienced by production deployment systems.

 If you use Jenkins for continuous integration or are looking for a good way to test scaling Docker, there are many plug-ins (*http://bit.ly/1gZvZW1*) for Docker, Mesos, and Kubernetes that are worth investigating.

Outside Dependencies

But what about those external dependencies we glossed over? Things like the database, or Memcache or Redis instances that we need to run our tests against our container? If our fictional company's application needs a database to run, or a Memcache or Redis instance, we need to solve that external dependency to have a clean test environment. It would be nice to use the container model to support that dependency. With some work, you can do this with tools like Docker Compose (*https://github.com/docker/compose*). Our build job could express some dependencies between containers, and then Compose will use Docker's link mechanism to connect them together. Linking is a mechanism where Docker exposes environment variables into a container to let you connect containers when you have more than one deployed to the same host. It can also add information to the */etc/hosts* file inside the container, enabling visibility between them.

Because Docker's link mechanism is limited to working on a single host, Compose is best for things like development and testing rather than production. But it has an expressive config syntax that's easy to understand and is great for this kind of testing. If you are interested in linking, Compose is your best option.

Even though containers are normally designed to be disposable, you may still find that standard testing is not always sufficient to avoid all problems and that you will want some tools for debuging running containers. In the next chapter, we will discuss some of the techniques that you can use to get information from your containers that will help diagnose problems that might crop up in production.

## CHAPTER 8

Debugging Containers

Once you've shipped an application to production, there will come a day when it's not working as expected. It's always nice to know ahead of time what to expect when that day comes. Debugging a containerized application is not all that different from debugging a normal process on a system.

First, we'll cover one of the easiest ways to see what's going on inside your containers. By using the docker top command, you can see the process list as your container understands it. It is also critical to understand that your application is not running in a separate system from the other Docker processes. They share a kernel, likely a filesystem, and depending on your container configuration, they may share network interfaces. That means you can get a lot of information about what your container is doing.

If you're used to debugging applications in a virtual machine environment, you might think you would need to enter the container to inspect in detail an application's memory or CPU use, or debug system calls. Not so! Despite feeling in many ways like a virtualization layer, processes in containers are just processes on the Docker host itself. If you want to see a process list across all of the Docker containers on a machine, you can just run ps with your favorite command-line options right on the server, for example. Let's look at some things you can do when debugging a containerized application.

Process Output

Docker has a built-in command for showing what's running inside a container: docker top <containerID>. This is nice because it works even from remote hosts as it's exposed over the Docker Remote API. This isn't the only way to see what's going on inside a container, but it's the easiest to use. Let's take a look at how that works here:

```
$ docker ps
CONTAINER ID     IMAGE          COMMAND       ...   NAMES
106ead0d55af     test:latest    /bin/bash     ...   clever_hypatia

$ docker top 106ead0d55af
UID        PID     PPID    C  STIME   TTY TIME      CMD
root       4548    1033    0  13:29   ?   00:00:00  /bin/sh -c nginx
root       4592    4548    0  13:29   ?   00:00:00  nginx: master process nginx
www-data   4593    4592    0  13:29   ?   00:00:00  nginx: worker process
www-data   4594    4592    0  13:29   ?   00:00:00  nginx: worker process
www-data   4595    4592    0  13:29   ?   00:00:00  nginx: worker process
www-data   4596    4592    0  13:29   ?   00:00:00  nginx: worker process
```

We need to know the ID of our container, which we get from docker ps. We then pass that to docker top and get a nice listing of what's running in our container, ordered by PID just as we'd expect from Linux ps output.

Some oddities exist here, though. The primary one of these is namespacing of user IDs and filesystems.

For example, a user might exist in a container's /etc/passwd that does not exist on the host machine. In the case where that user is running a process in a container, the ps output on the host machine will show a numeric ID rather than a user name. In some cases, two containers might have users squatting on the same numeric ID, or mapping to an ID that is a completely different user on the host system.

For example, if you had a production Docker server using CentOS 7 and ran the following commands, you would see that UID 7 is named halt:

```
$ id 7
uid=7(halt) gid=0(root) groups=0(root)
```

 Don't read too much into the UID number we are using here. It was chosen simply because it is used by default on both platforms but represents a different username.

If we then enter the standard Ubuntu container on that Docker host, you will see that UID 7 is set to lp in /etc/passwd. By running the following commands, you can see that the container has a completely different perspective of who UID 7 is:

```
$ docker run -ti ubuntu:latest /bin/bash
root@f86f8e528b92:/# grep x:7: /etc/passwd
lp:x:7:7:lp:/var/spool/lpd:/usr/sbin/nologin
root@f86f8e528b92:/# id lp
uid=7(lp) gid=7(lp) groups=7(lp)
root@409c2a8216b1:/# exit
```

If we then run `ps au` on the Docker host while that container is running as UID 7 (`-u 7`), we would see that the Docker host would show the container process as being run by `halt` instead of `lp`:

```
$ docker run -d -u 7 ubuntu:latest sleep 1000
5525...06c6
$ ps ua | grep sleep
 1185 halt     sleep 1000
 1192 root     grep sleep
```

This could be particulary confusing if a well-known user like `nagios` or `postgres` were configured on the host system but not in the container, yet the container ran its process with the same ID. This namespacing can make the `ps` output look quite strange. It might, for example, look like the `nagios` user on your Docker host is running the `postgresql` daemon that was launched inside a container, if you don't pay close attention.

 One solution to this is to dedicate a nonzero UID to your containers. On your Docker hosts, you can create a `container` user as UID 5000 and then create the same user in your base container images. If you then run all your containers as UID 5000 (`-u 5000`), you will not only improve the security of your system by not running container processes as UID 0, but you will also make the `ps` output on the Docker host easier to decipher by displaying the `container` user for all of your running container processes.

Likewise, because the process has a different view of the filesystem, paths that are shown in the `ps` output are relative to the container and not the host. In these cases, knowing it is in a container is a big win.

So that's how you use the Docker tooling to look at what's running in a container. But that's not the only way, and in a debugging situation, it might not be the best way. If you hop onto a Docker server and run a normal Linux `ps` to look at what's running, you get a full list of everything containerized and not containerized just as if they were all equivalent processes. There are some ways to look at the process output to make things a lot clearer. Debugging can be facilitated by looking at the Linux `ps` output in tree form so that you can see all of the processes descended from Docker. Here's what that can look like using the BSD command-line flags. We'll chop the output to just the part we care about:

```
$ ps axlfww
... /usr/bin/docker -d
...  \_ docker-proxy -proto tcp -host-ip 0.0.0.0 -host-port 6379 ...
...  \_ redis-server *:6379
...  \_ docker-proxy -proto tcp -host-ip 0.0.0.0 -host-port 27017 ...
...  \_ mongod
```

Many of the ps commands in the preceding example work only on true Linux distributions. Boot2Docker is based on Tiny Core Linux, which uses busybox and provides a stripped-down ps command.

Here you can see that we're running one Docker daemon and two instances of the docker-proxy, which we will discuss in more detail in "Network Inspection" on page 127. Everything else under those processes represents Docker containers. In this example, we have two containers. They show up as top-level processes under docker. In this case, we are running one Redis server in a container, and one MongoDB server in another container. Each container has a related docker-proxy process that is used to map the required network ports between the container and the host Docker server. It's pretty clear how they are related to each other, and we know they're running in a container because they are in docker's process tree. If you're a bigger fan of Unix SysV command-line flags, you can get a similar, but not as nice looking, tree output with ps -ejH:

```
$ ps -ejH
40643 ...    docker
43689 ...     docker
43697 ...     docker
43702 ...     start
43716 ...      java
46970 ...     docker
46976 ...     supervisord
46990 ...      supervisor_remo
46991 ...      supervisor_stdo
46992 ...      nginx
47030 ...       nginx
47031 ...       nginx
47032 ...       nginx
47033 ...       nginx
46993 ...      ruby
47041 ...       ruby
47044 ...       ruby
```

You can get a more concise view of the docker process tree by using the pstree command. Here, we'll use pidof to scope it to the tree belonging to docker:

```
$ pstree `pidof docker`
docker─┬─2*[docker───6*[{docker}]]
       ├─mongod───10*[{mongod}]
       ├─redis-server───2*[{redis-server}]
       └─18*[{docker}]
```

This doesn't show us PIDs and therefore is only useful for getting a sense of how things hang together in our containers. But this is pretty nice output when there are a lot of containers running on a host. It's far more concise and provides a nice high-level map of how things connect. Here we can see the same containers that were shown in the ps output above, but the tree is collapsed so we get multipliers like 10* when there are 10 duplicate processes.

We can actually get a full tree with PIDs if we run pstree, as shown here:

```
$ pstree -p `pidof docker`
docker(4086)─┬─docker(6529)─┬─{docker}(6530)
             │              ├─...
             │              └─{docker}(6535)
             ├─...
             ├─mongod(6675)─┬─{mongod}(6737)
             │              ├─...
             │              └─{mongod}(6756)
             ├─redis-server(6537)─┬─{redis-server}(6576)
             │                    └─{redis-server}(6577)
             ├─{docker}(4089)
             ├─...
             └─{docker}(6738)
```

This output provides us with a very good look at all the processes attached to Docker and what they are running. It is, however, difficult to see the docker-proxy in this output, since it is really just another forked docker process.

Process Inspection

If you're logged in to the Docker server, you can inspect running processes in many of the same ways that you would on the host. Common debugging tools like strace work as expected. In the following code, we'll inspect a unicor process running inside a Ruby webapp container:

```
$ strace -p 31292
Process 31292 attached - interrupt to quit
select(11, [10], NULL, [7 8], {30, 103848}) = 1 (in [10], left {29, 176592})
fcntl(10, F_GETFL)                = 0x802 (flags O_RDWR|O_NONBLOCK)
accept4(10, 0x7fff25c17b40, [128], SOCK_CLOEXEC) = -1 EAGAIN (...)
getppid()                         = 17
select(11, [10], NULL, [7 8], {45, 0})  = 1 (in [10], left {44, 762499})
fcntl(10, F_GETFL)                = 0x802 (flags O_RDWR|O_NONBLOCK)
accept4(10, 0x7fff25c17b40, [128], SOCK_CLOEXEC) = -1 EAGAIN (...)
getppid()                         = 17
```

You can see that we get the same output that we would from noncontainerized processes on the host. Likewise, an lsof shows us that the files and sockets that a process has open work as expected:

```
$ lsof -p 31292
COMMAND ...  NAME
ruby    ...  /data/app
ruby    ...  /
ruby    ...  /usr/local/rbenv/versions/2.1.1/bin/ruby
ruby    ...  /usr/.../iso_8859_1.so (stat: No such file or directory)
ruby    ...  /usr/.../fiber.so (stat: No such file or directory)
```

```
ruby    ...  /usr/.../cparse.so (stat: No such file or directory)
ruby    ...  /usr/.../libsasl2.so.2.0.23 (path dev=253,0, inode=1443531)
ruby    ...  /lib64/libnspr4.so (path dev=253,0, inode=655717)
ruby    ...  /lib64/libplc4.so (path dev=253,0, inode=655718)
ruby    ...  /lib64/libplds4.so (path dev=253,0, inode=655719)
ruby    ...  /usr/lib64/libnssutil3.so (path dev=253,0, inode=1443529)
ruby    ...  /usr/lib64/libnss3.so (path dev=253,0, inode=1444999)
ruby    ...  /usr/lib64/libsmime3.so (path dev=253,0, inode=1445001)
ruby    ...  /usr/lib64/libssl3.so (path dev=253,0, inode=1445002)
ruby    ...  /lib64/liblber-2.4.so.2.5.6 (path dev=253,0, inode=655816)
ruby    ...  /lib64/libldap_r-2.4.so.2.5.6 (path dev=253,0, inode=655820)
```

Note that the paths to the files are all relative to the container's view of the backing filesystem, which is not the same as the host view. Therefore, inspecting the version of the file on the host will not match the one the container sees. In this case, it's probably best to enter the container to look at the files with the same view that the processes inside it have.

It's possible to run the GNU debugger (gdb) and other process inspection tools in the same manner as long as you're root and have proper permissions to do so.

Controlling Processes

When you have a shell directly on the Docker server, you can treat containerized processes just like any other process running on the system. If you're remote, you might send signals with docker kill because it's expedient. But if you're already logged in to a Docker server for a debugging session or because the Docker daemon is not responding, you can just kill away like you would normally. Note that unless you kill the top-level process in the container, however, this will not terminate the container itself. That might be desirable if you were killing a runaway process, but might leave the container in an unexpected state if developers on remote systems expect that all the processes are running if they can see their container in docker ps.

These are just normal processes in many respects, and can be passed the whole array of Unix signals listed in the man page for the Linux kill command. Many Unix programs will perform special actions when they receive certain predefined signals. For example, nginx will reopen its logs when receiving a SIGUSR1 signal. Using the Linux kill command, it is possible to send any Unix signal to a container process on the local Docker server.

We consider it to be a best practice to run some kind of process control in your production containers. Whether it be systemd, upstart, runit, supervisor, or your own homegrown tools, this allows you to treat containers atomically even when they contain more than one process. You want docker ps to reflect the presence of the whole container and don't want to worry if one of the processes inside it has died. If you can assume that the presence of a container and absence of error logs means that things are working, it allows you to treat docker ps output as the truth about what's happening on your Docker systems. Because containers ship as a single artifact, this tends to be how people think of them. But you should only run things that are logically the same application in a single container. It is also a good idea to ensure that you understand the complete behavior of your preferred process control service, including memory or disk utilization, since this can impact your container's performance.

Network Inspection

Unlike process inspection, debugging containerized applications at the network level can be more complicated. Unless you are running Docker containers with the host networking option, which we will discuss in "Networking" on page 177, your containers will have their own IP addresses and therefore won't show up in all netstat output. Running netstat -an on the Docker server, for example, works as expected, as shown here:

```
$ sudo netstat -an
Active Internet connections (servers and established)
Proto Recv-Q Send-Q Local Address           Foreign Address         State
tcp        0      0 10.0.3.1:53             0.0.0.0:*               LISTEN
tcp        0      0 0.0.0.0:22              0.0.0.0:*               LISTEN
tcp6       0      0 :::23235                :::*                    LISTEN
tcp6       0      0 :::2375                 :::*                    LISTEN
tcp6       0      0 :::4243                 :::*                    LISTEN
tcp6       0      0 fe80::389a:46ff:fe92:53 :::*                    LISTEN
tcp6       0      0 :::22                   :::*                    LISTEN
udp        0      0 10.0.3.1:53             0.0.0.0:*
udp        0      0 0.0.0.0:67              0.0.0.0:*
udp        0      0 0.0.0.0:68              0.0.0.0:*
udp6       0      0 fe80::389a:46ff:fe92:53 :::*
```

Here we can see all of the interfaces that we're listening on. Our container is bound to port 23235 on IP address 0.0.0.0. That shows up. But what happens when we ask netstat to show us the process name that's bound to the port?

```
$ netstat -anp
Active Internet connections (servers and established)
Proto ... Local Address           Foreign Address State  PID/Program name
tcp   ... 10.0.3.1:53             0.0.0.0:*       LISTEN 23861/dnsmasq
```

```
tcp    ... 0.0.0.0:22                  0.0.0.0:*        LISTEN 902/sshd
tcp6   ... :::23235                    :::*             LISTEN 24053/docker-proxy
tcp6   ... :::2375                     :::*             LISTEN 954/docker
tcp6   ... :::4243                     :::*             LISTEN 954/docker
tcp6   ... fe80::389a:46ff:fe92:53 :::*                 LISTEN 23861/dnsmasq
tcp6   ... :::22                       :::*             LISTEN 902/sshd
udp    ... 10.0.3.1:53                 0.0.0.0:*               23861/dnsmasq
udp    ... 0.0.0.0:67                  0.0.0.0:*               23861/dnsmasq
udp    ... 0.0.0.0:68                  0.0.0.0:*               880/dhclient3
udp6   ... fe80::389a:46ff:fe92:53 :::*                        23861/dnsmasq
```

We see the same output, but notice what is bound to the port: docker-proxy. That's because Docker actually has a proxy written in Go that sits between all of the containers and the outside world. That means that when we look at output, we see only docker-proxy and that masks which container this is bound to. Luckily, docker ps shows us which containers are bound to which ports, so this isn't a big deal. But it's not necessarily expected, and you probably want to be aware of it before you're debugging a production failure.

If you're using host networking in your container, then this layer is skipped. There is no docker-proxy, and the process in the container can bind to the port directly.

Other network inspection commands work as expected, including tcpdump, but it's important to remember that docker-proxy is there, in between the host's network interface and the container.

Image History

When you're building and deploying a single container, it's easy to keep track of where it came from and what images it's sitting on top of. But this rapidly becomes unmanageable when you're shipping many containers with images that are built and maintained by different teams. How can you tell what images are actually underneath the one your container is running on? docker history does just that. You can see the image IDs that are layered into the image and the sizes and commands that were used to build them:

```
$ docker history centurion-test:latest
IMAGE          CREATED         CREATED BY                                  SIZE
ec64a324e9cc   7 months ago    /bin/sh -c #(nop) CMD [/bin/sh -c ngi      0 B
f38017917da1   7 months ago    /bin/sh -c #(nop) EXPOSE map[80/tcp:{      0 B
df0d88d6811a   7 months ago    /bin/sh -c #(nop) ADD dir:617ceac0be1      20.52 kB
b00af4e7a358   11 months ago   /bin/sh -c #(nop) ADD file:76c644211a      518 B
2d4b732ca5cf   11 months ago   /bin/sh -c #(nop) ADD file:7b7ef6cc04      239 B
b6f49406bcf0   11 months ago   /bin/sh -c echo "HTML is working" > /      16 B
f384626619d9   11 months ago   /bin/sh -c mkdir /srv/www                  0 B
5c29c073d362   11 months ago   /bin/sh -c apt-get -y install nginx       16.7 MB
d08d285012c8   11 months ago   /bin/sh -c apt-get -y install python-      42.54 MB
340b0525d10f   11 months ago   /bin/sh -c apt-get update                  74.51 MB
```

```
8e2b3cf3ca53   12 months ago   /bin/bash                                 1.384 kB
24ba2ee5d982   13 months ago   /bin/sh -c #(nop) ADD saucy.tar.xz in    144.6 MB
cc7385a89304   13 months ago   /bin/sh -c #(nop) MAINTAINER Tianon G     0 B
511136ea3c5a   19 months ago                                             0 B
```

This can be useful, for example, when determining that a container that is having a problem was actually built on top of the right base image. Perhaps a bug fix was a applied and the particular container in question didn't get it because it was still based on the previous base image. Unfortunately the ADD commands show a hash rather than the actual files, but they do show whether it was a directory or a file that was added, which can help you determine which statement in the Docker file is being referred to.

Inspecting a Container

In Chapter 4, we showed you how to read the docker inspect output to see how a container is configured. But underneath that is a directory on the host's disk that is dedicated to the container. Usually this is in */var/lib/docker/containers*. If you look at that directory, it contains very long SHA hashes, as shown here:

```
$ ls /var/lib/docker
106ead0d55af55bd803334090664e4bc821c76dadf231e1aab7798d1baa19121
28970c706db0f69716af43527ed926acbd82581e1cef5e4e6ff152fce1b79972
3c4f916619a5dfc420396d823b42e8bd30a2f94ab5b0f42f052357a68a67309b
589f2ad301381b7704c9cade7da6b34046ef69ebe3d6929b9bc24785d7488287
959db1611d632dc27a86efcb66f1c6268d948d6f22e81e2a22a57610b5070b4d
a1e15f197ea0996d31f69c332f2b14e18b727e53735133a230d54657ac6aa5dd
bad35aac3f503121abf0e543e697fcade78f0d30124778915764d85fb10303a7
bc8c72c965ebca7db9a2b816188773a5864aa381b81c3073b9d3e52e977c55ba
daa75fb108a33793a3f8fcef7ba65589e124af66bc52c4a070f645fffbbc498e
e2ac800b58c4c72e240b90068402b7d4734a7dd03402ee2bce3248cc6f44d676
e8085ebc102b5f51c13cc5c257acb2274e7f8d1645af7baad0cb6fe8eef36e24
f8e46faa3303d93fc424e289d09b4ffba1fc7782b9878456e0fe11f1f6814e4b
```

That's a bit daunting. But those are just the container IDs in long form. If you want to look at the configuration for a particular container, you just need to use docker ps to find its short ID, and then find the directory that matches:

```
$ docker ps
CONTAINER ID      IMAGE                          COMMAND              ...
106ead0d55af      kmatthias/centurion-test:latest   "/bin/sh -c nginx"  ...
```

You can look at the short ID from docker ps, then match it to the ls /var/lib/ docker output to see that you want the directory beginning with 106ead0d55af. If you need exact matching, you can do a docker inspect 106ead0d55af and grab the long ID from the output. As we discussed in Chapter 5, this directory contains some files that are bind-mounted directly into your container, like hosts:

```
$ cd /var/lib/docker/\
    containers/106ead0d55af55bd803334090664e4bc821c76dadf231e1aab7798d1baa19121
$ ls -la
total 32
drwx------  2 root root  4096 Jun 23  2014 .
drwx------ 14 root root 12288 Jan  9 11:33 ..
-rw-------  1 root root     0 Jun 23  2014 106ead0d55a...baa19121-json.log
-rw-r--r--  1 root root  1642 Jan 23 14:36 config.json
-rw-r--r--  1 root root   350 Jan 23 14:36 hostconfig.json
-rw-r--r--  1 root root     8 Jan 23 14:36 hostname
-rw-r--r--  1 root root   169 Jan 23 14:36 hosts
```

This directory is also where Docker stores the JSON file containing the log that is shown with the docker logs command, the JSON configuration that backs the docker inspect output (*config.json*), and the networking configuration for the container (*hostconfig.json*) are located.

Even if we're not able to enter the container, or if docker is not responding, we can look at how the container was configured. It's also pretty useful to understand what's backing that mechanism inside the container. Keep in mind that it's not a good idea to modify these files. Docker expects them to contain reality, and if you alter that reality, you're asking for trouble. But it's another avenue for information on what's happening in your container.

Filesystem Inspection

Docker, regardless of the backend actually in use, has a layered filesystem that allows it to track the changes in any given container. This is how the images are actually assembled when you do a build, but it is also useful when trying to figure out if a Docker container has changed anything, and if so, what. As with most of the core tools, this is built into the docker command-line tooling and is also exposed via the API. Let's take a look at what this shows us in Example 8-1. We'll assume that we already have the ID of the container we're concerned with.

Example 8-1. docker diff

```
$ sudo docker diff 89b8e19707df
C /var/log/redis
A /var/log/redis/redis.log
C /var/run
A /var/run/cron.reboot
A /var/run/crond.pid
C /var/lib/logrotate.status
C /var/lib/redis
A /var/lib/redis/dump.rdb
C /var/spool/cron
A /var/spool/cron/root
```

Each line begins with either A or C, which are just shorthand for added or changed. We can see that this container is running redis, that the redis log is being written to, and that someone or something has been changing the crontab for root. Logging to the local filesystem is not a good idea, especially for anything with high-volume logs. Being able to find out what is writing to your Docker filesystem can really help you understand where things are filling up, or give you a preview of what would be added if you were to build an image from it.

Further detailed inspection requires jumping into the container with docker exec or nsenter and the like in order to see what is exactly in the filesystem. But docker diff gives you a good place to start.

Moving Along

At this point, you can deploy and debug containers in your production environment, but how do you start to scale this for large applications? In the next chapter, we will explore some of the tools that are avaliable to help you scale Docker inside your data center and in the cloud.

## CHAPTER 9

Docker at Scale

One of Docker's major strengths is its ability to abstract away the underlying hardware and operating system so that your application is not constrained to any particular host or environment. It facilitates not just horizontally scaling a stateless application within your data center, but also across cloud providers without many of the traditional barriers to similar efforts. True to the shipping container metaphor, a container on one cloud looks like a container on another.

Many organizations will find cloud deployments of Docker very appealing because they can gain any of the immediate benefits of a scalable container-based platform without needing to completely build something in-house. But the barrier is low for creating your own clusters, and we'll cover some options for doing that shortly.

It is easy to install Docker on almost any Linux-based cloud instance. However, Docker and almost every major public cloud provider is actively developing tooling for intelligently deploying and managing Docker containers across a cluster. At the time of this writing, many of these projects are usable, but still in the early stages.

If you have your own private cloud, you can leverage a tool like Docker Swarm to deploy containers easily across a large pool of Docker hosts, or use the community tool Centurion or Helios to quickly facilitate multi-host deployments. If you have already experimented with Docker at scale and are looking to build something more like what the cloud providers themselves offer, then you should consider Kubernetes or Mesos, which we addressed in the last chapter.

The major public cloud providers have all made efforts to support containers natively on their offering. Some of the biggest efforts to implement Docker containers on the public cloud include:

- Amazon EC2 Container Service (*http://aws.amazon.com/ecs/*)
- Google Container Engine (*http://bit.ly/1R3wcvZ*)
- Red Hat OpenShift 3 (*https://www.openshift.com*)

Even cloud providers running on non-Linux operating systems like SmartOS and Windows are actively finding ways to support the Docker ecosystem:

- Joyent Triton (*http://bit.ly/1R3weUC*)
- Microsoft Azure (*http://bit.ly/1R3winh*)

In this chapter, we'll cover some options for running Docker at scale in your own data center, first with a pass through Docker Swarm and Centurion, and then take a dive into the Amazon EC2 Container Service (Amazon ECS). All of these examples will hopefully give you a view of how Docker can be succesfully leveraged to provide an incredibly flexible platform for your application workloads.

Docker Swarm

After first building the container runtime in the form of the Docker engine, the engineers at Docker turned to the problems of orchestrating a fleet of individual Docker hosts and effectively packing those hosts full of containers. The tool that evolved from this work is Docker Swarm. The idea behind Swarm is to present a single interface to the docker client tool, but have that interface be backed by a whole cluster rather than a single Docker daemon. Swarm doesn't concern itself with application configuration or repeatable deployments; it is aimed at clustering computing resources for wrangling by the Docker tools. It has grown a lot since its first release and now contains several scheduler plugins with different strategies for assigning containers to hosts, and with basic service discovery built in. But, it remains only one building block of a more complex solution.

Swarm is implemented as a single Docker container that acts as both the central management hub for your Docker cluster and also as the agent that runs on each Docker host. By deploying it to all of your hosts, you merge them into a single, cohesive cluster than can be controlled with the Swarm and Docker tooling.

 It is actually possible to compile Swarm as a standalone binary that can be run directly on a host if you prefer not to use the containerized version. But, as with any containerized application, the container is simpler to deploy. Here we'll cover the containerized deployment on a TLS-based Docker host utilizing port 2376.

Let's get a Swarm cluster up and running. As with any Docker deployment, the very first thing we should do is download the Swarm container onto our Docker host by running a `docker pull`, as shown here:

```
$ docker pull swarm
Using default tag: latest
latest: Pulling from library/swarm
844fab328d6a: Pull complete
d53941759232: Pull complete
3445c6fe19be: Pull complete
a3ed95caeb02: Pull complete
Digest: sha256:51a8eba9502f1f89eef83e10b9f457cfc67193efc3edf88b45b1e910dc48
Status: Downloaded newer image for swarm:latest
```

We now need to create our Docker cluster by running the Swarm container on our preferred Docker host.

```
$ docker run --rm swarm create
e480f01dd24432adc551e72faa37bddd
```

This command returns a hash that represents a unique identifier for your newly created Docker cluster, and is typically referred to as the cluster ID.

Docker Swarm needs to keep track of information about the cluster it will manage. When invoked, it needs to discover the hosts and their containers. The default method uses a token and a simple discovery API located on Docker Hub at *discovery.hub.docker.com*. But it also supports other discovery methods, including etcd (*https://github.com/coreos/etcd*) and Consul (*https://www.consul.io*).

We now want to deploy the Swarm manager to one of the Docker hosts in our cluster:

```
$ docker run -d -p 3376:3376 -t -v /var/lib/boot2docker:/certs:ro \
  swarm manage -H 0.0.0.0:3376 --tlsverify --tlscacert=/certs/ca.pem \
  --tlscert=/certs/server.pem --tlskey=/certs/server-key.pem \
  token://e480f01dd24432adc551e72faa37bddd
aba1c4d8e7eaad9bb5021fde3a32f355fad23b91bc45bf145b3f0f2d70f3002b
```

You can expose the Swarm manager on any port. In this case, we are using 3376, since 2375 and/or 2376 are already in use on the Docker host by the Docker server.

If we rerun `docker ps`, we will now see the Swarm manager running on our Docker host:

```
$ docker ps
... IMAGE COMMAND              ... PORTS                    ...
... swarm "/swarm manage -H 0.0" ... 2375/tcp, 0.0.0.0:3376->3376/tcp ...
```

To register a Docker host with our cluster, we need to run the Swarm container with the `join` argument. In the following command, we need to be sure and provide the address and port for our Docker host, and the token that we received when we first created the cluster:

```
$ docker run -d swarm join --addr=172.17.42.10:2376 \
    token://e480f01dd24432adc551e72faa37bddd
e96afd3b3f8e360ac63ec23827560bafcc44695a8cdd82aec8c44af2f2fe6910
```

> Remember that your Docker port in the command above may be different, depending on wether you are using TLS or not. Typically 2375 or 2376 is the correct value. Our example assumes that you are using TLS.

The `swarm join` command launches the Swarm agent on our Docker host and then returns the full hash to the agent container. If we now run `docker ps` against our Docker host we will see both the Swarm manager and the Swarm agent running. You can also see that the short hash for the agent matches the first 12 characters of the full hash that we received from the previous command:

```
$ docker ps
CONTAINER ID IMAGE COMMAND              ... PORTS                    ...
e96afd3b3f8e swarm "/swarm join --addr=1" ... 2375/tcp                 ...
aba1c4d8e7ea swarm "/swarm manage -H 0.0" ... 0.0.0.0:3376->3376/tcp, 2375/tcp
```

> At this point, we have a single host cluster. Under normal circumstances, we would want to add additional Docker hosts to the cluster, and you can do this very easily by starting a second Docker host using your preferred tool of choice, like `docker-machine`, `vagrant`, etc.

We can list all of the nodes in our cluster by running:

```
$ docker run --rm swarm list token://e480f01dd24432adc551e72faa37bddd
172.17.42.10:2376
```

The diagram in Figure 9-1 gives a good overview of the components that make up the Docker Swarm cluster.

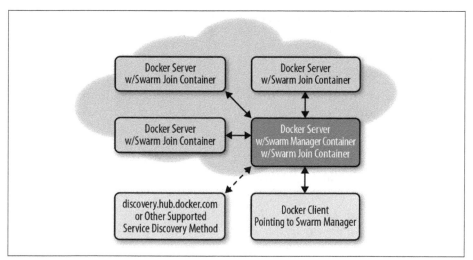

Figure 9-1. Swarm Manager controlling Docker cluster

At this point we can start using docker to interact with our Docker cluster, instead of with an individual host. By setting the DOCKER_HOST environment variable to the IP address and port that our Swarm manager is running on, we can now run normal Docker commands against our Swarm-based Docker cluster, as shown here:

 If your local development environment and Docker Swarm evirionment are not both using the same TLS settings, you might need to adjust the $DOCKER_TLS_VERIFY, $DOCKER_TLS, and $DOCKER_CERT_PATH environment variables when switching between them.

```
$ export DOCKER_HOST="tcp://172.17.42.10:3376"((("docker", "info")))
$ docker info
Containers: 6
Images: 1
Role: primary
Strategy: spread
Filters: health, port, dependency, affinity, constraint
Nodes: 1
 local: 192.168.99.100:2376
   ∟ Status: Healthy
   ∟ Containers: 6
   ∟ Reserved CPUs: 0 / 1
   ∟ Reserved Memory: 0 B / 1.021 GiB
   ∟ Labels: executiondriver=native-0.2, kernelversion=4.1.17-boot2docker,
     operatingsystem=Boot2Docker 1.10.1 (TCL 6.4.1); master : b03e158 -
     Thu Feb 11 22:34:01 UTC 2016, provider=virtualbox, storagedriver=aufs
   ∟ Error: (none)
   ∟ UpdatedAt: 2016-02-15T19:39:05Z
```

```
Kernel Version: 4.1.17-boot2docker
Operating System: linux
CPUs: 1
Total Memory: 1.021 GiB
Name: e480f01dd244
```

The above output from `docker info` shows some basic details about all of the nodes in our cluster.

We can now run an nginx (*http://nginx.org*) container in our new cluster, by using the following command:

```
$ docker run -d nginx
5519a2a379668ceab685a1d73d7692dd0a81ad92a7ef61f0cd54d2c4c95d3f6e
```

Running `docker ps` again will now show that we have a container running within the context of the cluster.

```
$ docker ps
CONTAINER ID   IMAGE    COMMAND                ... NAMES
5519a2a37966   nginx    "nginx -g 'daemon off" ... local/furious_jennings
```

An interesting thing to note is that the container name (*berserk_hodgkin*) is now prefixed by the name of the node (*local*) that it is running on. If we look back at the output from `docker info`, we will see the node name listed there, like this:

```
local: 172.17.42.10:2376
```

If we now run `docker ps -a`, we will see an interesting behavior. In addition to containers that are not running, we will also see containers that are running outside the scope of the cluster (like the swarm containers, themselves) and therefore are "unknown" to the cluster, although still actually running on one of our hosts.

```
$ docker ps -a
... IMAGE COMMAND                 PORTS                                           ...
... nginx "nginx -g 'daemon off"  80/tcp, 443/tcp                                 ...
... swarm "/swarm manage -H 0.0"  2375/tcp, 192.168.99.100:3376->3376/tcp ...
... swarm "/swarm join --addr=1"  2375/tcp                                        ...
...
```

 Although Swarm does not list its own images in standard `docker ps` output, it will happily let you `docker stop` the Swarm management or agent containers, which will, in turn, break things. Don't do that.

This covers the basics of using Docker Swarm and should help get you started building your own Docker cluster for deployment.

When you are done using Swarm, you will need to reset your DOCKER_HOST environment variable to point directly at your Docker host. If your host is using TLS, then you will also need to set DOCKER_TLS_VERIFY, DOCKER_TLS, and DOCKER_CERT_PATH back to their previous values.

Centurion

Centurion (*https://github.com/newrelic/centurion*), which we discussed in Chapter 8, is one of many tools that enables repeatable deployment of applications to a group of hosts. Unlike Swarm, which treats the cluster as a single machine, you tell Centurion about each host you want it to know about. Its focus is on guaranteeing repeatability of container creation and simplifying zero-down-time deployment. It assumes that a load balancer sits in front of your application instances. It is an easy first step in moving from traditional deployment to a Docker workflow.

We could equally be covering Spotify's Helios here, or Ansible's Docker tooling, but we believe that Centurion is the simplest of these tools to get up and running. You are encouraged to see if there are tools that are a better fit for your deployment needs, but this section will hopefully give you a taste of what you might achieve as a first step.

Let's look at deploying a simple application with Centurion. Here we'll deploy the public nginx container as our web application. It won't do much, but will serve up a welcome page that we can see in a browser. You could easily switch in your custom application. The only requirement is that it be deployed to a registry.

Before we can deploy, we have to satisfy the dependencies for the tool and get it installed. Centurion depends on having the Docker command-line tool present and requires that you have Ruby 1.9 or higher so you'll want to make sure you have a system with these installed. Centurion can run on Linux or Mac OS X. Windows support is untested. Packages are available via yum or apt-get on all popular Linux distributions. Generally, any distribution with a kernel new enough to run Docker will ship with packages that meet this requirement. On recent Mac OS X versions, you will already have the right version of Ruby. If you are on an older release, you can install a recent Ruby with Homebrew. Most Linux distributions that are capable of running Docker also ship with a modern enough Ruby to run Centurion. You can check if you have Ruby installed and if you have a version new enough like this:

```
$ ruby -v
ruby 2.2.1p85 (2015-02-26 revision 49769) [x86_64-darwin12.0]
```

Here, we have Ruby 2.2.1, which is plenty new enough. Once you have Ruby running, install Centurion with the Ruby package manager:

```
$ gem install centurion
Fetching: logger-colors-1.0.0.gem (100%)
Successfully installed logger-colors-1.0.0
Fetching: centurion-1.8.5.gem (100%)
Successfully installed centurion-1.8.5
Parsing documentation for logger-colors-1.0.0
Installing ri documentation for logger-colors-1.0.0
Parsing documentation for centurion-1.8.5
Installing ri documentation for centurion-1.8.5
Done installing documentation for logger-colors, centurion after 0 seconds
2 gems installed
```

You can now invoke `centurion` from the command line to make sure it's available:

```
$ centurion --help
Options:
  -p, --project=<s>           project (blog, forums...)
  -e, --environment=<s>       environment (production, staging...)
  -a, --action=<s>            action (deploy, list...) (default: list)
  -i, --image=<s>             image (yourco/project...)
  -t, --tag=<s>               tag (latest...)
  -h, --hosts=<s>             hosts, comma separated
  -d, --docker-path=<s>       path to docker executable (default: docker)
  -n, --no-pull               Skip the pull_image step
  --registry-user=<s>         user for registry auth
  --registry-password=<s>     password for registry auth
  -o, --override-env=<s>      override environment variables, comma separated
  -l, --help                  Show this message
```

There are a lot of options there, but right now we're just making sure that it's installed and working. If Centurion is not yet available and you get an error, we can add it to our path:

```
$ gempath=`gem environment | grep "INSTALLATION DIRECTORY" | awk '{print $4}'`
$ export PATH=$gempath/bin:$PATH
```

You should now be able to invoke `centurion  --help` and see the output of the help.

To begin with, we'll just make a directory in which we'll store the Centurion configuration. If this were your own application, this might be the application's directory, or it might be a directory in which you store all the deployment configs for all of your applications. We encourage that pattern for larger installations. Since we're just going to deploy the public `nginx` container, let's create a directory to house our configs. Then we'll change into it and tell Centurion to scaffold a basic config for us with the `centurionize` tool:

```
$ mkdir nginx
$ cd nginx
```

```
$ centurionize -p nginx
Creating /Users/someuser/apps/nginx/config/centurion
Writing example config to /Users/someuser/apps/nginx/config/centurion/
    nginx.rake
Writing new Gemfile to /Users/someuser/apps/nginx/Gemfile
Adding Centurion to the Gemfile

Remember to run `bundle install` before running Centurion

Done!
```

We can ignore the Gemfile stuff for now and just open the config it generated for us. You might take a look at it to see what it put in place in order to get an idea of what Centurion can do. The scaffolded config contains examples of how to use many of the features of Centurion. We'll just edit it down to the basics we care about:

```
namespace :environment do
  desc 'Staging environment'
  task :staging do
    set_current_environment(:staging)
    set :image, 'nginx'

    env_vars MY_ENV_VAR: 'something important'

    host_port 10234, container_port: 80

    host 'docker1'
    host 'docker2'
  end
end
```

Centurion supports multiple environments in the same config. Here we're just going to deploy to *staging*. We could add as many as we like. The default file also uses a pattern where common configurations between environments are put into a *common* section that is called by each of the environments. For demonstration purposes, we cut this config down to a bare minimum.

What we now have is a config that will let us deploy the *nginx* image from the public registry to two hosts, docker1 and docker2, while setting the environment variable MY_ENV_VAR to some text and mapping port 80 inside the container to the public port 10234. It supports any number of environment variables, hosts, ports, or volume mounts. The idea is to store a repeatable configuration for your application that can be stamped out onto as many Docker hosts as needed.

Centurion supports a rolling deployment model out of the box for web applications. It will cycle through a set of hosts, taking one container down at a time to keep the application up during deployment. It uses a defined health check endpoint on a container to enable rolling deployments. By default, this is "/" and that's good enough for us with our simple welcome page application. Nearly all of this is configurable, but we'll keep it simple.

We're ready, so let's deploy this to staging. We'll tell Centurion to use the `nginx` project, the `staging` environment, and to do a web application zero-downtime deployment with `rolling_deploy`. Centurion will initiate a `docker pull` on the hosts in parallel, then on each host in turn it will create a new container, tear down the old one, and start up the new one. We'll cut down the very verbose output to get a clearer idea of the process:

```
$ centurion -p nginx -e staging -a rolling_deploy
...
I, [2015... #51882]  INFO -- : Fetching image nginx:latest IN PARALLEL
I, [2015... #51882]  INFO -- : Using CLI to pull
I, [2015... #51882]  INFO -- : Using CLI to pull
4f903438061c: Pulling fs layer
1265e16d0c28: Pulling fs layer
0cbe7e43ed7f: Pulling fs layer
...
** Invoke deploy:verify_image (first_time)
** Execute deploy:verify_image
I, [2015... #51882]  INFO -- : ----- Connecting to Docker on docker1 -----
I, [2015... #51882]  INFO -- : Image 224873bd found on docker1
...
I, [2015... #51882]  INFO -- : ----- Connecting to Docker on docker2 -----
I, [2015... #51882]  INFO -- : Image 224873bd found on docker2
...
I, [2015... #51882]  INFO -- : ----- Connecting to Docker on docker1 -----
I, [2015... #51882]  INFO -- : Stopping container(s):
[{"Command"=>"nginx -g 'daemon off;'", "Created"=>1424891086,
"Id"=>"6b77a8dfc18bd6822eb2f9115e0accfd261e99e220f96a6833525e7d6b7ef723",
"Image"=>"2485b0f89951", "Names"=>["/nginx-63018cc0f9d268"],
"Ports"=>[{"PrivatePort"=>443, "Type"=>"tcp"}, {"IP"=>"172.16.168.179",
"PrivatePort"=>80, "PublicPort"=>10234, "Type"=>"tcp"}],
"Status"=>"Up 5 weeks"}]
I, [2015... #51882]  INFO -- : Stopping old container 6b77a8df
(/nginx-63018cc0f9d268)
I, [2015... #51882]  INFO -- : Creating new container for 224873bd
I, [2015... #51882]  INFO -- : Starting new container 8e84076e
I, [2015... #51882]  INFO -- : Waiting for the port to come up
I, [2015... #51882]  INFO -- : Found container up for 1 seconds
W, [2015... #51882]  WARN -- : Failed to connect to http://docker1:10234/,
no socket open.
I, [2015... #51882]  INFO -- : Waiting 5 seconds to test the / endpoint...
I, [2015... #51882]  INFO -- : Found container up for 6 seconds
I, [2015... #51882]  INFO -- : Container is up!
...
** Execute deploy:cleanup
I, [2015... #51882]  INFO -- : ----- Connecting to Docker on docker1 -----
I, [2015... #51882]  INFO -- : Public port 10234
I, [2015... #51882]  INFO -- : Removing old container e64a2796 (/sad_kirch)
I, [2015... #51882]  INFO -- : ----- Connecting to Docker on docker2 -----
```

```
I, [2015... #51882]  INFO -- : Public port 10234
I, [2015... #51882]  INFO -- : Removing old container dfc6a240 (/prickly_morse)
```

What we see happening here is pulling the requested image, verifying that it pulled properly, and then connecting to the hosts to stop the old container, create a new one, start it, and health-check it until it's up. At the very end, it cleans up the old containers so they don't hang around forever.

Now we have the container up and running on both docker1 and docker2. We can connect with a web browser by hitting *http://docker2:10234* or the same URI on docker1. In real production, you'll want a load balancer configured to sit in front of these hosts and point your clients to either of the instances. There is nothing dynamic to this setup, but it gets your application deployed with all the basic benefits of Docker for a minimal investment of time.

That's all there is to it for a basic setup. Centurion supports a lot more than this, but you can start to get the sense of the kinds of things some of the community tooling can support.

This class of tooling is very easy to get started with and will get you to a production infrastructure quickly. But growing your Docker deployment to a vast scale will likely involve a distributed scheduler, or one of the cloud providers. In that vein, let's look at Amazon's new service.

Amazon EC2 Container Service

One of the most popular cloud providers is Amazon via their AWS offering. Support for running containers natively has existed in Elastic Beanstalk since mid-2014. But that service assigns only a single container to an Amazon instance, which means that it's not ideal for short-lived or lightweight containers. EC2 itself is a great platform for hosting your own Docker environment, though, and because Docker is powerful, you don't necessarily need much on top of your instances to make this a productive environment to work in. But Amazon has spent a lot of engineering time building a service that treats containers as first-class citizens: the EC2 Container Service.

This section assumes that you have access to an AWS account and some familiarity with the service. Amazon provides detailed documentation online (*http://amzn.to/1F9dHlG*) that covers everything required to bootstrap an EC2 container install, including signing up for AWS, creating a user, creating a Virtual Private Cloud (VPC), etc.

The container service offering is an orchestration of several parts. You first define a cluster, then put one or more EC2 instances running Docker and Amazon's special agent into the cluster, and then push containers into the cluster. The agent works with the ECS service to coordinate your cluster and schedule containers to hosts.

IAM Role Setup

In AWS, Identity and Access Management (IAM) roles are used to control what actions a user can take within your cloud environment. We need to make sure we can grant access to the right actions before moving on with the EC2 Container Service.

To work with the EC2 Container Service, you need a role that consists of a policy with the privileges:

```
{
  "Version": "2012-10-17",
  "Statement": [
    {
      "Effect": "Allow",
      "Action": [
        "ecs:CreateCluster",
        "ecs:RegisterContainerInstance",
        "ecs:DeregisterContainerInstance",
        "ecs:DiscoverPollEndpoint",
        "ecs:Submit*",
        "ecs:Poll"
      ],
      "Resource": [
        "*"
      ]
    }
  ]
}
```

 In this example, we are only giving out the specific ecs privileges that we need for normal interaction with the service. `ecs:Crea teCluster` is optional if the cluster you will be registering the EC2 container agent with already exists.

AWS CLI Setup

Amazon supplies comand-line tools that make it easy to work with their API-driven infrastructure. You will need to install version 1.7 or higher of the AWS Command Line Interface (CLI) tools. Amazon has detailed documentation (*http://amzn.to/1PCpPNA*) that covers installation of their tools, but the basic steps are as follows.

Installation

Mac OS X. In Chapter 3, we discussed installing Homebrew. If you previously did this, you can install the AWS CLI using the following commands:

```
$ brew update
$ brew install awscli
```

Windows. Amazon provides a standard MSI installer for Windows, which can be downloaded from Amazon S3 for your architecture:

- 32-Bit Windows (*https://s3.amazonaws.com/aws-cli/AWSCLI32.msi*)

- 64-Bit Windows (*https://s3.amazonaws.com/aws-cli/AWSCLI64.msi*)

Other. The Amazon CLI tools are written in Python. So on most platforms, you can install the tools with the Python `pip` package manager by running the following from a shell:

```
$ pip install awscli
```

Some platforms won't have `pip` installed by default. In that case, you can use the `easy_install` package manager, like this:

```
$ easy_install awscli
```

Configuration

Quickly verify that your AWS CLI version is at least 1.7.0 with the following command:

```
$ aws --version
aws-cli/1.10.1 Python/2.7.10 Darwin/15.3.0 botocore/1.3.23
```

To quickly configure the AWS CLI tool, ensure that you have access to your AWS Access Key ID and AWS Secret Access Key, and then run the following. You will be prompted for your authentication information and some preferred defaults:

```
$ aws configure
AWS Access Key ID [None]: EXAMPLEEXAMPLEEXAMPLE
AWS Secret Access Key [None]: ExaMPleKEy/7EXAMPL3/EXaMPLeEXAMPLEKEY
Default region name [None]: us-east-1
Default output format [None]: json
```

You can quickly test that the CLI tools are working correctly by running the following command to list the IAM users in your account:

```
$ aws iam list-users
```

Assuming everything went according to plan and you chose JSON as your default output format, you should get something like the return shown here:

```
{
    "Users": [
        {
            "UserName": "myuser",
            "Path": "/",
            "CreateDate": "2015-01-15T18:30:30Z",
            "UserId": "EXAMPLE123EXAMPLEID",
```

```
            "Arn": "arn:aws:iam::01234567890:user/myuser"
        }
    ]
}
```

Container Instances

The first thing you need to do after installing the required tools is to create at least a single cluster that your Docker hosts will register with when they are brought online.

> The default cluster name is imaginatively named "default." If you keep this name, you do not need to specify --cluster-name in many of the commands that follow.

The first thing we need to do is start a cluster in the container service. We'll then push our containers into the cluster once it's up and running. For these examples, we will start by creating a cluster called "testing":

```
$ aws ecs create-cluster --cluster-name testing
{
    "cluster": {
        "clusterName": "testing",
        "status": "ACTIVE",
        "clusterArn": "arn:aws:ecs:us-east-1:0123456789:cluster/testing"
    }
}
```

You will now need to create an instance via the Amazon console. You could use your own AMI with the ECS agent and Docker installed, but Amazon provides one that we'll use here. This is almost always the way you'll want to use it since most of your custom code will ship in Docker containers anyway, right? So we'll deploy that AMI and configure it for use in the cluster. Consult Amazon's detailed documentation (*http://amzn.to/1PCqQFn*) for this step.

> If you are creating a new EC2 instance, be sure and note the IP address that it is assigned so that you can connect to it later.

As we mentioned, it is also possible to take an existing Docker host within your EC2 environment and make it compatible with the EC2 Container Service. To do this, you need to connect to the EC2 instance and ensure that you are running Docker version 1.3.3 or greater, and then deploy the Amazon ECS Container

Agent (*http://amzn.to/1PCqT4a*) to the local Docker host with the proper environment variable configured for your setup, as shown here:

```
$ sudo docker --version
Docker version 1.4.1, build 5bc2ff8

$ sudo docker run --name ecs-agent -d \
-v /var/run/docker.sock:/var/run/docker.sock \
-v /var/log/ecs/:/log -p 127.0.0.1:51678:51678 \
-e ECS_LOGFILE=/log/ecs-agent.log \
-e ECS_LOGLEVEL=info \
-e ECS_CLUSTER=testing \
amazon/amazon-ecs-agent:latest
```

Once you have at least a single instance running and registered into your cluster, you can check it by running:

```
$ aws ecs list-container-instances --cluster testing
{
    "containerInstanceArns": [
        "arn:aws:ecs:us-east-1:01234567890:
            container-instance/zse12345-12b3-45gf-6789-12ab34cd56ef78"
    ]
}
```

If the above output does not include a UID, then the ECS AMI or custom Docker host running the amazon-ecs-agent is not properly connected to the cluster. Carefully reread the preceding section and make sure that you did not skip any steps.

Taking the UID from the end of the previous command's output, we can request even more details about the container instance with the command shown here:

```
$ aws ecs describe-container-instances --cluster testing \
    --container-instances zse12345-12b3-45gf-6789-12ab34cd56ef78
{
    "failures": [],
    "containerInstances": [
        {
            "status": "ACTIVE",
            "registeredResources": [
                {
                    "integerValue": 1024,
                    "longValue": 0,
                    "type": "INTEGER",
                    "name": "CPU",
                    "doubleValue": 0.0
                },
                {
                    "integerValue": 3768,
                    "longValue": 0,
                    "type": "INTEGER",
```

```
                "name": "MEMORY",
                "doubleValue": 0.0
            },
            {
                "name": "PORTS",
                "longValue": 0,
                "doubleValue": 0.0,
                "stringSetValue": [
                    "2376",
                    "22",
                    "51678",
                    "2375"
                ],
                "type": "STRINGSET",
                "integerValue": 0
            }
        ],
        "ec2InstanceId": "i-aa123456",
        "agentConnected": true,
        "containerInstanceArn": "arn:aws:ecs:us-east-1:
          01234567890:container-instance/
          zse12345-12b3-45gf-6789-12ab34cd56ef78",
        "remainingResources": [
            {
                "integerValue": 1024,
                "longValue": 0,
                "type": "INTEGER",
                "name": "CPU",
                "doubleValue": 0.0
            },
            {
                "integerValue": 3768,
                "longValue": 0,
                "type": "INTEGER",
                "name": "MEMORY",
                "doubleValue": 0.0
            },
            {
                "name": "PORTS",
                "longValue": 0,
                "doubleValue": 0.0,
                "stringSetValue": [
                    "2376",
                    "22",
                    "51678",
                    "2375"
                ],
                "type": "STRINGSET",
                "integerValue": 0
            }
        ]
    }
```

```
    ]
}
```

It is interesting to note that the output includes both the container instance's registered resources, as well as its remaining resources. When you have multiple instances, this information helps the service determine where to deploy containers within the cluster.

Tasks

Now that our container cluster is up and running, we need to start putting it to work. To do this, we need to create at least one task definition. The Amazon EC2 Container Service defines the phrase "task definition" as a list of containers grouped together.

To create your first task definition, open up your favorite editor, copy in the following JSON, and then save it as *starwars-task.json* in your home directory, as shown here:

```
[
  {
    "name": "starwars",
    "image": "rohan/ascii-telnet-server:latest",
    "essential": true,
    "cpu": 50,
    "memory": 128,
    "portMappings": [
      {
        "containerPort": 23,
        "hostPort": 2323
      }
    ],
    "environment": [
      {
        "name": "FAVORITE_CHARACTER",
        "value": "Boba Fett"
      },
      {
        "name": "FAVORITE_EPISODE",
        "value": "V"
      }
    ],
    "entryPoint": [
      "/usr/bin/python",
      "/root/ascii-telnet-server.py"
    ],
    "command": [
      "-f",
      "/root/sw1.txt"
    ]
  }
]
```

In this task definition, we are saying that we want to create a task called starwars that will be based on the Docker image rohan/ascii-telnet-server:latest (*http://bit.ly/1PCrfI2*). This Docker image launches a Python-based telnet server that serves the Ascii Art version of the movie Star Wars (*http://www.asciimation.co.nz*) to anyone who connects.

In addition to typical variables included in a Dockerfile or via the `docker run` command, we define some constraints on memory and CPU usage for the container, in addition to telling Amazon whether this container is essential to the task. The `essential` flag is useful when you have multiple containers defined in a task, and not all of them are required for the task to be successful. If `essential` is true and the container fails to start, then all the containers defined in the task will be killed and the task will be marked as failed.

To upload this task definition to Amazon, we run a command similar to that shown here:

```
$ aws ecs register-task-definition --family starwars-telnet \
  --container-definitions file://$HOME/starwars-task.json

{
    "taskDefinition": {
        "taskDefinitionArn": "arn:aws:ecs:us-east-1:
          01234567890:task-definition/starwars-telnet:1",
        "containerDefinitions": [
            {
                "environment": [
                    {
                        "name": "FAVORITE_EPISODE",
                        "value": "V"
                    },
                    {

                        "name": "FAVORITE_CHARACTER",
                        "value": "Boba Fett"
                    }
                ],
                "name": "starwars",
                "image": "rohan/ascii-telnet-server:latest",
                "cpu": 50,
                "portMappings": [
                    {
                        "containerPort": 23,
                        "hostPort": 2323
                    }
                ],
                "entryPoint": [
                    "/usr/bin/python",
                    "/root/ascii-telnet-server.py"
                ],
```

```
                "memory": 128,
                "command": [
                    "-f",
                    "/root/sw1.txt"
                ],
                "essential": true
            }
        ],
        "family": "starwars-telnet",
        "revision": 1
    }
}
```

We can then list all of our task definitions by running the following:

```
$ aws ecs list-task-definitions

{
    "taskDefinitionArns": [
        "arn:aws:ecs:us-east-1:01234567890:task-definition/starwars-telnet:1"
    ]
}
```

Now we are ready to run our first task in our cluster. This is easily achieved with the command here:

```
$ aws ecs run-task --cluster testing --task-definition starwars-telnet:1 \
  --count 1

{
    "failures": [],
    "tasks": [
        {
            "taskArn": "arn:aws:ecs:us-east-1:
              01234567890:task/b64b1d23-bad2-872e-b007-88fd6ExaMPle",
            "overrides": {
                "containerOverrides": [
                    {
                        "name": "starwars"
                    }
                ]
            },
            "lastStatus": "PENDING",
            "containerInstanceArn": "arn:aws:ecs:us-east-1:
              01234567890:container-instance/
              zse12345-12b3-45gf-6789-12ab34cd56ef78",
            "desiredStatus": "RUNNING",
            "taskDefinitionArn": "arn:aws:ecs:us-east-1:
              01234567890:task-definition/starwars-telnet:1",
            "containers": [
                {
                    "containerArn": "arn:aws:ecs:us-east-1:
                      01234567890:container/
                      zse12345-12b3-45gf-6789-12abExamPLE",
```

```
                "taskArn": "arn:aws:ecs:us-east-1:
                  01234567890:task/b64b1d23-bad2-872e-b007-88fd6ExaMPle",
                "lastStatus": "PENDING",
                "name": "starwars"
            }
        ]
    }
  ]
}
```

The count argument allows us to define how many copies of this task we want deployed into our cluster. For this job, one is enough.

 The task-definition value is a name followed by a number (starwars-telnet:1). The number is the revision. If you edit your task and reregister it with the aws ecs register-task-definition command, you will get a new revision, which means that you will want to reference that new revision in your aws ecs run-task. If you don't change that number, you will continue to launch containers using the older JSON. This versioning makes it very easy to roll back changes and test new revisions without impacting all future instances.

In the output from the previous command, it is very likely that the lastStatus key displayed a value of PENDING.

You can now describe that task to ensure that it has transitioned into a RUNNING state by locating the task Arn from the previous output and then executing the code shown here:

```
$ aws ecs describe-tasks --cluster testing \
  --task b64b1d23-bad2-872e-b007-88fd6ExaMPle

{
    "failures": [],
    "tasks": [
        {
            "taskArn": "arn:aws:ecs:us-east-1:
              01234567890:task/b64b1d23-bad2-872e-b007-88fd6ExaMPle",
            "overrides": {
                "containerOverrides": [
                    {
                        "name": "starwars"
                    }
                ]
            },
            "lastStatus": "RUNNING",
            "containerInstanceArn": "arn:aws:ecs:us-east-1:
              017663287629:container-instance/
              zse12345-12b3-45gf-6789-12ab34cd56ef78",
            "desiredStatus": "RUNNING",
```

```
            "taskDefinitionArn": "arn:aws:ecs:us-east-1:
              01234567890:task-definition/starwars-telnet:1",
            "containers": [
                {
                    "containerArn": "arn:aws:ecs:us-east-1:
                      01234567890:container/
                      zse12345-12b3-45gf-6789-12abExamPLE",
                    "taskArn": "arn:aws:ecs:us-east-1:
                      01234567890:task/b64b1d23-bad2-872e-b007-88fd6ExaMPle",
                    "lastStatus": "RUNNING",
                    "name": "starwars",
                    "networkBindings": [
                        {
                            "bindIP": "0.0.0.0",
                            "containerPort": 23,
                            "hostPort": 2323
                        }
                    ]
                }
            ]
        }
    ]
}
```

After verifying that the lastStatus key is set to RUNNING, we should be able to
test our container.

Testing the Task

You will need either netcat (*http://nc110.sourceforge.net*) or a telnet client
installed on your system to connect to the container.

Installing NetCat/Telnet

Mac OS X. Mac OS X ships with a copy of netcat in */usr/bin/nc*, but you can also
install it via Homebrew:

```
$ brew install netcat
```

In this case, you will find the binary is called netcat rather than nc.

Debian-based system.
```
$ sudo apt-get install netcat
```

RedHat-based systems.
```
$ sudo yum install nc
```

Windows. Windows comes with a supported telnet client, but it is typically not
installed by default. You can launch an administrative command prompt and
type a single command to install the telnet client.

1. Click Start and under search, type **CMD**.

2. Right-click CMD and click Run as administrator.

3. If prompted, enter your Administrator password.

4. In the command prompt that launches, type the following command to enable the telnet client:

```
$ pkgmgr /iu:"TelnetClient"
```

Connecting to the container

We can now test the containerized task using either netcat or telnet. Launch a command prompt and then run the following commands. Be sure to replace the IP address with the address assigned to your EC2 instance.

When you connect to the container, you should see an ASCII version of the Star Wars movie (*http://www.asciimation.co.nz*) playing on your console.

netcat.

```
$ clear
$ nc 192.168.0.1 2323
```

To exit, simply press Ctrl-C.

telnet.

```
$ clear
$ telnet 192.168.0.1 2323
```

To exit, press Ctrl-], and in the telnet prompt, type **quit**, then press Enter.

Stopping the Task

We can list all the tasks running in our cluster using the following command:

```
$ aws ecs list-tasks --cluster testing

{
    "taskArns": [
        "arn:aws:ecs:us-east-1:
          01234567890:task/b64b1d23-bad2-872e-b007-88fd6ExaMPle"
    ]
}
```

We can further describe the task by reusing the aws ecs describe-tasks command:

```
$ aws ecs describe-tasks --cluster testing \
  --task b64b1d23-bad2-872e-b007-88fd6ExaMPle

...
```

Finally, we can stop the task by running:

```
$ aws ecs stop-task --cluster testing \
  --task b64b1d23-bad2-872e-b007-88fd6ExaMPle

{
...
        "lastStatus": "RUNNING",
...
        "desiredStatus": "STOPPED",
...
}
```

If we describe the task again, we should now see that the lastStatus key is set to STOPPED:

```
$ aws ecs describe-tasks --cluster staging_cluster \
  --task b64b1d23-bad2-872e-b007-88fd6ExaMPle

{
...
        "lastStatus": "STOPPED",
...
        "desiredStatus": "STOPPED",
...
}
```

And finally, listing all the tasks in our cluster should return an empty set.

```
$ aws ecs list-tasks --cluster testing

{
    "taskArns": []
}
```

At this point, we can start creating more complicated tasks that tie multiple containers together and rely on the EC2 Container Service tooling to deploy the tasks to the most idle hosts in our cluster.

Wrap-Up

After reading this chapter, you should have a good idea of the type of tools you can use to create a truly dynamic Docker cluster for your applications to live in. With Docker's highly portable container format and its ability to abstract away so much of the underlying Linux system, it is easy to move your applications fluidly between your data center and as many cloud providers as you want.

## CHAPTER 10

Advanced Topics

In this chapter, we'll do a quick pass through some of the more advanced topics. We're going to assume that you have a pretty good hold on Docker by now and that you've already got it in production or at least you're a regular user. We'll talk some more about deployment tools, networking, orchestration, security, and advanced configuration.

Some of this chapter covers configurable changes you can make to your Docker installation. These can be useful. But Docker has good defaults and the defaults are much better tested and usually more robust than the alternatives. Keep in mind that this is early production release software and things are moving fast. The defaults have the most eyeballs on them and therefore have had the largest number of bug fixes. You should stick to the defaults on your operating system unless you have a good reason to change them and have educated yourself on what those changes mean to you.

Pluggable Backends

Docker has a very clean external interface and, in part because it's largely a single static Go binary, it looks pretty monolithic. But there's actually a lot going on under the covers that is configurable, and the two kinds of backends are a good example. With Docker, you can easily swap both how Docker interacts with the underlying filesystem and how it talks to the kernel about containers! Those are powerful switches and you'll want to know what they do before throwing them. First we'll talk about execution drivers, then the filesystem backends.

Execution Driver

Docker is not the mechanism for talking to the Linux kernel and managing the life cycle of containers. It seems like this might be true, because Docker knows how to do the right things out of the box. That's because it ships with a container engine known as the execution driver. This driver is exposed as a standard API, and while the driver has to be built into Docker at compile time, they were originally switchable at runtime with a simple command-line argument. By default, Docker ships with the "native" driver enabled. Before the release of Docker 1.10, you could change the execution driver to the LXC (Linux Container) driver with a simple command-line argument when you started Docker:

```
docker daemon -e lxc
```

This is no longer possible in current releases, but is still interesting to discuss, since it illuminates some of the ways that Docker interacts with the underlying system. If you were to change your execution driver, it would most likely drastically affect how Docker interacts with the kernel and might even introduce additional runtime dependencies to your environment.

Docker Engine now ships with "native" as the only available execution driver. The native driver has seen the heaviest development and is tightly controlled by Docker, while other execution drivers often suffered from quality control issues. Useful functionality, like the /stats endpoint on the API (which we talked about in Chapter 8), is only available on the native execution driver. So let's find out what your system is running by using docker info:

```
$ docker info
Containers: 18
Images: 286
Storage Driver: aufs
 Root Dir: /var/lib/docker/aufs
 Backing Filesystem: extfs
 Dirs: 323
Execution Driver: native-0.2
Kernel Version: 3.8.0-35-generic
Operating System: Ubuntu precise (12.04.3 LTS)
CPUs: 1
Total Memory: 987.9 MiB
Name: ubuntu
ID: UNKL:ZFZ5:ELSF:DU7Z:WJBM:NVPO:WDUZ:BO53:UFAD:KARC:NSSH:ZA5Q
```

We've shown this before, but hopefully after this chapter you'll have a better idea of what that means. This Ubuntu server is running the "native-0.2" execution driver. The native driver is versioned so that in theory you could compile your Docker against different versions of libcontainer and have it exercise only the functionality that's available in that version of the library. Unless you are building Docker from source and intentionally changing things, these will always be correctly matched for you and are therefore nothing to worry about.

native, lxc, windows, etc.

Originally the Docker project leveraged work done by the Linux Containers Project (LXC) (*https://linuxcontainers.org*) to control container life cycles. LXC was the one and only execution driver until the release of Docker 0.9 and the newly added support for a standardized execution driver API. This was done with the intention of bringing many other virtualization layers into the fold, including non-container engines. It was envisioned that things like FreeBSD jails and Solaris Zones might appear as execution drivers (*http://bit.ly/1PCtdIj*). We haven't seen that really play out so far. The LXC driver is no more, and now Docker automatically utilizes either the native or windows execution drivers (*http://bit.ly/1PCtfQs*) that ship with Docker.

Because LXC was not a part of the Docker project, it was hard for Docker to ensure that the LXC project didn't introduce changes that caused issues with Docker. It also made it challenging for Docker to ensure that important changes required in the next LXC release were prioritized.

As a result, in version 0.9, the LXC execution driver was replaced with libcontainer (*https://github.com/docker/libcontainer*), a Docker-native Go library for working with containers, namespaces, and cgroups. All modern Docker builds use libcontainer as the default backend.

Containers configured with different execution drivers are not compatible with each other. You will need to recreate containers when swapping the execution driver.

Storage

Backing all of the images and all of the containers on your Docker server is a storage backend that handles reading and writing all of that data. Docker has some strenuous requirements on its storage backend: it has to support layering, the mechanism by which Docker tracks changes and reduces both how much disk a container occupies and how much is shipped over the wire to deploy new images. Using a copy-on-write strategy, Docker can start up a new container from an existing image without having to copy the whole image. The storage backend supports that. The storage backend is what makes it possible to export images as groups of changes in layers, and also lets you save the state of a running container. In most cases, you need the kernel's help in doing this efficiently. That's because the filesystem view in your container is generally a union of all of the layers below it, which are not actually copied into your container. Instead, they are made visible to you, and only when you make changes does anything get written to your container's own filesystem.

Docker relies on an array of possible kernel drivers to handle the layering. The Docker codebase contains code that can handle interaction with all of these backends, and the decision about which to use can be configured on daemon restart. So let's take a look at what is available and some of the pluses and minuses of each.

AUFS, Device Mapper, BTRFS, vfs, etc.

Various backends have different limitations that may or may not make them your best choice. In some cases, your choices of which backend to use are limited by what your distribution of Linux actually supports. Using drivers that are built in to the kernel that your distribution ships with will make life ever so much easier. It's generally best to stay near the tested path here as well. We've seen all manner of oddities from various backends since Docker's release. And, as usual, the common case is always the best supported one. Different backends also report different statistics up through the Docker Remote API (/info endpoint). This is potentially useful for monitoring your Docker systems.

AUFS

The original backend, and at the time of this writing the officially recommended one, is AUFS: a union filesystem driver with reasonable support on various popular Linux distributions. It was never accepted into the mainline kernel, however, and this has limited its availability on various distributions. It is not supported on recent versions of RedHat, Fedora, or CentOS, for example. It is not shipped in the standard Ubuntu distribution, but is in the Ubuntu linux-image-extra package.

Its status as a second-class citizen in the kernel has lead to the development of many of the other backends now available. Older, but still recent, versions of AUFS had a limitation of 42 layers, which might constrain how you build base images if you are running on such a version. If you are shipping images for public consumption, you should definitely keep this limitation in mind because even if you don't have it, someone else probably does. The current limit in Docker for AUFS is 127 layers, which is probably well more than you should ever use for performance reasons. AUFS has been a pretty good performer on recent kernels and is quite well-tested with Docker.

devicemapper

RedHat's various distributions have not supported AUFS recently, so RedHat contributed (*http://red.ht/1PCwg34*) a backend to the Docker project based on devicemapper, which is a heavily tested layer of the Linux kernel that underpins things like LVM, disk encryption, and other software RAID implementations.

The Docker backend was written quickly to just get some support for Docker into RedHat-based distributions, and at first had some major flaws. Most of these have been addressed now and it's reasonably stable. But even in later versions of Docker, it has been shown to be only somewhat reliable in production. Unlike AUFS, which can usually be unloaded from the kernel and then reloaded, devicemapper often has other kernel modules that depend on it. That means that the worst failure modes currently require a reboot of the whole server on which Docker is running. Performance is reasonable, but no one would call it speedy when using the loopback mode (the default). It does support using disk partitions raw, which should be faster. It does not have much tolerance for having anything at all written into the container during runtime. It's the default choice on RedHat/CentOS distributions before Red-Hat/CentOS 7.

BTRFS

btrfs (*http://bit.ly/1PCwkQw*) is fundamentally a copy-on-write filesystem, which means it's a pretty good fit for the Docker image model. On systems that don't support AUFS and where the btrfs driver is present, it's the default backend. This includes, for example, RHEL and CentOS 7. It also works on various Ubuntu versions. Like AUFS and unlike devicemapper, Docker is using the backend in the way it was intended. That means it's both pretty stable in production and also a good performer. It scales reasonably to thousands of containers on the same system. A major drawback for Red Hat–based systems is that btrfs does not support SELinux. If you have btrfs available, we currently recommend it as the most stable backend for production. The space is changing rapidly, however, and new backends keep becoming available.

vfs

The vfs driver is the simplest, and slowest, to start up of the supported drivers. It doesn't really support copy-on-write. Instead, it makes a new directory and copies over all of the existing data. It was originally intended for use in tests and for mounting host volumes. It is very slow to create new containers, but runtime performance is native, which is a real benefit. It is very simple in mechanism, which means there is less to go wrong. Docker, Inc., does not recommend it for production use so you should proceed with caution if you think it's the right solution for your production environment.

overlayfs

overlayfs is now the union filesystem driver that is supported in the mainline Linux kernel as of version 3.18 (*http://bit.ly/1zFjGhH*). That's good news for its long-term support. It also means that it's likely to get a lot of attention to performance and will be available on most Linux distributions once they catch up with version 3.18 and higher kernels. It is a bit like AUFS but fundamentally simpler underneath, which leads to very strong performance. The

Docker backend is still under active development, but we expect it to be a good option going forward.

 The Docker community is frequently improving support for a variety of filesytems. For example, ZFS support was added in Docker 1.7 and XFS is the new default filesystem for devimapper-backed systems in Docker 1.9. For more details about the supported filesystems, take a look at the official documentation (*https://docs.docker.com/engine/userguide/storagedriver/*).

 Storage backends can have a big impact on the performance of your containers. And if you swap the backend on your Docker server, all of your existing images will disappear. They are not gone, but they will not be visible until you switch the driver back. Caution is advised.

You can use docker info to see which storage backend your system is running. It will also tell you what the underlying filesystem is in cases where there is one. In some cases, like with devicemapper on raw partitions or with btrfs, there won't be a different underlying filesystem.

Like with execution drivers, storage backends can be swapped via command-line arguments to docker on startup. If we wanted to switch our Ubuntu system from AUFS to devicemapper, we would do that like this:

```
$ docker daemon --storage-driver=devicemapper
```

That will work on pretty much any Linux system that can support Docker because devicemapper is almost always present. You will need to have the actual underlying dependencies in place for the other drivers. For example, without AUFS in the kernel—usually via a kernel module—Docker will not start up with AUFS set as the storage driver.

Getting the right storage driver for your systems and deployment needs is one of the more important technical items to get right when taking Docker to production. Be conservative; make sure the path you choose is well-supported in your kernel and distribution.

Containers in Detail

While we all talk about Linux containers as a single entity, they are implemented through several separate mechanisms that all work together: Control Groups (cgroups), namespaces, and SELinux/AppArmor. cgroups provide for resource limits, namespaces allow for processes to use identically named resources and isolate them from each other's view of the system, and SELinux/AppArmor provides strong security isolation. We'll talk about SELinux and AppArmor in a bit. But what do cgroups and namespaces do for you?

Control Groups (cgroups)

Operations teams have often aimed for one server per intensive task. So, for example, you don't run your applications on the database server because they have competing resource demands and their resource usage could grow unbounded and come to dominate the server, starving neighbors of performance.

On real hardware systems, this could be quite expensive and so solutions like virtual servers are very appealing, in part because you can share expensive hardware between competing applications, and the virtualization layer would handle your resource partitioning. While it saves money, this is a reasonably expensive way to go about it if you don't need all the other separation provided by virtualization, because running multiple kernels introduces a reasonable overhead on the applications. Maintaining virtual machines is also not the cheapest solution. All the same, cloud computing has shown that it's immensely powerful and with the right tooling, incredibly effective.

But if the only kind of isolation you needed was resource partitioning, wouldn't it be great if you could do that on the same kernel? For many years, you could assign a "niceness" value to a process and it would give the scheduler hints about how you wanted this process to be treated in relation to others. But it wasn't possible to impose hard limits like those that you get with virtual machines. And niceness is not at all fine-grained: I can't give something more I/O and less CPU than other processes. This fine-grained control, of course, is one of the promises of Docker, and the mechanism that it uses to do that is cgroups, which predate Docker and were invented to solve just that problem.

Control Groups, or cgroups for short, allow you to set limits on resources for processes and their children. This is the mechanism that Docker uses to control limits on memory, swap, and CPU resources. They are built in to the Linux kernel and originally shipped back in 2007 in Linux 2.6.24. The official kernel documentation (*http://bit.ly/1PCxJ9y*) defines them as "a mechanism for aggregating/ partitioning sets of tasks, and all their future children, into hierarchical groups with specialized behaviour." It's important to note that this setting applies to a process and all of the children that descend from it. That's exactly how containers are structured.

Every Docker container is assigned a cgroup that is unique to that container. All of the processes in the container will be in the same group. This means that it's easy to control resources for each container as a whole without worrying about what might be running. If a container is redeployed with new processes added, you can have Docker assign the same policy and it will apply to all of them.

We talked previously about the cgroups hooks exposed by Docker via the Remote API. This allows you to control memory, swap, and disk usage. But there are lots of other things you can limit with cgroups, including the number of I/O operations per second (iops) a container can have, for example. You might find that in your environment you need to use some of these levers to keep your containers under control, and there are a few ways you can go about doing that. cgroups by their nature need to do a lot of accounting of resources used by each group. That means that when you're using them, the kernel has a lot of interesting statistics about how much CPU, RAM, disk I/O, and so on. that your processes are using. So Docker uses cgroups not just to limit resources but also to report on them. These are many of the metrics you see, for example, in the output of `docker stats`.

The /sys filesystem

The primary way to control cgroups in a fine-grained manner, even if you configured them with Docker, is to manage them yourself. This is the most powerful method because changes don't just happen at creation time—they can be done on the fly.

On systems with `systemd`, there are command-line tools like `systemctl` that you can use to do this. But since cgroups are built into the kernel, the method that works everywhere is to talk to the kernel directly via the `/sys` filesystem. If you're not familiar with `/sys`, it's a filesystem that directly exposes a number of kernel settings and outputs. You can use it with simple command-line tools to tell the kernel how to behave in a number of ways.

It's important to note that this method of configuring cgroups controls for containers only works directly on the Docker server and is not available remotely via any API. If you use this method, you'll need to figure out how to script this for your own environment.

> Changing cgroups values yourself, outside of any Docker configuration, breaks some of the repeatability of Docker deployment. Unless you tool changes into your deployment process, settings will go away when containers are replaced.

Let's use an example of changing the CPU cgroups settings for a container we already have running. First we need to get the long ID of the container, and then we need to find it in the `/sys` filesystem. Here's what that looks like:

```
$ docker ps --no-trunc
CONTAINER ID IMAGE          COMMAND       CREATED      STATUS     NAMES
dcbbaa763... 0415448f2cc2  "supervisord" 3 weeks ago Up 2 days romantic_morse
```

Here we've had `docker ps` give us the long ID in the output, and the ID we want is "dcbbaa763daff1dc0a91e7675d3c93895cb6a6d83371e25b7f0bd62803ed8e86". You can see why Docker normally truncates this. In the examples we're going to truncate it, too, to make it at least a little readable and fit into the constraints of a printed page. But you need to use the long one!

Now that we have the ID, we can find our container's cgroup in the /sys filesystem. Cgroups are laid out so that each kind of setting is grouped into a module and that module is exposed at a different place in the /sys filesystem. So when we look at CPU settings, we won't see blkio settings, for example. You might take a look around in the /sys to see what else is there. But for now we're looking at the CPU controller, so let's inspect what that gives us. You need *root* access on the system to do this because you're manipulating kernel settings:

```
$ ls /sys/fs/cgroup/cpu/docker/dcbbaa763daf
cgroup.clone_children   cpu.cfs_period_us   cpu.rt_runtime_us   notify_on_release
cgroup.event_control    cpu.cfs_quota_us    cpu.shares          tasks
cgroup.procs            cpu.rt_period_us    cpu.stat
```

> The exact path above will change a bit depending on the Linux distribution your Docker server is running on and what the hash of your container is. For example, on CoreOS, the path would look something like this: /sys/fs/cgroup/cpu/system.slice/ docker-8122be2d7a67a52e949582f6d5 cb2771a8469ab20ecf7b6915e9217d92ddde98.scope/

You can see that under cgroups, there is a docker directory that contains all of the Docker containers that are running on this host. You can't set cgroups for things that aren't running because they apply to running processes. This is an important point that you should consider. Docker takes care of reapplying cgroups settings for you when you start and stop containers. Without that mechanism, you are somewhat on your own.

Back to our task. Let's inspect the CPU shares for this container. Remember that we earlier set these via the Docker command-line tool. But for a normal container where no settings were passed, this setting is the default:

```
$ cat /sys/fs/cgroup/cpu/docker/dcbbaa763daf/cpu.shares
1024
```

1024 CPU shares means we are not limited at all. Let's tell the kernel that this container should be limited to half that:

```
$ echo 512 > /sys/fs/cgroup/cpu/docker/dcbbaa763daf/cpu.shares
$ cat /sys/fs/cgroup/cpu/docker/dcbbaa763daf/cpu.shares
512
```

There you have it. We've changed the container's settings on the fly. This method is very powerful because it allows you to set any cgroups setting at all for the container. But as we mentioned earlier, it's entirely ephemeral. When the container is stopped and restarted, the setting is reset to the default:

```
$ docker stop dcbbaa763daf
dcbbaa763daf
$ cat /sys/fs/cgroup/cpu/docker/dcbbaa763daf/cpu.shares
cat: /sys/fs/.../cpu.shares: No such file or directory
```

You can see that the directory path doesn't even exist any more now that the container is stopped. And when we start it back up, the directory comes back but the setting is back to 1024:

```
$ docker start dcbbaa763daf
dcbbaa763daf
$ cat /sys/fs/cgroup/cpu/docker/dcbbaa763daf/cpu.shares
1024
```

If you were to change these kinds of settings in a production system via the /sys fileystem directly, you'd want to tool that directly. A daemon that watches the docker events stream and changes settings at container startup, for example, is a possibility. Currently, the community has not contributed much rich tooling to this aspect. It's likely that Docker will eventually expand the native driver's functionality to allow this level of configuration.

 As of Docker 1.6, it is possible to create custom cgroups outside of Docker and then attach a new container to that cgroup using the --cgroup-parent argument to docker create.

Kernel Namespaces, User Namespaces

Inside each container, you see a filesystem, network interfaces, disks, and other resources that all appear to be unique to the container despite sharing the kernel with all the other processes on the system. The network interface on the actual machine, for example, is a single shared resource. But to your container it looks like it has the run of an entire network interface to itself. This is a really useful abstraction: it's what makes your container feel like a machine all by itself. The way this is implemented in the kernel is with namespaces. Namespaces take a single global resource and make it appear as a single owned resource to the container.

Rather than just having a single namespace, however, containers have a namespace on each of the six types of resources that are currently namespaced in the kernel: mounts, UTS, IPC, PID, network, and user namespaces. We'll explain all of those in a minute. But essentially when you talk about a container, you're talking about a number of different namespaces that Docker sets up on your behalf. So what do they all do?

Mount namespaces

Docker uses these primarily to make your container look like it has its entire own filesystem namespace. If you've ever used a chroot jail, this is its tougher cousin. It looks a lot like a chroot jail but goes all the way down to the kernel so that even mount and unmount system calls are namespaced. If you use docker exec or nsenter to get into a container, you'll see a filesystem rooted on "/". But we know that this isn't the actual root partition of the system. It's the mount namespaces that make that possible.

UTS namespaces

Named for the kernel structure they namespace, and ultimately from the "Unix Timesharing System," UTS namespaces give your container its own hostname and domain name. This is also used by older systems like NIS to identify which domain a host belongs to. When you enter a container and see a hostname that is not the same as the machine on which it runs, it's this namespace that makes that happen.

> With the release of Docker Engine 1.7, it is now possible to have a container use its host's UTS namespace, by specifying the --uts=host option when launching the container with docker run.

IPC namespaces

These isolate your container's System V IPC and POSIX message queue systems from those of the host. Some IPC mechanisms use filesystem resources like named pipes, and those are covered by the mount namespace. The IPC namespace covers things like shared memory and semaphores that aren't filesystem resources but which really should not cross the container wall.

PID namespaces

We already showed you that you can see all of the processes in containers in the Linux ps output on the host Docker server. But inside the container, processes have a totally different PID. This is the PID namespace in action. A process has a unique PID in each namespace to which it belongs. If you look in /proc inside a container, or run ps, you will only see the processes inside the container's PID namespace.

Network namespaces

This is what allows your container to have its own network devices, ports, etc. When you run docker ps and see the bound ports for your container, you are seeing ports from both namespaces. Inside the container your nginx might be bound to port 80, but that's on the namespaced network interface. This namespace makes it possible to have what seems to be a completely separate network stack for your container.

User namespaces

These provide isolation between the user and group IDs inside a container and those on the Docker host. Earlier when we looked at `ps` output outside the container and inside and saw different user IDs, this is how that happened. A new user inside a container is not a new user on the Docker host's main namespace, and vice versa. There are some subtleties here, though. For example, root in a user namespace is not necessarily root on the main system. Some of this work is reasonably new to the Linux kernel and there are concerns about security leakage, which we'll talk about in a bit.

 Docker Engine 1.10 added the `--userns-remap` argument to the `docker daemon` command, so that it is easier to run all containers within a user and group context that is unprivileged on the host system. This protects the host from various potential security exploits. For more information about this topic, read through the official `docker daemon` documentation (*https://docs.docker.com/ engine/reference/commandline/daemon/*).

So namespaces provide the visual, and in many cases functional, isolation that makes a container look like a virtual machine even though it's on the same kernel. Let's explore what some of that namespacing that we just described actually looks like.

Exploring Namespaces

One of the easiest to demonstrate is the UTS namespace, so let's use `docker exec` to get a shell in a container and take a look. From within the docker server, run the following:

```
$ hostname
docker2
$ docker exec -i -t 28970c706db0 /bin/bash -l
# hostname
28970c706db0
```

Although `docker exec` will work from a remote system, here we `ssh` into the Docker server itself in order to demonstrate that the hostname of the server is different from inside the container.

That `docker exec` command line gets us an interactive process (`-i`) and allocates a pseudo-tty (`-t`), and then executes `/bin/bash` while executing all the normal login process in the bash shell (`-l`). Once we have a terminal open inside the container's namespace, we ask for the hostname and get back the container ID. That's the default hostname for a Docker container unless you tell Docker to name it otherwise. This is a pretty simple example, but it should clearly show that we're not in the same namespace as the host.

Another example that's easy to understand and demonstrate is with PID namespaces. Let's log in to the Docker server again, take a look at the process list of one of our containers, and then get the same list from inside the container:

```
$ docker exec -i -t 28970c706db0 /bin/bash -l
# ps -ef
UID        PID  PPID  C STIME TTY          TIME CMD
root         1     0  0 22:20 ?        00:00:00 /bin/bash
root        22     0  0 22:53 ?        00:00:00 /bin/bash -l
# exit
logout
$ ps axlf
...
46049     1   20    0 706552 18228 futex_ Ssl  ?         2:16 /usr/bin/docker -d
46135 46049  20    0  18104  1892 n_tty_ Ss+ pts/0     0:00  \_ /bin/bash
```

What we can see here is that from inside our container, the original command run by Docker from the CMD in our Dockerfile is /bin/bash and it has been assigned the PID 1 inside the container. You might recall that this is the PID normally used by the init process on Unix systems. In this case, the /bin/bash we started to create the container in the first place is the first PID, so it gets ID 1. But in the Docker host's main namespace, we do a little work to find our container's processes and we see the PID there is not 1, it's 46135 and it's a child of the docker daemon, which is PID 46049.

The other namespaces work in essentially the same manner and you probably get the idea by now. It's worth pointing out here that when we were working with nsenter back in Chapter 4, we had to pass a pretty arcane (at that point) set of arguments to the command when we ran it to enter a container from the Docker server. Let's look at that command line now:

```
$ sudo nsenter --target $PID --mount --uts --ipc --net --pid
root@3c4f916619a5:/#
```

After explaining namespaces in detail, this probably makes a lot more sense to you. You're telling nsenter exactly which of the namespaces you want to enter. It can also be educational to use nsenter to only enter parts of the namespace of a throwaway container to see what you get. In the example above, we enter all of the namespaces we just talked about.

When it comes down to it, namespaces are the primary thing that make a container look like a container. Combine them with cgroups and you have a reasonably robust isolation between processes on the same kernel.

Security

We've spent a good bit of space now talking about how Docker contains applications, allows you to constrain resources, and uses namespaces to give the container a view of the world that is unique to the container. We also briefly mentioned the need for SELinux/AppArmor. One of the wins for containers is the ability to replace virtual machines in a number of cases. So let's take a look at what isolation we really get, and what we don't.

How Secure Is Your Container?

You are undoubtedly aware by now that the isolation you get from a container is not as strong as that from a virtual machine. We've been reinforcing the idea from the start of this book that containers are just processes running on the Docker server. Despite the isolation provided by namespaces, containers are not as secure as you might imagine if the idea of a lightweight virtual machine persists.

One of the big boosts in performance for containers, and one of the things that makes them lightweight, is that they share the kernel of the Docker server. This is also the source of the greatest security concerns around Docker containers. The main reason is that not everything in the kernel is namespaced. We talked about all of the namespaces that exist and how the container's view of the world is constrained by the namespaces it runs in. But there are still lots of places in the kernel where really no isolation exists. And namespaces only constrain you if you can't tell the kernel to give you access to a different one.

For purposes of security, containers are more secure than an application on the host directly because cgroups (if you use them), and namespaces provide some isolation from the host's core resources. But you must not think of containers as a substitute for good security practices. If you think about how you would run an application on a production system, that is really how you should run your containers. If your application would run as a non-privileged user in a non-container environment, then it should be run in the same manner inside the container, for example. You can tell Docker to run your whole container as a non-privileged user, and in production deployments, this is probably what you want to do. You can't, unfortunately, enforce that Docker start all containers as non-privileged users at this time. But starting them that way yourself, or at least dropping privileges inside the running application as soon as possible, is a good idea.

Let's look at some security risks and controls.

UID 0

The first and most overarching security risk in a container is that the *root* user in the container is actually the *root* user on the system. There are extra constraints on *root* in a container, and namespaces do a good job of isolating *root* in the container from the most dangerous parts of the /proc and /sys filesystems, for example. But generally speaking you have *root* access so if you can get access to resources outside of your namespace, then the kernel will see you as *root*. And Docker starts all services in containers as *root* by default which means you are then responsible for managing privilege in your applications just like you are on any Linux system. Let's explore some of the limits on *root* access and look at some obvious holes. This is not intended to be an exhaustive statement on container security, but rather to give you a healthy understanding of some of the classes of security risks.

First, we'll fire up a container and get a bash shell using the public Ubuntu image shown in the following code. Then we'll see what kinds of access we have:

```
$ sudo docker run -t -i ubuntu /bin/bash
root@808a2b8426d1:/# lsmod
Module                  Size  Used by
xt_nat                 12726  2
xt_tcpudp              12603  8
veth                   13244  0
xt_addrtype            12713  2
xt_conntrack           12760  1
iptable_filter         12810  1
acpiphp                24119  0
ipt_MASQUERADE         12759  4
aufs                  191008  14
iptable_nat            12909  1
nf_conntrack_ipv4      14538  2
nf_defrag_ipv4         12729  1 nf_conntrack_ipv4
nf_nat_ipv4            13316  1 iptable_nat
nf_nat                 26158  4 ipt_MASQUERADE,nf_nat_ipv4
nf_conntrack           83996  6 ipt_MASQUERADE,nf_nat
ip_tables              27473  2 iptable_filter,iptable_nat
x_tables               29938  7 ip_tables,xt_tcpudp
bridge                101039  0
floppy                 70206  0
...
```

We've cut the output down a bit, but what we're looking at here is a new container that we started and we've just asked the kernel to tell us what modules are loaded. That's not too surprising: a normal user can do that. But it does reinforce that we're talking to the same Linux kernel. If you run this listing on the Docker server itself, it will be identical. So we can see the kernel modules; what happens if we try to unload the floppy module?

```
root@808a2b8426d1:/# rmmod floppy
rmmod: ERROR: ... kmod_module_remove_module() could not remove 'floppy': ...
rmmod: ERROR: could not remove module floppy: Operation not permitted
```

That's the same error message we would get if we were a nonprivileged user telling the kernel what to do. This should give you a good sense that the kernel is doing its best to prevent us from doing things we shouldn't. And because we're in a limited namespace, we also can't get the kernel to give us access to the top-level namespace either. We're really relying on there being no bugs in the kernel that allow us to escalate that, however, because if we do, we're *root* and can change things.

We can contrive a simple example of how things can go wrong by starting a bash shell in a container that has had the Docker server's /etc bind mounted into the container's namespace. Keep in mind that anyone who can start a container on your Docker server can do what we're about to do any time they like because you can't configure Docker to prevent it:

```
$ docker run -i -t -v /etc:/host_etc ubuntu /bin/bash
root@e674eb96bb74:/# more /host_etc/shadow
root:!:16230:0:99999:7:::
daemon:*:16230:0:99999:7:::
bin:*:16230:0:99999:7:::
sys:*:16230:0:99999:7:::

...
irc:*:16230:0:99999:7:::
nobody:*:16230:0:99999:7:::
libuuid:!:16230:0:99999:7:::
syslog:*:16230:0:99999:7:::
messagebus:*:16230:0:99999:7:::
kmatthias:$1$aTAYQT.j$3xamPL3dHGow4ITBdRh1:16230:0:99999:7:::
sshd:*:16230:0:99999:7:::
lxc-dnsmasq:!:16458:0:99999:7:::
```

Here we've used the -v switch to Docker to tell it to mount a host path into the container. The one we've chosen is /etc, which is a dangerous thing to do. But it serves to prove a point: we are root in the container and root has file permissions in this path. So we can look at the real /etc/shadow file any time we like. There are plenty of other things you could do here, but the point is that by default you're only partly constrained.

 It is a bad idea to run your container processes with UID 0. This is because any exploit that allows the process to somehow escape its namespaces will expose your host system to a fully privileged process. You should always run your standard containers with a non-privileged UID.

Privileged containers

There are times when you need your container to have special kernel capabilities (*http://bit.ly/1F9loIz*) that would normally be denied to the container. This could include many things like mounting a USB drive, modifying the network configuration, or creating a new Unix device.

In the following code, we try to change the MAC address of our container:

```
$ docker run --rm -ti ubuntu /bin/bash
root@b328e3449da8:/# ip link ls
1: lo: <LOOPBACK,UP,LOWER_UP> mtu 65536 qdisc noqueue state ...
    link/loopback 00:00:00:00:00:00 brd 00:00:00:00:00:00
9: eth0: <BROADCAST,UP,LOWER_UP> mtu 1500 qdisc noqueue state ...
    link/ether 02:42:0a:00:00:04 brd ff:ff:ff:ff:ff:ff
root@b328e3449da8:/# ip link set eth0 address 02:0a:03:0b:04:0c
RTNETLINK answers: Operation not permitted
root@b328e3449da8:/# exit
```

As we can see, it doesn't work. This is because the underlying Linux kernel blocks the nonprivileged container from doing this, which is exactly what we normally want. However, assuming that we need this functionality for our container to work as intended, the easiest way to significantly expand a container's privileges is by launching it with the `--privileged=true` argument:

```
$ docker run -ti --rm --privileged=true ubuntu /bin/bash
root@88d9d17dc13c:/# ip link ls
1: lo: <LOOPBACK,UP,LOWER_UP> mtu 65536 qdisc noqueue state ...
    link/loopback 00:00:00:00:00:00 brd 00:00:00:00:00:00
9: eth0: <BROADCAST,UP,LOWER_UP> mtu 1500 qdisc noqueue state ...
    link/ether 02:42:0a:00:00:04 brd ff:ff:ff:ff:ff:ff
root@88d9d17dc13c:/# ip link set eth0 address 02:0a:03:0b:04:0c
root@88d9d17dc13c:/# ip link ls
1: lo: <LOOPBACK,UP,LOWER_UP> mtu 65536 qdisc noqueue state ...
    link/loopback 00:00:00:00:00:00 brd 00:00:00:00:00:00
9: eth0: <BROADCAST,UP,LOWER_UP> mtu 1500 qdisc noqueue state ...
    link/ether 02:0a:03:0b:04:0c brd ff:ff:ff:ff:ff:ff
root@88d9d17dc13c:/# exit
```

In the preceding output, you will notice that we no longer get the error and the `link/ether` entry for eth0 has been changed.

The problem with using the `--privileged=true` argument is that you are giving your container very broad privileges, and in most cases you likely only need one or two kernel capabilities to get the job done.

If we explore our privileged container some more, we will discover that we have capabilities that have nothing to do with changing the MAC address. I can even do things that could cause issue with both Docker and the host system. In the following code, we are going to create a memory swapfile[1] and enable it:

```
$ docker run -ti --rm --privileged=true ubuntu /bin/bash
root@0ffcdd8f7535:/# dd if=/dev/zero of=/swapfile1 bs=1024 count=100
100+0 records in
100+0 records out
102400 bytes (102 kB) copied, 0.00046004 s, 223 MB/s
root@0ffcdd8f7535:/# mkswap /swapfile1
```

---

[1] Swapfiles are used to virtually extend your system's memory capacity by giving it access to a large file for additional storage space.

```
Setting up swapspace version 1, size = 96 KiB
no label, UUID=fc3d6118-83df-436e-867f-87e9fbce7692
root@00ffcdd8f7535:/# swapon /swapfile1
root@00ffcdd8f7535:/# swapoff /swapfile1
root@00ffcdd8f7535:/# exit
exit
```

 In the previous example, if you do not disable the swapfile before exiting your container, you will leave your Docker host in a bad state where Docker can't destroy the container because your host is accessing a swapfile that is inside the container's filesystem.

In that case, the error message will look something like this:

```
FATAL [0049] Error response from daemon:
Cannot destroy container 0ff...670:
 Driver overlay failed to remove root filesystem 0ff...670:
 remove /var/lib/docker/overlay/0ff...670/upper/swapfile1:
 operation not permitted
```

You can fix this from the Docker server by running:

```
$ sudo swapoff /var/lib/docker/overlay/0ff...670/upper/swapfile1
```

So as we've seen, it is possible for people to do bad things in a fully privileged container.

To change the MAC address, the only kernel capability we actually need is CAP_NET_ADMIN. Instead of giving our container the full set of privileges, we can give it this one privilege by launching our Docker container with the --cap-add argument, as shown here:

```
$ docker run -ti --rm --cap-add=NET_ADMIN ubuntu /bin/bash
root@852d18f5c38d:/# ip link set eth0 address 02:0a:03:0b:04:0c
root@852d18f5c38d:/# ip link ls
1: lo: <LOOPBACK,UP,LOWER_UP> mtu 65536 qdisc noqueue state ...
    link/loopback 00:00:00:00:00:00 brd 00:00:00:00:00:00
9: eth0: <BROADCAST,UP,LOWER_UP> mtu 1500 qdisc noqueue state ...
    link/ether 02:0a:03:0b:04:0c brd ff:ff:ff:ff:ff:ff
root@852d18f5c38d:/# exit
```

You should also notice that although we can change the MAC address, we can no longer use the swapon command inside our container.

```
$ docker run -ti --rm --cap-add=NET_ADMIN ubuntu /bin/bash
root@848aa7924594:/# dd if=/dev/zero of=/swapfile1 bs=1024 count=100
100+0 records in
100+0 records out
102400 bytes (102 kB) copied, 0.000575541 s, 178 MB/s
root@848aa7924594:/# mkswap /swapfile1
Setting up swapspace version 1, size = 96 KiB
no label, UUID=3b365d90-8116-46ad-80c5-24341299dc41
root@848aa7924594:/# swapon /swapfile1
```

```
swapon: /swapfile1: swapon failed: Operation not permitted
root@848aa7924594:/# exit
```

By using both the `--cap-add` and `--cap-drop` arguments to `docker run`, you can finely control the Linux kernel capabilities that your container has.

SELinux, AppArmor

Earlier we talked about how containers are a combination of two or three things: cgroups, namespaces, and SELinux or AppArmor. We're going to talk about the latter two systems now. They allow you to apply security controls that extend beyond those normally supported by Unix systems. SELinux originally came out of the US National Security Agency and supports very fine-grained control. AppArmor is an effort to achieve many of the same goals without the level of complication involved in SELinux. It actually predates SELinux, having first appeared in 1998 in the Immunix Linux distribution. Novell, SuSE, and Canonical have been some of its recent champions.

Docker ships by default with reasonable profiles enabled on platforms that support them. This means that on Ubuntu systems, AppArmor is enabled and configured, and on CentOS/RHEL/Fedora systems, SELinux is. You can further configure these profiles to prevent things like what we've just done in Chapter 9, and if you're running Docker in production, you should do a risk analysis and determine if this is something you should look at. Here's a quick outline of the benefits we're getting from these systems.

They provide what is known as Mandatory Access Control. This is a class of security system where a system-wide security policy grants users (or "initiators") access to a resource (or "target"). What this allows you to do is to prevent anyone, including root, from accessing a part of the system that they should not have access to. You can apply the policy to a whole container so that all processes are constrained. Many chapters would be required to give a very clear overview of how to configure these systems in detail. The default profiles are doing things like blocking access to parts of the /proc and /sys filesystems that would be dangerous to expose in the container, even though they show in the container's namespace. They also provide more narrowly scoped mount access to prevent containers from getting ahold of mount points they should not see.

If you are considering using Docker containers in production, you should make certain that the systems you are running have AppArmor or SELinux enabled and running. For the most part, both systems are reasonably equivalent. But in the Docker context, one notable limitation of SELinux is that it only works fully on systems that support filesystem metadata, which means that it won't work for you on BTRFS-backed Docker daemons, for example. Only the devicemapper backend currently fully supports SELinux. Unfortunately, that backend is also not currently very stable for production. The OverlayFS backend is going to support

...s shortly. AppArmor, on the other hand, does not use filesystem metadata and ...o works on all of the Docker backends. Which one you use is going to be somewhat distribution-centric, so you may be forced to choose a filesystem backend based on which distribution you run.

How Secure Is the Docker Daemon?

From a security standpoint, the Docker daemon is the only completely new risk you are introducing to the network. Your containerized applications are not less secure and are at least a little more secure than they would be if deployed outside of containers. But without the containers, you would not be running the daemon. You can run Docker such that it doesn't expose any ports on the network. In this model, you'd need to do something like set up an SSH tunnel to each Docker server if you wanted to control the containers. That's not very useful, so nearly everyone will expose one or more ports on the local network.

The default configuration for Docker on all the distributions we're familiar with leave Docker isolated from the network with only a local Unix socket exposed. Since you cannot remotely administer Docker when it is set up this way, many people add the nonencrypted port 2375 to the configuration. This is great for getting going with Docker, and depending on your security analysis it might be all right for you. But it's probably not what you should do in any environment where you need a reasonable level of security.

You can do a few things to tighten Docker down that make sense in most production environments. But no matter what you do, you are relying on the Docker daemon itself to be resilient against things like buffer overflows and race conditions, two of the more common classes of security vulnerabilities. This is true of any network service. The risk is perhaps a little higher from Docker because it has access to control all of your applications, and because of the privileges required, it has to run as root.

The basics of locking Docker down are common with many other network daemons: encrypt your traffic and authenticate users. The first is reasonably easy to set up on Docker and the second is not as easy. If you have certificates you can use for protecting HTTP traffic to your hosts, such as a wildcard cert for your domain, you can turn on TLS support to encrypt all of the traffic to your Docker servers. This is a good step. The Docker documentation (*https://docs.docker.com/articles/https/*) will walk you through doing this.

Authorization is more complicated: Docker does not provide any kind of fine-grained authorization: you either have access or you don't. But the authentication control it does provide is reasonably strong: signed certificates. Unfortunately this also means that you don't get a cheap step from no authentication to some authentication without also having to set up your own certificate authority in most cases. If your organization already has one, then you are in luck. Certificate management needs to be implemented carefully in any organization both to keep them secure and to distribute them efficiently. So, given that, here are the basic steps:

1. Set up a method of generating and signing certificates.
2. Generate certificates for the server and clients.
3. Configure Docker to require certificates with `--tlsverify`.

Detailed instructions on getting a server and client set up, as well as a simple certificate authority are included in the Docker documentation (*https://docs.docker.com/articles/https/*).

Because it's a daemon that runs with privilege, and because it has direct control of your applications, it's probably not a good idea to expose Docker directly on the Internet. If you need to talk to your Docker hosts from outside your network, you should consider something like a VPN or an SSH tunnel to a jump host.

Networking

Early on we described the layers of networking that are in place between a Docker container and the real live network. Let's take a closer look at how that works. Figure 10-1 shows a drawing of a typical Docker server, where there are three containers running on their private network, shown on the right. One of them has a public port (TCP port 10520) that is exposed on the Docker server. We'll track how an inbound request gets to the Docker container and also how a Docker container can make an outbound connection to the external network.

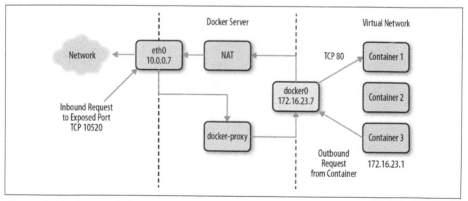

Figure 10-1. Swarm Manager controlling Docker cluster

If we have a client somewhere on the network that wants to talk to the nginx server running on TCP port 80 inside Container 1, the request will come into the eth0 interface on the Docker server. Because Docker knows this is a public port, it has spun up an instance of docker-proxy to listen on port 10520. So our request is passed to the docker-proxy process, which then makes the request to the correct container address and port on the private network. Return traffic from the request flows through the same route.

Outbound traffic from the container follows a different route, in which the docker-proxy is not involved at all. In this case, Container 3 wants to contact a server on the public Internet. It has an address on the private network of 172.16.23.1 and its default route is the docker0 interface 172.16.23.7. So it sends the traffic there. The Docker server now sees that this traffic is outbound and it has traffic forwarding enabled. And since the virtual network is private, it wants to send the traffic from its own public address instead. So the request is passed through the kernel's network address translation layer (NAT) and put onto the external network via the eth0 interface on the server. Return traffic passes through the same route. Note that the NAT is one-way, so containers on the virtual network will see real network addresses in response packets.

You've probably noted that it's not a simple configuration. It's a fair amount of mechanism, but it makes Docker seem pretty transparent. It's also a contributor to the security posture of the Docker stack because the containers are namespacd into their own network namespace, are on their own private network, and don't have access to things like the main system's DBus or IPTables.

Let's take a look at what is happening at a more detailed level. The interfaces that show up in ifconfig or ip addr show in the Docker container are actually virtual Ethernet interfaces on the Docker server's kernel. They are then mapped into the network namespace of the container and given the names that you see inside the container. Let's take a look at what we see when running ip addr show on a Docker server. We'll shorten the output a little for clarity and typesetting issues, as shown here:

```
$ ip addr show
1: lo: <LOOPBACK,UP,LOWER_UP>
    link/loopback 00:00:00:00:00:00 brd 00:00:00:00:00:00
    inet 127.0.0.1/8 scope host lo
    inet6 ::1/128 scope host
       valid_lft forever preferred_lft forever
2: eth0: <BROADCAST,MULTICAST,UP,LOWER_UP>
    link/ether 00:0c:29:b2:2a:21 brd ff:ff:ff:ff:ff:ff
    inet 172.16.168.178/24 brd 172.16.168.255 scope global eth0
    inet6 fe80::20c:29ff:feb2:2a21/64 scope link
       valid_lft forever preferred_lft forever
4: docker0: <BROADCAST,MULTICAST,UP,LOWER_UP>
    link/ether 56:84:7a:fe:97:99 brd ff:ff:ff:ff:ff:ff
    inet 172.17.42.1/16 scope global docker0
    inet6 fe80::5484:7aff:fefe:9799/64 scope link
       valid_lft forever preferred_lft forever
112: vethf3e8733: <BROADCAST,UP,LOWER_UP>
```

```
        link/ether b6:3e:7a:ba:5e:1c brd ff:ff:ff:ff:ff:ff
        inet6 fe80::b43e:7aff:feba:5e1c/64 scope link
            valid_lft forever preferred_lft forever
```

What that is telling us is that we have the normal loopback interface, our real Ethernet interface eth0, and then the Docker bridge interface, docker0, that we described earlier. This is where all the traffic from the Docker containers is picked up to be routed outside the virtual network. The surprising thing in this output is that vethf3e8733 interface. When Docker creates a container, it creates two virtual interfaces, one of which sits on the server-side and is attached to the docker0 bridge, and one that is exposed into the container's namespace. What we're seeing here is the server side interface. Notice how it doesn't show up as having an IP address assigned to it? That's because this interface is just joined to the bridge. This interface will also have a totally different name in the container's namespace as well.

It would be entirely possible to run a container without the whole networking configuration that Docker puts in place for you. And the docker-proxy can be somewhat throughput limiting for very high-volume data services. So what does it look like if we turn it off? Since the beginning, Docker has let you do this on a per-container basis with the --net=host command-line switch. There are times, like when you want to run high throughput applications, where you might want to do this. But you lose some of Docker's flexibility when you do it. Even if you never need or want to do this, it's useful to expose how the mechanism works underneath.

 Like other things in this chapter, this is not a setting you should take lightly. It has operational and security implications that might be outside your tolerance level. It can be the right thing to do, but you should consider the repercussions.

Let's start a container with --net=host and see what happens, as shown here:

```
$ docker run -i -t --net=host ubuntu /bin/bash
$ ip addr show
1: lo: <LOOPBACK,UP,LOWER_UP>
    link/loopback 00:00:00:00:00:00 brd 00:00:00:00:00:00
    inet 127.0.0.1/8 scope host lo
    inet6 ::1/128 scope host
        valid_lft forever preferred_lft forever
2: eth0: <BROADCAST,MULTICAST,UP,LOWER_UP>
    link/ether 00:0c:29:b2:2a:21 brd ff:ff:ff:ff:ff:ff
    inet 172.16.168.178/24 brd 172.16.168.255 scope global eth0
    inet6 fe80::20c:29ff:feb2:2a21/64 scope link
        valid_lft forever preferred_lft forever
3: lxcbr0: <BROADCAST,MULTICAST,UP,LOWER_UP>
    link/ether fe:59:0b:11:c2:76 brd ff:ff:ff:ff:ff:ff
    inet 10.0.3.1/24 brd 10.0.3.255 scope global lxcbr0
```

```
    inet6 fe80::fc59:bff:fe11:c276/64 scope link
        valid_lft forever preferred_lft forever
4: docker0: <BROADCAST,MULTICAST,UP,LOWER_UP>
    link/ether 56:84:7a:fe:97:99 brd ff:ff:ff:ff:ff:ff
    inet 172.17.42.1/16 scope global docker0
    inet6 fe80::5484:7aff:fefe:9799/64 scope link
        valid_lft forever preferred_lft forever
112: vethf3e8733: <BROADCAST,UP,LOWER_UP>
    link/ether b6:3e:7a:ba:5e:1c brd ff:ff:ff:ff:ff:ff
    inet6 fe80::b43e:7aff:feba:5e1c/64 scope link
        valid_lft forever preferred_lft forever
```

That should look pretty familiar. That's because when we run a container with the host networking option, we're just in the host's network namespace. Note that we're *also* in the server's UTS namespace. Our server's hostname is "docker2," so let's see what the container's hostname is:

```
$ hostname
docker2
```

If we do a mount to see what's mounted, though, we see that Docker is still maintaining our /etc/resolv.conf, /etc/hosts, and /etc/hostname. Interestingly, the /etc/hostname simply contains the server's hostname. Just to prove that we can see all the normal networking on the Docker server, let's look at netstat -an and see if we can see the docker daemon running:

```
$netstat -an | grep 2375
tcp6       0      0 :::2375                  :::*                LISTEN
```

So we are indeed in the server's network namespace. What all of this means that if we were to launch a high-throughput network service, we would be able to expect network performance from it that is essentially native. But it also means we could bind to ports that would collide with those on the server, so if you do this you should be careful about how you allocate port assignments.

With the release of Docker 1.7, the --userland-proxy flag was added to Docker Engine. When you set this flag to false while launching the Docker daemon (--userland-proxy=false), Docker will completely disable the userland-proxy and instead rely on hairpin NAT functionality to route traffic between local containers. It is likely that this will eventually become the preferred approach, once it has been proven to be reliable.

In Docker 1.9, a new network subcommand was added to the docker client. This subcommand allows you to view and manipulate the Docker network layers and how they are attached to containers that are running on the system.

Listing the networks available from Docker's perspective is easily accomplished with the following command:

```
# docker network ls
NETWORK ID          NAME            DRIVER
c37e1476e9c1        none            null
d7f88e502765        host            host
15dd2b3b16b1        bridge          bridge
```

You can then find out more details about any individual network by using the docker network inspect command along with the network ID:

```
# docker network inspect 15dd2b3b16b1
[
    {
        "Name": "bridge",
        "Id": ...,
        "Scope": "local",
        "Driver": "bridge",
        "IPAM": {
            "Driver": "default",
            "Config": [
                {
                    "Subnet": "172.18.0.0/16"
                }
            ]
        },
        "Containers": {
            "...": {
                "EndpointID": "...",
                "MacAddress": "04:42:ab:26:03:52",
                "IPv4Address": "172.18.0.2/16",
                "IPv6Address": ""
            }
        },
        "Options": {
            "com.docker.network.bridge.default_bridge": "true",
            "com.docker.network.bridge.enable_icc": "true",
            "com.docker.network.bridge.enable_ip_masquerade": "true",
            "com.docker.network.bridge.host_binding_ipv4": "0.0.0.0",
            "com.docker.network.bridge.name": "docker0",
            "com.docker.network.driver.mtu": "1500"
        }
    }
]
```

Docker networks can be created and removed, as well as attached and detached from individual containers by using the network subcommand.

There is a lot more you can configure with the Docker network layer. However, the defaults, host networking, and userland-proxyless mode, are the ones that you're most likely to use or encounter in the wild. Some of the other things you can configure, for example, are the DNS servers used, the resolver options, the default gateways the containers use, and much more. The networking section of

The Docker documentation (*https://docs.docker.com/articles/networking/*) gives an overview of how to do some of these things.

 For advanced network configuration of Docker, check out Weave (*https://github.com/zettio/weave*)—a virtual network tool for spanning containers across multiple Docker hosts. And if you are going to be using Kubernetes, take a look at CoreOS's flannel (*https://github.com/coreos/flannel*), which is an `etcd`-backed network fabric for containers.

## CHAPTER 11

Designing Your Production Container Platform

When implementing any core technology in production, the most mileage is often gained by designing a resilient platform that is forgiving of the unexpected issues that will eventually occur. When used as intended, with close attention to detail, Docker can be an incredibly powerful tool. As a young technology that is going through very rapid growth cycles, you are bound to trigger frustrating bugs in Docker and its interactions with the underlying kernel.

If, instead of simply deploying Docker into your environment, you take the time to build a well-designed container platform on top of Docker, you can enjoy the many benefits of a Docker-based workflow while protecting yourself from some of the sharper exposed edges that typically exist in such a high-velocity project.

Like all other technology, Docker doesn't magically solve all your problems. To reach its true potential, organizations must make very conscious decisions about why and how they are going to use it. For very small projects, it is possible to use Docker in a very simple manner; however, if you plan to support a large project that can scale with demand, it quickly becomes important to ensure that you are making very deliberate decisions about how your applications and platform are designed. This ensures that you can maximize the return on your investment in the technology. Taking the time to design your platform with intention can also make it much easier to modify your production workflow over time. A well-designed Docker platform will ensure that your software is running on a dynamic foundation that can easily be upgraded as technology and processes develop over time.

Below we will explore some of the leading thinking about how container platforms should be designed to improve the resiliency and supportability of the overall platform.

The Twelve-Factor App

In November of 2011, Adam Wiggins, cofounder of Heroku, and his colleagues, released an article called "The Twelve-Factor App." (*http://12factor.net*) This document describes a series of 12 distilled practices that come from the experiences of Heroku engineers on how to design applications that will thrive and grow in a modern Software-as-a-Service (SaaS) environment.

Although not required, applications built with these 12 steps in mind are ideal candidates for the Docker workflow. Below we explore each of these steps and why they can, in numerous ways, help improve your development cycle.

Codebase

A single codebase tracked in revision control.

Many instances of your application will be running at any given time, but they should all come from the same code repository. Each and every Docker image of an application should be built from a single source code repository that contains all the code required to build the Docker container. This ensures that the code can easily be rebuilt, and that all third-party requirements are well defined within the repository, if not actually directly included.

What this means is that building your application shouldn't require stitching together code from multiple source repositories. That is not to say that you can't have a dependency on an artifact from another repo. But it does mean that there should be a clear mechanism for determining which pieces of code were shipped when you built your application. Docker's ability to simplify dependency management is much less useful if building your application requires pulling down mutiple source code repositories and copying pieces together. And it's not repeatable unless you know the magic incantation.

Dependencies

Explicitly declare and isolate dependencies.

Never rely on the belief that a dependency will be made available via some other avenue, like the operating system install. Any dependencies that your application requires should be well-defined in the code base and pulled in by the build process. This will help ensure that your application will run when deployed, without relying on libraries being installed by other processes. This is particularly important within a container since the container's processes are isolated from the rest of the host operating system and will usually not have access to anything outside the container image's filesystem.

The Dockerfile and language-dependent configuration files like Node's *package.json* or Ruby's *Gemfile* should define every nonexternal dependency required by your application. This ensures that your image will run correctly on any ~~tem to which it is deployed.~~ Gone will be the days when you deploy and run yo ~~application~~ only to find out that important libraries are missing or installed wit ~~wrong version.~~ This has huge reliability and repeatability advantages, and very positive ramifications for system security. If you update the OpenSSL or libyaml libraries that your Dockerized application uses to fix a security issue, you can be assured that it will always be running with that version wherever you deploy that particular application.

It is also important to note that most Docker base images are actually much larger than they need to be. Remember that your application process will be running on a shared kernel, and the only files that you actually need inside your base image are ones that the process will require to run. It's good that the container makes this repeatable. But it can sometimes mask hidden dependencies. Although people often start with a minimal install of Ubuntu or CentOS, these images still contain a lot of operating system files that your process almost certainly does not need, or possibly some that you rely on and don't realize it. You need to be in charge of your dependencies, even when containerizing your application.

A good way to shed light on the depth of your application's dependency tree is to compare it to a container for a statically linked program written in a language like Go or C. They don't need any libraries or command-line binaries. To explore what one of these ultra-light containers might look like, let's run a statically linked Go program in a container by executing the following command:

```
$ docker run --publish=8085:8080 --detach=true \
  --name=static-helloworld adejonge/helloworld:latest
365cc5ddb0c40a50763217c66be26959933028631ef24a60a7da9944971587a3
```

Keep a copy of the long ID hash for your container, because you will need it in a moment. If you now point a local web browser at port 8085 on your Docker server (i.e., *http://172.17.42.10:8085/*) you would see the message:

```
Hello World from Go in minimal Docker container
```

Contrary to everything we've looked at in this book so far, this very minimal container does not contain a shell or SSH. This means we can't use ssh, nsenter, or docker exec to examine it. Instead we can examine the container's filesystem by logging directly into the Docker server via ssh, and then looking into the container's filesystem itself. To do that, we need to find the filesystem on the server's disk. We do this by first running docker info to determine the root directory for the storage driver.

```
$ docker info
...
Storage Driver: aufs
```

```
Root Dir: /mnt/sda1/var/lib/docker/aufs
...
```

 The `Docker Root Dir` and the `Root Dir` are not the same things. We specifically want the `Root Dir` listed under `Storage Driver`.

By combining the Docker root directory and the container hash into a file path, it is possible to view the container's filesystem from the Docker server. You might need to poke around in the storage driver's root directory a bit to determine the exact location of the container filesystems. In our case, it is under the additional directory called `mnt`.

If we now list the files in that directory, we will discover that the number of files in this container is incredibly small:

```
$ ls -R /mnt/sda1/var/lib/docker/aufs/mnt/36...a3
/mnt/sda1/var/lib/docker/aufs/mnt/36...a3:
dev/        etc/        helloworld  proc/        sys/

/mnt/sda1/var/lib/docker/aufs/mnt/36...a3/dev:
console  pts/    shm/

/mnt/sda1/var/lib/docker/aufs/mnt/36...a3/dev/pts:

/mnt/sda1/var/lib/docker/aufs/mnt/36...a3/dev/shm:

/mnt/sda1/var/lib/docker/aufs/mnt/36...a3/etc:
hostname    hosts       mtab        resolv.conf

/mnt/sda1/var/lib/docker/aufs/mnt/36...a3/proc:

/mnt/sda1/var/lib/docker/aufs/mnt/36...a3/sys:
```

You can see that in addition to `console` device and basic `/etc` files, the only other file is the `helloworld` binary, which contains everything our simple web application needs to run on a modern Linux kernel, and hence from within a container.

In addition to the filesystem layers used by Docker, keeping your containers stripped down to the bare necessities is another great way to keep your images slim and your `docker pull` commands fast. It's much harder to do with interpreted languages living in a container. But the point is that you should try to keep as minimal a base layer as needed so that you can reason about your dependencies. Docker helps you package them up, but you still need to be in charge of them.

Config

Store configuration in environment variables, not in files checked into the code bas

This makes it simple to deploy the exact same code base to different environ-ments, like staging and production, without maintaining complicated configura-tion in code or rebuilding your container for each environment. This keeps your code base much cleaner by keeping environment-specific information like data-base names and passwords out of your source code repository. More importantly though, it means that you don't bake deployment environment assumptions into the repository, and because of that it is extremely easy to deploy your applications anywhere that it might be useful. You also need to be able to test the same image you will ship to production. You can't do that if you have to build an image for each environment with all of its configuration baked in.

As discussed in Chapter 5, this can be achieved by launching docker run com-mands that leverage the -e command-line argument. Using -e APP_ENV=*produc tion* tells Docker to set the environment variable *APP_ENV* to the value "production" within the newly launched container.

For a real-world example, let's assume we pulled the image for the chat robot hubot with the HipChat (*https://www.hipchat.com/*) adapter installed. We'd issue something like the following command to get it running:

```
docker run \
  -e BIND_ADDRESS="0.0.0.0"
  -e ENVIRONMENT="development" \
  -e SERVICE_NAME="hubot" \
  -e SERVICE_ENV="development" \
  -e EXPRESS_USER="hubot" \
  -e EXPRESS_PASSWORD="Chd273gdExAmPl3wlkjdf" \
  -e PORT="8080" \
  -e HUBOT_ADAPTER="hipchat" \
  -e HUBOT_ALIAS="/" \
  -e HUBOT_NAME="hubot" \
  -e HUBOT_HIPCHAT_JID="someroom@chat.hipchat.com" \
  -e HUBOT_HIPCHAT_PASSWORD='SOMEEXAMPLE' \
  -e HUBOT_HIPCHAT_NAME="hubot" \
  -e HUBOT_HIPCHAT_ROOMS="anotherroom@conf.hipchat.com" \
  -e HUBOT_HIPCHAT_JOIN_ROOMS_ON_INVITE="true" \
  -e REDIS_URL="redis://redis:6379" \
  -d --restart="always" --name hubot hubot:latest
```

Here we are passing a whole set of environment variables into the container when it is created. When the process is launched in the container, it will have access to these environment variables so that it can properly configure itself at runtime. These configuration items are now an external dependency that we can inject at runtime.

the case of a Node.js application like hubot, you could then write the following code to make decisions based on these environment variables:

```
switch(process.env.ENVIRONMENT){
        case 'development':
            console.log('Running in development');

        case 'staging':
            console.log('Running in staging');

        case 'production':
            console.log('Running in production');

        default:
            console.log('Assuming that I am running in development');
    }
```

Keeping specific configuration information out of your source code makes it very easy to deploy the exact same container to multiple environments, with no changes and no sensitive information committed into your source code repository. Crucially, it supports testing your container images thoroughly before deploying to production by allowing the same image to be used in both environments.

Backing Services

Treat backing services as attached resources.

Local databases are no more reliable than third-party services, and should be treated as such. Applications should handle the loss of an attached resource gracefully. By implementing graceful degradation in your application and ensuring that you never assume that any resource, including filesystem space, is available, your application will continue to perform as many of its functions as it can, even when external resources are unavailable.

This isn't something that Docker helps you with directly, and although it is always a good idea to write robust services, it is even more important when you are using containers. High availability is most often achieved through horizontal scaling and rolling deployments when using containers, instead of relying on the live migration of long-running process, like on traditional virtual machines. This means that specific instances of a service will often come and go over time and your service should be able to handle this gracefully.

Additionally, because Docker containers have limited filesystem resources, you can't simply rely on having some local disk available. You need to plan that into your application's dependencies and handle it explicitly.

Build, Release, Run

Strictly separate build and run stages.

Build the code, release it with the proper configuration, and then deploy it. This ensures that you maintain control of the process and can perform any single step without triggering the whole workflow. By ensuring that each of these steps are self-contained in a distinct process, it allows you to tighten the feedback loop and react more quickly to any problems within the deployment flow.

As you design your Docker workflow, you want to ensure that each step in the deployment process is clearly separated. It is perfectly fine to have a single button, that builds a container, tests it, and then deploys it, assuming that you trust your testing processes—but you don't want to be forced to rebuild a container simply in order to deploy it to another environment.

Docker supports the twelve-factor ideal well in this area because there is a clean hand-off point between building an image and shipping it to production: the registry. If your build process generates images and pushes them to the registry, then deployment can simply be pulling the image down to servers and running it.

Processes

Execute the app as one or more stateless processes.

All shared data must be accessed via a stateful backing store, so that application instances can easily be redeployed without losing any important session data. You don't want to keep critical state on disk in your ephemeral container, nor in the memory of one of its processes. Containerized applications should always be considered ephemeral. A truly dynamic container environment requires the ability to destroy and recreate containers at a moment's notice. This flexibility helps enable the rapid deployment cycle and outage recovery demanded by modern, Agile workflows.

As much as possible, it is preferable to write applications that do not need to keep state longer than the time required to process and respond to a single request. This ensures that the impact of stopping any given container in your application pool is very minimal. When you must maintain state, the best approach is to use a remote datastore like Redis, PostgreSQL, Memcache, or even Amazon S3, depending on your resiliency needs.

Port Binding

Export services via port binding.

Your application needs to be addressable by a port specific to itself. Applications should bind directly to a port to expose the service and should not rely on an external daemon like inetd to handle that for them. You should be certain that when you're talking to that port, you're talking to your application. Most modern web platforms are quite capable of directly binding to a port and servicing their own requests.

Exposing a port from your container, as discussed in Chapter 4, can be achieved by launching docker run commands that use the -p command-line argument. Using -p 80:8080 would tell Docker to proxy the container's port 8080 on the host's port 80.

The statically linked Go hello world container that we discussed in "Dependencies" on page 184 is a great example of this because the container contains nothing but our application to serve its content to a web browser. We did not need to include any additional web servers, which would require additional configuration, add additional complexity, and increase the number of potential failure points in our system.

Concurrency

Scale out via the process model.

Design for concurrency and horizontal scaling within your applications. Increasing the resources of an existing instance can be difficult and hard to reverse. Adding and removing instances as scale fluctuates is much easier and helps maintain flexibility in the infrastructure. Launching another container on a new server is incredibly inexpensive compared to the effort and expense required to add resources to an underlying virtual or physical system. Designing for horizontal scaling allows the platform to react much faster to changes in resource requirements.

This is where tools like swarm, mesos, and kubernetes really begin to shine. Once you have implemented a Docker cluster with a dynamic scheduler, it is very easy to add three more instances of a container to the cluster as load increases, and then to later remove two instances of your application from the cluster as load starts to decrease again.

Disposability

Maximize robustness with fast startup and graceful shutdown.

Services should be designed to be ephemeral. We already talked a little bit about this when talking about external state. But dynamic horizontal scaling, rolling deploys, and responding to unexpected problems require applications that can quickly and easily be started or shut down. Services should respond gracefully to a SIGTERM signal from the operating system and even handle hard failures with aplomb. Most importantly, we shouldn't need to care if any given container for our application is up and running. As long as requests are being served, developer should be freed from being concerned about the health of any gi single component within the system. If an individual node is behaving poor. turning it off or redeploying it should be an easy decision that doesn't entail lon planning sessions and concerns about the health of the rest of the cluster.

As discussed in Chapter 8, Docker sends standard Unix signals to containers when it is stopping or killing them, therefore it is possible for any containerized application to detect these signals and take the appropriate steps to shut down gracefully.

Development/Production Parity

Keep development, staging, and production as similar as possible.

The same processes and artifacts should be used to build, test, and deploy services into all environments. The same people should do the work in all environments, and the physical nature of the environments should be as similar as reasonably possible. Repeatability is incredibly important. Almost any issue discovered in production points to a failure in the process. Every area where production diverges from staging is an area where risk is being introduced into the system. These inconsistencies ensure that you are blind to certain types of issues that could occur in your production environment until it is too late to proactively deal with them.

In many ways, this repeats the essence of a few of the early recommendations. However, the specific point here is that any environment divergence introduces risks, and although these differences are common in many organizations, they are much less necessary in a containerized environment. Docker servers can normally be created so that they are identical in all of your environments and environment-based configuration changes, and should typically only affect which endpoints your service connects to without specifically changing the applications behavior.

Logs

Treat logs as event streams.

Services should not concern themselves with routing or storing logs. Instead, events should be streamed, unbuffered, to STDOUT for handling by the hosting process. In development, STDOUT can be easily viewed, while in staging and production, the stream can be routed to anything, including a central logging service. Different environments have different exceptions for log handling. This logic should never be hard-coded into the application. By streaming everything to STDOUT, it is possible for the top-level process manager to handle the logs via chever method is best for the environment, and this allows the application veloper to focus on core functionality.

n Chapter 6, we discussed the docker logs command which collects the output from your container's STDOUT and records them as logs. If you write logs to random files within the container's filesystem, you will not have easy access to them. It is also possible to send logs to a local or remote logging system using things like rsyslog, heka, or fluentd.

If you use a process manager or init system, like upstart, systemd, or supervisord with the remote-logging plug-in, it is usually very easy to direct all process output to STDOUT and then have your process monitor capture it and send it to a remote logging host.

Admin Processes

Run admin/management tasks as one-off processes.

One-off administration tasks should be run via the exact same code base and configuration that the application uses. This helps avoid problems with synchronization and code/schema drift problems. Oftentimes, management tools exist as one-off scripts or live in a completely different code base. It is much safer to build management tools within the application's code base, and utilize the same libraries and functions to perform required work. This can significantly improve the reliability of these tools by ensuring that they leverage the same code paths that the application relies on to perform its core functionality.

What this means is that you should never rely on random cron-like scripts to perform administrative and maintenance functions. Instead, include all of these scripts and functionality in your application code base. Assuming that these don't need to be run on every instance of your application, you can launch a special short-lived container whenever you need to run a maintenance job, which simply executes the one job, reports its status somewhere, and then exits.

Twelve-Factor Wrap-Up

While it wasn't written as a Docker-specific manifesto, almost all of this can be applied to writing and deploying applications on a Docker platform. This is in part because "The Twelve-Factor App" document heavily influenced the design of Docker, and in part because the manifesto itself codified many of the best practices promoted by modern software architects.

The Reactive Manifesto

Riding alongside "The Twelve-Factor App," another pertinent document was released in July of 2013 by Jonas Bonér (*http://bit.ly/1F9pHng*), cofounder and

CTO of Typesafe: "The Reactive Manifesto." (*http://www.reactivemanifest.*
Jonas originally worked with a small group of contributors to solidify a manir
that discusses how the expectations for application resiliency have evolved o
the last few years, and how applications should be engineered to react in a pre
dictable manner to various forms of interaction, including events, users, load,
and failures (*http://bit.ly/1F9pMHJ*).

In the Manifesto, it states that "Reactive Systems" are responsive, resilient, elastic,
and message-driven.

Responsive

The system responds in a timely manner if at all possible.

In general, this means that the application should respond to requests very
quickly. User simply don't want to wait, and there is almost never a good reason
to make them. If you have a containerized service that renders large PDF files,
design it so that it immediately responds with a *job submitted* message so that the
user can go about his day, and then provide a message or banner that informs the
user when the job is finished and where he can download the resulting PDF.

Resilient

The system stays responsive in the face of failure.

When your application fails for any reason, the situation will always be worse if
the application becomes unresponsive. It is much better to handle the failure
gracefully, and dynamically reduce the application's functionality or even display
a simple but clear problem message to the user while reporting the issue internally.

Elastic

The system stays responsive under varying workload.

With Docker, this is achieved by dynamically deploying and decommissioning
containers as requirements and load fluctuate so that your application is always
able to handle server requests quickly, without deploying a lot of underutilized
resources.

Message Driven

*Reactive systems rely on asynchronous message-passing to establish a boundary
between components.*

Although not directly addressed by Docker, the idea here is that there are times
when an application can become busy or unavailable. If you utilize asynchronous

age-passing between your services, you can help ensure that your service
not lose requests and that these will be processed as soon as possible.

n Summary

All four of these design features require application developers to design graceful
degradation and a clear separation of responsibilities into their applications. By
treating all dependencies as attached resources, properly designed, dynamic container environments allow you to easily maintain n+2 status across your application stack, reliably scale individual services in your environment, and quickly
replace unhealthy nodes.

The core ideas in "The Reactive Manifesto" merge very nicely with "The Twelve-
Factor App" and the Docker workflow. These documents successfully attempt to
frame many of the most important discussions about the way you need to think
and work if you want to be successful in meeting new expectations in the industry. The Docker workflow provides a practical way to implement many of these
ideas in any organization in a completely approachable way.

## CHAPTER 12

Conclusion

We've had a pretty good tour through what Docker is and isn't, and how it can benefit you and your organization. We also mapped some of the common pitfalls. We have tried to impart to you many of the small pieces of wisdom that we picked up from running Docker in production. Our personal experience has shown that the promise of Docker is realistically achievable, and we've seen significant benefits in our organization as a result. Like other powerful technologies, Docker is not without its downsides, but the net result has been a big positive for us, our teams, and our organization. If you implement the Docker workflow and integrate it into the processes you already have in your organization, there is every reason to believe that you can benefit from it as well. So let's quickly review the problems that Docker is designed to help you solve and some of the power it brings to the table.

The Challenges

In traditional deployment workflows, there are all manner of required steps that significantly contribute to the overall pain felt by teams. Every step you add to the deployment process for an application increases the overall risk inherent in shipping it to production. Docker combines a workflow with a simple tool set that is targeted squarely at addressing these concerns. Along the way, it aims your development process toward some industry best practices, and its opinionated approach leads to better communication and more robustly crafted applications. Some of the specific problems that Docker can help mitigate include:

- Outdated build and release processes that require multiple levels of handoff between development and operations teams.

he giant build-deploy step required by many frontend sites that require
set compilation, or dynamic languages that need dependencies to be
sembled together.

vergent dependency versions required by applications that need to share
e same hardware.

anaging multiple Linux distributions in the same organization.

ailding one-off deployment processes for each application you put into
oduction.

- The constant need to patch dependencies for security vulnerabilities while
running your application in production.

By using the registry as a handoff point, Docker eases and simplifies communication between operations and development teams, or between multiple development teams on the same project. By bundling all of the dependencies for an
application into one shipping artifact, Docker eliminates concerns about which
Linux distribution developers want to work on, which versions of libraries they
need to use, and how they compile their assets or bundle their software. It isolates
operations teams from the build process and puts developers in charge of their
dependencies.

The Docker Workflow

Docker's workflow helps organizations tackle really hard problems—some of the
same problems that DevOps processes are aimed at solving. A major problem in
incorporating DevOps successfully into a company's processes is that many people have no idea where to start. Tools are often incorrectly presented as the solution to what are fundamentally process problems. Adding virtualization,
automated testing, deployment tools, or configuration management suites to the
environment often just changes the nature of the problem without delivering a
resolution.

It would be easy to dismiss Docker as just another tool making unfulfillable
promises about fixing your business processes, but that would be selling it short.
Where Docker's power meets the road is in the way that its natural workflow
allows applications to travel through their whole life cycle, from conception to
retirement, within one ecosystem. That workflow is often opinionated, but it follows a path that simplifies the adoption of some of the core principles of DevOps.
It encourages development teams to understand the whole life cycle of their
application, and allows operations teams to support a much wider variety of
applications on the same runtime environment. And that delivers value across
the board.

Minimizing Deployment Artifacts

Docker alleviates the pain induced by sprawling deployment artifacts. It does th̶
by defining the result of a build as a single artifact, the Docker image, which con̶
tains everything your Linux application requires to run, and it executes it within
a protected runtime environment. Containers can then be easily deployed on
modern Linux distributions. But because of the clean split between Docker client
and server, developers can build their applications on non-Linux systems and still
participate in the Linux container environment remotely.

Leveraging Docker allows software developers to create Docker images that,
starting with the very first proof of concept release, can be run locally, tested with
automated tools, and deployed into integration or production environments
without ever rebuilding them. This ensures that the application will run in production in the exact same environment in which it was built and tested. Nothing
needs to be recompiled or repackaged during the deployment workflow, which
significantly lowers the normal risks inherent in most deployment processes. It
also means that a single build step replaces a typically error-prone process that
involves compiling and packaging multiple complex components for distribution.

Docker images also simplify the installation and configuration of an application
by ensuring that every single piece of software that an application requires to run
on a modern Linux kernel is contained in the image, with nothing else that might
cause dependency conflicts in many environments. This makes it trivial to run
multiple applications that rely on different versions of core system software on
the exact same server.

Optimizing Storage and Retrieval

Docker leverages filesystem layers to allow containers to be built from a composite of multiple images. This shaves a vast amount of time and effort off of many
deployment processes by shipping only significant changes across the wire. It also
saves considerable disk space by allowing multiple containers to be based on the
same lower-level OS image, and then utilizing a copy-on-write process to write
new or modified files into a top layer. This also helps in scaling an application by
simply starting more copies on the same servers without the need to push it
across the wire for each new instance.

To support image retrieval, Docker leverages the image registry for hosting
images. While not revolutionary on the face of it, the registry actually helps split
team responsibilities clearly along the lines embraced by DevOps principles.
Developers can build their application, test it, ship the final image to the registry,
and deploy the image to the production environment, while the operations team
can focus on building excellent deployment and cluster management tooling that

s from the registry, runs reliably, and ensures environmental health. Opera-
ns teams can provide feedback to developers and see it tested at build time
ther than waiting to find problems when the application is shipped to produc-
.ion. This enables both teams to focus on what they do best without a multi-
phased handoff process.

The Payoff

As teams become more confident with Docker and its workflow, the realization
often dawns that containers create an incredibly powerful abstraction layer
between all of their software components and the underlying operating system.
Done correctly, organizations can begin to move away from the legacy need to
create custom physical servers or virtual machines for most applications, and
instead deploy fleets of identical Docker hosts that can then be used as a large
pool of resources to dynamically deploy their applications to, with an ease that
was never before so smooth.

When these process changes are successful, the cultural impact within a software
engineering organization can be dramatic. Developers gain more ownership of
their complete application stack, including many of the smallest details, which
would typically be handled by a completely different group. Operations teams are
simultaneously freed from trying to package and deploy complicated dependency
trees with little or no detailed knowledge of the application.

In a well-designed Docker workflow, developers compile and package the application, which makes it much easier to become more operationally focused and
ensure that their application is running properly in all environments, without
being concerned about significant changes introduced to the application environment by the operations teams. At the same time, operations teams are freed from
spending most of their time supporting the application and can focus on creating
a robust and stable platform for the application to run on. This dynamic creates a
very healthy environment where teams have clearer ownership and responsibilities in the application delivery process, and friction between the teams is significantly decreased.

Getting the process right has a huge benefit to both the company and the customers. With organizational friction removed, software quality is improved, processes are streamlined, and code ships to production faster. This all helps free the
organization to spend more time providing a satisfying customer experience and
delivering directly to the broader business objectives. A well-implemented
Docker-based workflow can greatly help organizations achieve those goals.

The Final Word

You are now armed with knowledge that we hope can help you with the pro
of getting Docker into production. We encourage you to experiment with Doc
on a small scale on your laptop or in a VM to develop a strong understanding
how all of the pieces fit together, and then consider how you might begin to
implement it yourself. Every organization or individual developer will follow a
different path determined by their own needs and competencies. If you're looking for guidance on how to start, we've found success in tackling the deployment
problem first with simpler tools, and then moving on to things like service discovery and distributed scheduling. Docker can be made as complicated as you
like, but as with anything, starting simple usually pays off.

We hope you can now go forth with the knowledge we've imparted and make
good on some of the promise for yourself.

Index

the Authors

Kane is currently a Lead Site Reliability Engineer at New Relic. He has had
...ng career in production operations, with many diverse roles, in a broad range
...industries. He has spoken about subjects like alerting fatigue and hardware
...utomation at various meet-ups and technical conferences, including Velocity.

Sean spent most of his youth living overseas, and exploring what life has to offer,
including graduating from the Ringling Bros. and Barnum & Bailey Clown Col-
lege, completing two summer internships with the US Central Intelligence
Agency, and building the very first web site in the state of Alaska. He gratefully
lives in the US Pacific Northwest with his wife and children and loves traveling
and still photography.

Karl Matthias is a Principal Systems Engineer with Nitro Software. He has
worked as a developer, systems administrator, and network engineer for everything from startups to Fortune 500 companies. After a few years at startups in
Germany and the UK followed by a stint at home in Portland, Oregon, he and his
family recently landed in Dublin, Ireland. When not devoting his time to things
digital, he can be found herding his two daughters, shooting film with vintage
cameras, or riding one of his bicycles.

Colophon

The animal on the cover of *Docker: Up and Running* is a blue whale (*Balaenoptera
musculus*). Blue whales can grow up to 100 feet in length, and 200 tons in weight,
making them the largest animals on Earth, and the largest animals to ever exist.
At birth, a blue whale calf is as large as an adult hippopotamus, and can gain up
to 200 pounds a day. When fully grown, blue whales are long and thin, with a
small dorsal fin, two flippers at their side, and a horizontal tail, also known as a
"fluke." Blue whales are named for their bluish-grey coloring.

Blue whales are migratory and can be found in every ocean. They generally feed
in colder polar regions, and then head to warmer tropical waters to give birth.
Blue whales usually travel alone or in pairs, and communicate through a series of
complex vocalizations. As a member of the balaenopteridae or rorqual family,
blue whales feed by straining their prey through bony plates in their mouth
known as baleen. Their diet consists almost entirely of krill, a small crustacean
similar to shrimp. They can eat up to 7,900 pounds of krill a day, and require 1.5
million kilocalories of energy every day. Because of their speed and size, blue
whales have practically no natural predators.

Blue whales were once widespread, with a population estimated in the hundreds
of thousands, While they were initially too large and fast for whalers to capture,
the invention of the harpoon gun in the late 1800s enabled whalers to success-

fully hunt blue whales. Decades of whaling followed, causing a signifi... lation decline. An international ban on the hunting of blue whales was e... 1966, allowing their numbers to recover, although they remain endangere...

Many of the animals on O'Reilly covers are endangered; all of them are impo... to the world. To learn more about how you can help, go to *htt...* *animals.oreilly.com.*

The cover image is from *British Quadrupeds*. The cover fonts are URW Type-writer and Guardian Sans. The text font is Adobe Minion Pro; the heading font is Adobe Myriad Condensed; and the code font is Dalton Maag's Ubuntu Mono.

Learn from experts.
ınd the answers you need.

Sign up for a **10-day free trial** to get **unlimited access** to all of the content on Safari, including Learning Paths, interactive tutorials, and curated playlists that draw from thousands of ebooks and training videos on a wide range of topics, including data, design, DevOps, management, business—and much more.

Start your free trial at:
oreilly.com/safari

(No credit card required.)

©2016 O'Reilly Media, Inc. O'Reilly is a registered trademark of O'Reilly Media, Inc. D2565

CPSIA information can be obtained
at www.ICGtesting.com
Printed in the USA
BVHW09s1659050718
520790BV00013B/264/P